Perceived Organizational Support

Perceived Organizational Support

FOSTERING ENTHUSIASTIC AND PRODUCTIVE EMPLOYEES

Robert Eisenberger
Florence Stinglhamber

AMERICAN PSYCHOLOGICAL ASSOCIATION
WASHINGTON, DC

Published by
American Psychological Association
750 First Street, NE
Washington, DC 20002
www.apa.org

To order
APA Order Department
P.O. Box 92984
Washington, DC 20090-2984
Tel: (800) 374-2721; Direct: (202) 336-5510
Fax: (202) 336-5502; TDD/TTY: (202) 336-6123
Online: www.apa.org/pubs/books
E-mail: order@apa.org

In the U.K., Europe, Africa, and the Middle East, copies may be ordered from
American Psychological Association
3 Henrietta Street
Covent Garden, London
WC2E 8LU England

Typeset in Meridien by Circle Graphics, Inc., Columbia, MD

Printer: Maple-Vail Book Manufacturing, Inc., York, PA
Cover Designer: Berg Design, Albany, NY

The opinions and statements published are the responsibility of the authors, and such opinions and statements do not necessarily represent the policies of the American Psychological Association.

Library of Congress Cataloging-in-Publication Data

Eisenberger, Robert.
  Perceived organizational support : fostering enthusiastic and productive employees / Robert Eisenberger and Florence Stinglhamber. — 1st ed.
    p. cm.
  Includes bibliographical references and index.
  ISBN-13: 978-1-4338-0933-0
  ISBN-10: 1-4338-0933-8
1. Industrial relations. 2. Employees. 3. Organizational behavior. 4. Employee motivation.
5. Organizational effectiveness. 6. Organizational sociology. I. Stinglhamber, Florence. II. Title.

  HD6971.E54 2011
  658.3'14—dc22

                                    2010032283

British Library Cataloguing-in-Publication Data
A CIP record is available from the British Library.

Printed in the United States of America
First Edition

doi: 10.1037/12318-000

For Lynn M. Shore and Lois Tetrick, whose basic contributions to the study of perceived organizational support began from Day 1 and whose friendship and advice I have cherished over the past quarter century.
—Robert Eisenberger

For Olivier and our wonderful daughters, Clara and Alice, whose love, encouragement, and indulgence convinced me even further that support is a central tenet of life in general.
—Florence Stinglhamber

Contents

Perceived
Organizational
Support

Introduction

Consider the organization for which you work. To what extent do you agree with each of the following statements?

- My organization values my contribution to its well-being.
- My organization really cares about my well-being.
- My organization fails to appreciate any extra effort from me.
- My organization cares about my general satisfaction at work.
- My organization would ignore any complaint from me.
- Even if I did the best job possible, my organization would fail to notice.
- My organization takes pride in my accomplishments at work.
- My organization shows very little concern for me.

Research with tens of thousands of employees indicates that if you are like the great majority of others, how much you agree with any one of the statements is highly predictive of your agreement with the remaining statements. Perhaps you noticed a common theme running through the items. All the statements concern your work organization's valuation of you or, to be more exact, how much you believe your organization values your contributions and cares about your well-being. The favorableness of such *perceived organizational support* has far-reaching consequences for employees and the organizations for which they work.

Hundreds of carefully controlled studies indicate the benefits of perceived organizational support for employees. Employees with high perceived organizational support experience their working lives in more favorable ways. They have a more positive mood at work, are more satisfied with their jobs, believe they make important contributions, experience less stress, and are less conflicted between work and family life. Employees with high perceived support are also more favorably inclined toward their organization. They have a stronger positive emotional bond to the organization, identify more with the organization, and trust it more. They find their jobs to be more central to their lives, and they are more engaged in the work itself.

Perceived organizational support influences multiple workplace behaviors. Employees who feel supported show superior performance in standard job activities and voluntary actions that help the organization meet its objectives. They show less withdrawal from active participation in organizational activities by such actions as coming to work late, staying home, or quitting. They are less likely to violate organizational norms by mistreating others or damaging equipment. They are more creative, more cooperative with safety campaigns, and more likely to accept new information technology. If they deal with customers, they provide better service.

Research on perceived organizational support has been accelerating, with more than 350 scientific studies, a website (http://www. psychology.uh.edu/pos), and 600,000 references on the Internet. Why the intense interest? The answer, we believe, is that viewing the organization's supportiveness from the employees' perspective provides an effective tool for understanding employees psychological well-being, positive orientation toward the organization, and behavioral outcomes helpful to the organization. And researchers know a great deal about the causes of perceived organizational support.

Yet, there is no one place a student, researcher, human resource professional, or business person can go for a comprehensive review of the findings on perceived organizational support. Current reviews of these findings are limited to technical articles in research journals and book chapters about particular aspects of the topic. The present book is intended to fill the need for a general review of the research on perceived organizational support that will be useful to all those who would like to understand the benefits to employees and organizations of treating employees supportively. We examine the major findings concerning antecedents and consequences of perceived organizational support and their explanation. Rather than appealing to piecemeal explanations, we have used *organizational support theory,* which was designed to organize and explain the development, nature, and outcomes of perceived organizational support. We have also provided practical steps that managers can take to enhance perceived organizational support.

Before the discovery of perceived organizational support and related concepts, many insightful chief executives and managers intuitively understood that recognizing and rewarding employees' contributions had considerable benefits for their firms. Other executives emphasized the importance of caring about employees' well-being. Two decades ago, my colleagues and I (Eisenberger, Huntington, Hutchison, & Sowa, 1986) found that employees were forming a general belief that involved the extent to which the organization both values their contributions and cares about their well-being. We found that most employees valued such perceived organizational support highly and responded to it in a variety of positive ways. Thus, perceived organizational support helped explain managers' insights into ways to promote the dedication and efforts of employees.

We had been carrying out research on what makes employees committed to their work organization. We were led to the concept of perceived organizational support on the basis that although most managers are concerned with employees' commitment to them, most employees are concerned with the organization's positive valuation of themselves. Perhaps much could be learned about working life by considering the relationship between employees and their work organization from the employees' viewpoint. Perceived organizational support represents employees' attempts to assess their valuation by the organization.

Organizational support theory allows for an understanding of employees' favorable reactions to positive treatment by the organization. In brief, the theory holds that employees personify the organization, thinking of it as having lifelike qualities, including benevolent or malevolent intentions toward them. Employees value perceived organizational support because it meets their socioemotional needs (e.g., approval, esteem, affiliation, emotional support) and indicates the organization is ready to provide them help when needed and reward their increased efforts. As a consequence, perceived organizational support contributes to employees' happiness; identification with, and emotional commitment to, the organization; and felt obligation to help the organization reach its objectives. Voluntary and consistent support from the organization is especially valued because it signifies the organization's strong positive valuation of the employee. Organizational support theory, backed by evidence, provides practical steps that organizations can take to promote perceived organizational support and its positive consequences.

Following the discovery of perceived organizational support, I (Eisenberger) and a few colleagues at different universities, especially Lynn Shore and Lois Tetrick, began carrying out studies on the topic.

The measurement of perceived organizational support turned out to be surprisingly easy because various ways of asking employees about the organization's valuation of their contributions and concern about their welfare produced a single overriding perception; employees felt generally supported by the organization to a small, moderate, or high degree. Later, many other investigators became interested and began to study perceived organizational support among employees in such diverse occupations as manufacturing, banking, pharmaceuticals, insurance, postal services, education, medicine, law enforcement, and the military.

We highlight what we believe to be the major research findings of this research through the prism of organizational support theory. With such a large and diverse literature, we cannot cover every topic. We have included what appear to be the most important antecedents and consequences of perceived organizational support. This book differs from most business books because, although we certainly include many illustrative examples based on informal observations, we also draw on decades of scholarly research by organizational psychologists and business school researchers regarding the benefits of treating employees supportively. We, as well as many others who carry out research on employee motivation and satisfaction, have had our views shaped by our experiences with managers and employees. But the true strength of the present argument rests on the conceptual understanding brought about by a large body of careful research on perceived organizational support.

The scientific study of employee motivation and satisfaction has moved beyond informal reports and toward a systematic evidence-based understanding. These studies are typically carried out either with large numbers of employees drawn from a variety of organizations or from a single organization that agrees to participate on condition that its identity be shielded, which is a standard provision designed to protect proprietary information and guard against bad publicity. We supplement these carefully controlled studies with illustrative examples from organizations well known for treating employees in an especially favorable or unfavorable manner. In the former group are such companies as Costco, Google, Southwest Airlines, Wegmans (markets), Smucker's (jams and jellies), SAS (software), Genentech (biotechnology), NetApp (information technology), and W. L. Gore & Associates (breathable waterproof clothing). For comparison, we examine organizations that have a recent history of giving low support to employees, such as Wal-Mart and U.S. Airways. Although we provide examples with well-known companies and many personal experiences drawn from employment, research, and consulting, the basis for our understanding is the large number of scientific studies on perceived organizational support.

Chapter 1 places perceived organizational support in a historical context by examining two conflicting fundamental views by management concerning the worth of employees. The *marginal capital* view takes most employees to be minor, replaceable cogs in an industrial machine, whereas the *human capital* view claims that most employees are capable of making important contributions to organizations' long-term success, especially when given appropriate developmental experiences. The first chapter considers the increasing dominance of the marginal capital view over the past few decades yet notes the considerable success of a significant minority of organizations emphasizing the human capital view.

Chapter 2 introduces organizational support theory as a basis for understanding the antecedents and consequences of perceived organizational support. Fundamental to the theory is the norm of reciprocity, which creates a felt obligation to repay the organization for perceived organizational support with increased efforts to help achieve its objectives. Also, the fulfillment of socioemotional needs, such as esteem and emotional support, owing to perceived organizational support, increases employees' identification with, and emotional bond to, the organization.

Chapter 3 considers the antecedents of perceived organizational support. Notable for their powerful influence are work experiences involving fairness, organizational politics, and rewards.

Chapter 4 examines organizational agents that provide perceived organizational support, including upper level managers, supervisors, and social networks. We consider the important role of leadership in the development of perceived organizational support. The chapter also reports on extensions of organizational support theory to targets of support not involving typical employee–employer relationships, including the military, union members, customers, and volunteers.

Chapter 5 views the role of perceived organizational support in employees' happiness (subjective well-being), including positive mood, satisfaction in the workplace, self-esteem, reduced stress, and a more satisfying balance between work and home life.

Chapter 6 considers the contribution of perceived organizational support to employees' positive orientation toward their organization and work. Employees with high perceived organizational support identify more with, and are more emotionally committed to, their employer; are more involved in their jobs; and are more engaged in their work.

Chapter 7 examines the previously mentioned diverse kinds of positive behavioral outcomes of perceived organizational support that help the organization reach its objectives.

Chapter 8 presents practical approaches to increase perceived organizational support: (a) Managers can engage in supportive behaviors and promote human resources policies; (b) organizations can train managers to be more supportive; and (c) CEOs and top managers can establish a supportive organizational culture.

Chapter 9 summarizes what researchers have learned about perceived organizational support and considers useful ways to further expand this knowledge.

We write for all those who would like to better understand the relationship between how employees are treated and what employees, in turn, give back to the organization. This is an important issue not only for our colleagues in academia and business but also for general readers who are concerned about the deterioration of treatment of employees in many companies. We hope to show that when capitalism functions as it should, with rewards to managers for enhancing the long-term effectiveness of organizations, enlightened self-interest dictates the supportive treatment of employees. Knowledge of how employees respond to supportive treatment is an important first step in this direction.

The Supportive Organization

C ynthia Andrews, a petite, humorous 54-year-old, was making a comfortable living as a computer trainer for a highly profitable national bank with headquarters in upstate Delaware. As a 12-year veteran of the firm, Cynthia's achievements and industriousness earned her consistently superior performance evaluations. One warm spring morning, she picked up the newspaper from her driveway and read that the bank's CEO had announced that he was going to cut costs with a 5% reduction in the workforce. Later in the day, Cynthia's boss called her into his office and said, "You've been doing fine work, but we've got to make cuts somewhere. So we have to let you go. The good news is that we are able to keep you here for another few weeks."

Several days later, Cynthia was introduced to a nervous, recently hired young man named George, whom she was asked to train to take over her responsibilities. While chatting with George, Cynthia learned that he had graduated not long ago from college with mediocre grades and would be paid one third the amount of her salary. Thus, the downsizing was accompanied by the hiring of new, less experienced employees who would settle for a low salary.

Bob Jervis is a slim, tall 24-year-old who runs a mile each day after he finishes work at a Google-type Internet company. Although he has been with the organization only 2 years, Bob feels he is a valued member of a cohesive, creative work team. The company stresses dedication, which often involves working overtime to complete projects on time. In return, management takes great care to show its appreciation for employees' contributions and concern for their well-being. Workers are invited to provide suggestions for the company's products, and useful ideas are publicized and adopted. Most high-level positions are filled from within the company, and layoffs and voluntary turnover are rare. Although wages are no higher than the industry average, fringe benefits include a comprehensive medical plan and payments for higher education. Bob's company is especially solicitous of employees' individual problems and needs, such as taking time off to pursue advanced education or caring for an ill relative. Bob admires the company and appreciates the high regard it displays for him and his coworkers. He feels both a desire and an obligation to give the company his best.[1]

The treatment that Cynthia and Bob have received is representative of two conflicting contemporary views concerning the valuation of employees. The *marginal capital* view, illustrated by Cynthia's treatment, characterizes typical employees as low-value, disposable cogs in the industrial machine—losers who lack the talent and drive to achieve the status of the high-level managers. This approach holds that most job holders can be likened to ill-programmed robots. On the positive side, they are able to follow simple commands and have an opposable thumb so they can handle tools. On the other hand, they have low innate talent, are ignorant, fail to stay on task, have no ambition, and are frequently burdened by illnesses associated with their unhealthy life styles that produce absenteeism. It follows that the organization should expend just enough resources on the marginal majority of employees to keep turnover below an acceptable limit while discarding employees as soon as they can be replaced by lower paid newcomers or by new, more efficient technology.

The marginal capital approach often involves a *command-and-control strategy* in which management attempts to simplify and rigidify employees' jobs. For example, telesales representatives may be given a script to follow strictly. Customer service representatives are often required to carry out a series of fixed steps when dealing with customer problems, being careful not to think above their pay grade. After all, trying to teach these employees anything of value, given their lack of talent, is deemed pointless. Additionally, the size of the workforce is repeatedly reduced to save money, and employees are given increasingly more work to make up for understaffing. Such treatment of employees is consistent with the presumption that recipients of poorly paid, poorly

---

[1]Names and some details regarding several individuals have been changed to disguise their identities at their request.

designed, unpleasant work deserve such poor treatment because they lack the talent and ambition to find any better job.

By contrast, the *human capital* view, suggested by Bob's treatment, considers most employees as having the potential to warrant the organization's investment of time and resources to develop superior talents and skills. Because the human capital approach emphasizes the development of employees' talents and skills and the importance of their contributions, employees understand that their efforts will be appreciated and rewarded and that if they do a good job, they will be replaced only with great reluctance. The marginal and human capital views are mirrored by conflicting portrayals of ideal organizations in the popular media. Relying heavily on glowing accounts of organizations that have become successful, some business books, magazines, and newspapers promote the notion that ruthless efficiency, involving poor treatment for the majority of employees, is necessary for high profitability. In contrast, other authors are drawn to corporate success stories that encourage employee loyalty, initiative, and creativity (see Figure 1.1).

In this book, we examine the effects of high and low supportiveness on employees' psychological well-being, the favorableness of their orientation toward the organization, and behavioral outcomes beneficial for the organization. A key discovery concerning employees' reactions to their treatment by the organization is that they form a general view concerning the extent to which the organization values their contributions and cares about their well-being. Such *perceived organizational support* has an important influence on employees' engagement with the organization.

Many experiences strongly influence employees' satisfaction, motivation, and commitment at work. Effective leaders can provide the resources employees need to better carry out their jobs and provide a sense of accomplishment. They can inspire employees to identify with the goals of the organization. Organizations can take care to treat employees fairly and to pay employees what they deserve. Yet, a review of the research literature found that perceived organizational support contributed more to employees' positive feelings about the organization than did any of these other work experiences (Meyer, Stanley, Herscovitch, & Topolnytsky, 2002). The reason is that these and other important favorable employee experiences work through perceived organizational support to enhance satisfaction, motivation, and commitment. Perceived organizational support provides a means by which organizations can do well for themselves by doing well for their employees. The principles governing the establishment of perceived organizational support can be applied at all levels of the organizational hierarchy: supervisors thinking about how to treat subordinates, midlevel managers designing human resource policies, and CEOs and top-level managers shaping the organizational culture and designing organizational strategies.

FIGURE 1.1

	Marginal capital view	Human capital view
Premise	Most employees. . . Lack innate talent Are ignorant Lack motivation Are costly and of little added value	Most employees. . . Have high innate talent Can become very effective when properly trained and motivated Are a key component of organizational success
Consequences		
Development and training	Emphasis on narrow training for specific tasks	Emphasis on training that develops talents and expands skills
Use of employees' skills	Emphasis on simplification and standardization	Emphasis on full use of employee skills in furtherance of organizational objectives
Work experiences	Poor pay, work overload, use of punishment rather than rewards	Recognition for superior performance and cultivation of employees identification with organization
Job security	Employees discarded as soon as they can be replaced by lower paid newcomers or new technology	Attempt to retain well-performing employees even during economic downturns

Marginal capital versus human capital views of employees.

Positive Versus Negative Valuations of Employees

Our understanding of the way in which perceived organizational support operates is based on a theory of employee–organization relationships, called *organizational support theory,* the major tenets of which are backed by many carefully controlled studies. The founders of supportive organizations, such as Costco, Google, Southwest Airlines, and Whole Foods, had an intuitive feel for the value of organizational support, and we use such companies as examples throughout this book. Because positive examples work best with distinguishing negative cases, we also discuss organizations such as Wal-Mart and U.S. Airways that have been as unsupportive in their treatment of employees as the former group has been supportive.

Southwest Airlines is a good example of a company with the kind of policies useful for instilling high perceived organizational support. Southwest Airlines employees show far greater satisfaction and commitment than those of other major airlines despite the absence of better pay or fringe benefits. Southwest communicates its high valuation of employees' contributions by such means as the following:

- Employees' ideas for improving organizational effectiveness and employee welfare are actively solicited and the better ones are enacted;
- employees are given the authority to bypass many regulations to solve difficult employee problems;
- good faith attempts to solve problems are encouraged, and those that fail do not get punished; and
- a team spirit is encouraged in which the contributions of each type of job and each employee to Southwest's success are emphasized.

These points are not some gimmick by Southwest to convince employees that the company cares about them. The talents and skills of employees in all jobs at Southwest are used to enhance the airline's performance and customer service. For example, Southwest's excellent on-time record depends on the cooperation of employees in varied jobs to get fliers checked in quickly, seated quickly, the plane cleaned and serviced quickly, and the baggage moved quickly. High marks for customer service come from favorable treatment of employees and stem from customer contacts with a diversity of employees from desk agents to stewards.

A recognized leader in customer satisfaction, based in part on the superb service the air carrier gives fliers, Southwest deals effectively with unexpected problems that frequently crop up in air travel. Southwest, through its employees, conveys a jaunty enthusiasm for air travel. The company treats its customers with great consideration. The enthusiasm of the staff may not make flying fun—no one can do that anymore—but Southwest leaves its customers in a better mood at the end of its flights than any other major airline.

By contrast, fliers of U.S. Airways often complain about the treatment they receive from employees who themselves are passing on the poor treatment and lack of support they have received from the carrier. To take one notorious example, on Christmas weekend in 2004, thousands of customers experienced long delays with hundreds of cancelled flights and massive amounts of undelivered luggage. Although Midwestern storms were a major part of the problem, another factor involved the anger of hundreds of U.S. Airways employees who called in sick ("Christmas Nightmare," 2004). Forced to take repeated pay cuts to help the financially suffering airline, the employees were angered by the absence of any reduction in the generous compensation packages of top management (White, 2004). Management had sent the message that they themselves deserved high pay but the majority of employees deserved pay cuts.

There is a basic divide between organizations, such as Southwest Airlines, that value rank and file employees as human capital versus those that devalue them as a wasteful expense. These contrary human and marginal capital perspectives are embodied in the ways two highly successful discount retailers, Costco and Wal-Mart, view their employees. As of this writing, Wal-Mart has 1.4 million employees worldwide, with revenues of $258 billion, making it the world's largest corporation. The company's innovative use of information technology to track inventory, its dogged application of its enormous purchasing power to strike favorable deals with suppliers, and its low pay and heavy workload for lower level employees have allowed it to offer low prices that few competitors can match (Head, 2004).

At Wal-Mart, rest breaks and brief conversations concerning private issues are considered time theft, warranting disciplinary action. Wal-Mart has been found guilty of stealing their employees' time, working them during breaks or after clocking out (Saporito, 2007). As of this writing, the majority of Wal-Mart employees' salaries fall below federally established poverty guidelines. Medical insurance is subsidized to only a limited degree (Head, 2004) and requires a long waiting period (Zimmerman, 2004). The newest, improved plan instituted after devastating negative publicity carries a $2,000 deductible for a cashier making $17,000 a year (Saporito, 2007). These policies make it difficult for Wal-Mart to sustain a loyal labor force; about half its employees quit each year (Fishman, 2006).

The high attrition rate at Wal-Mart leaves behind a minority who seem to be genuinely happy working there. These are most likely heavily represented by two groups. First, there are older individuals with an additional source of income, such as Social Security, and who have limited interests in leisure activities. These older employees find that pleasantly greeting customers or performing other mundane tasks helps provide welcome social interaction and supplemental income. Second, there are teenage employees without dependents who may find it relatively easy to support themselves on Wal-Mart wages. For these youngsters, lacking a substantial work history, the pay may not seem all that low, and the 10% employee discount may appear to be attractive. But for many, if not most employees, low wages and continual demands for extra work in less time make Wal-Mart an unpleasant place to work— hence, the 50% voluntary annual turnover rate.

Costco, another highly profitable discount retailer, has a much more positive attitude toward those they employ. With more upscale merchandise than carried by Wal-Mart, this chain grew from one store in 1983 to 432 in 2007. Its operation is similar to Wal-Mart's, offering a limited number of brands at considerably discounted prices. However, in contrast to Wal-Mart, Costco pays its employees well, has only a short waiting period for health insurance, and contributes generously to insurance premiums (Zimmerman, 2004). Costco employees speak of being treated with respect and care. For example, Teamster union negotiators are not known for their generous comments toward management. However, following a 4-month negotiation on behalf of 13,000 unionized Costco warehouse employees, a union representative commented, "I think they are a company that proves you can treat your employees well and still be successful" (Frey, 2004).

According to Richard Galanti, Costco's chief financial officer,

> From day one, we've run the company with the philosophy that if we pay better than average, provide a salary that people can live on, have a positive environment and good benefits, we'll be able to hire better people, they'll stay longer and be more efficient. (Morgenson, 2004)

The Teamsters union, delighted with Costco's welcome of unionization and high wages, enthusiastically quoted CEO Jim Sinegal: "I don't see what's wrong with an employee earning enough to be able to buy a house or having a health plan for the family" (Flanigan, 2004). As a result of favorable treatment, employee theft, a major problem for most large retailers, occurs at an extremely low level at Costco (Morgenson, 2004). Also, Costco's productivity per employee is higher than Wal-Mart's, and its turnover rate among workers is only about half that of Wal-Mart's (Holmes & Zellner, 2004).

Wal-Mart's treatment of employees has become more common for large companies than Costco's. Indeed, Wal-Mart is one of the most, if not the most, admired U.S. corporations by the business community (Head, 2005). American business stands in awe of Wal-Mart's ability to keep labor cost low even if the overworked, poorly paid workforce provides poor customer service. The stock market generally rewards companies such as Wal-Mart for downsizing, thereby increasing the workload of remaining employees. This occurs because investors are primarily interested in anticipated short-term profits, even at the cost of a company's future ability to carry out basic functions, such as innovation in products and services or effective customer service.

Business executives are not so arrogant as to openly claim that they prefer to pay their employees poorly, provide meager health benefits, and require an unreasonable workload. These conditions are defended as a matter of necessity. CEOs cite the free market as both the cause and future cure of these difficulties. Their companies, they claim, are obligated to their shareholders, not to employees. Furthermore, businesses feel they must remain competitive or risk failure. Even when companies lay off full-time employees and replace them with poorly compensated part-time or temporary employees, the argument runs that the

U.S. economy, and therefore the labor force as a whole, will benefit from the company's health. By such brutal efficiencies, the line of reasoning holds that company will prosper and ultimately deliver that prosperity to employees as well as shareholders.

However, the benefits of a poorly paid workforce must be weighed against the implicit costs to the company, community, and nation. First, consumers are generally unaware of how the low prices found at Wal-Mart and other large companies that pay employees poorly come at a cost to the community: Consumers pay through higher taxes for the tax breaks and road construction often used by local governments to lure the businesses and for the social welfare programs needed for poorly paid workers. Second, employees who receive such low wages have little buying power to fuel the economy. The economy can be propelled through mortgages and credit card debt for only so long. Third, poor treatment of employees results in poor customer service. Everyone experiences long lines at airports, long waits when phoning call centers, and delays for medical treatment and tests. Fourth, companies suffer financially when disgruntled employees apply themselves to their narrowly defined job functions rather than protecting the organization from harm and thinking creatively and innovatively about what they can do to aid the organization. The emphasis on short-term profits by corporate executives at the expense of long-term gain is a formula for failed, rather than successful, long-run competition.

The Unsupported Worker

With the advent of strong global competition in the 1970s, U.S. employees began to experience a worsening of treatment at most organizations relative to the steady gains they had made during and following the second World War. Several years ago, I was on the shop floor of a U.S. automaker that had been steadily losing market share to foreign competitors. The company had asked for the employees' help: Unless increases in wages and fringe benefits could be eliminated in the new contract, massive layoffs would be necessary for the company to survive. With an understanding that shared sacrifice would be necessary to help the company through its travails, the workers had voted in favor of a contract that would fail to keep up with the cost of living. That morning, something was amiss. Clusters of employees were forming—some individuals were speaking angrily, others waving their fists. Top management had just announced that several thousand managers would receive substantial pay raises. "Never, never again," fumed a 20-year veteran, "will I trust anything management says." Another, younger employee remarked, "They care more for those incompetents who got us into this mess—not us." The message seemed clear: High-level managers believed that they deserved bonuses no matter the car maker's financial distress; ordinary employees were a drag on the company who deserved only to share its burdens.

The increasing disparity in wages and benefits between upper management and most employees is also found in successful businesses. Employee productivity, or the output of goods and services produced per hour worked, has greatly increased since the early 1970's, while real wages (controlling for inflation) for the majority of U.S. employees have not. Top managers benefited from rising productivity, profits, and stock prices with record increases in salary, bonuses, and stock options. However, the typical male worker's income, adjusted for inflation, is about the same as his father's was. Household income increased modestly, but mainly because of the greater number of women entering the workforce. Reduced health and economic benefits provided by companies adds to these economics pressures (Head, 2004; "Now Bringing Home the Leaner Bacon," 2006). (During the 1990's, average household job average household net worth fell by 4% [Irwin, 2010].) In short, even before the recent economic bust, America's economic expansion left most employees behind.

The gulf between the compensation for most employees and top management has reached unparalleled heights. Top managers receive record pay, whether they are successful or not. To take one of many examples, Barry Diller made $295 million in 2005 as CEO of his diverse conglomerate IAC/Interactive even though stockholders lost money in the preceding 5 years. The large amounts paid to top managers had only a small influence on the corporate bottom line in the past. Today, they have grown so large that they drain off a significant portion of major organization's profits. With their own benefits no longer rising in real terms, many employees are concluding that their organization thinks little of their contributions to its success and has little concern for their welfare.

Unreasonable work pressure is another signal of an uncaring management. Increasingly, organizations use technological advances and workforce reductions to squeeze greater effort from employees. Real-time computer control and monitoring is used to enforce faster speeds in a growing number of jobs. Call center employees have their time per call monitored, requiring completion of increasing numbers of calls per hour. This is readily apparent for consumers whose calls to many customer service centers are received by poorly trained personnel who are pressured to get the caller off the line as soon as possible.

New technology is often used as an excuse to reduce a company's workforce, leaving the survivors to do more work than they did before. Wal-Mart's highly effective merchandise tracking and delivery systems channel just-on-time merchandise deliveries to store work crews that are deliberately understaffed. Profit is maximized by working employees to the breaking point. At Wal-Mart, employees are told they must finish their often unreasonable workload at the end of the day no matter how difficult the job (Fishman, 2006).

Higher level jobs are not immune from increased work brought about by technology. By providing an excuse for eliminating traditional support jobs, such as secretarial help, the computer has made many professional jobs harder. Now, managers, professors, chemists, and engineers are often required to prepare reports, manuscripts, proposals, and presentations on their own. Computer and portable communication devices make more work, not less, and make it easier to demand completion of work assignments at night and weekends.

Ageism, managers' perception that older employees are less competent and less motivated, contributes to unfavorable treatment of veteran employees in many organizations. Older workers are much less likely than younger workers to have training and development opportunities at work to update their knowledge and skills or acquire new ones (Armstrong-Stassen & Ursel, 2009). Many would like to gradually reduce the amount of work they are doing, but few are given the flexibility of doing so. The U.S. has always been a vibrant society, welcoming new ideas provided by young scientists, inventors, engineers, and advertisers. But the emphasis on youth has been tempered by a respect for veteran insiders' accumulated knowledge and skills. However, the emphasis on short-term financial gains over the past several decades works against this useful balance.

Rapid promotion paths for young managers often places individuals in power who view their own career trajectory as evidence that those who have occupied the same job a long time are has-beens. Thus, veteran employees, who receive high pay because of accumulated yearly tenure, are often seen as an unnecessary drain on profit. A top Wal-Mart executive complained that "the cost of an associate with 7 years of tenure is almost 55% more than the cost of an associate with 1 year of tenure, yet there is no difference in his or her productivity" (Leonhardt, 2007). In April 2007, Circuit City, a retailer of consumer electronics, laid off 8% of its veteran workforce on the grounds that they were being paid too much money because of seniority, with the intention of replacing these employees with new, lower paid employees (Leonhardt, 2007). As implicit guarantees of long-term employment have frayed, nervousness concerning job security has particularly affected veteran employees. Older employees understand that finding a job elsewhere, should they be laid off, will be particularly difficult.

Higher level managers can achieve short-term profits, albeit at the expense of the long-term welfare of the organization, by replacing well-paid veteran employees with less-experienced and often poorly trained young people who will accept low pay. To promote this policy, it has become common in recent years to lay off experienced workers or offer them early retirement bonuses. Discrimination against older workers may be illegal under federal law, but any clever manager can disguise such discrimination by making the layoff of older workers appear to be the inadvertent consequence of a seemingly reasonable lay-off scheme. This emphasis on cost savings has spread to school systems and colleges where veteran teachers and professors are often given early retirement bonuses so that their positions can be filled by brand new teachers and researchers willing to be paid less.

News concerning layoffs of veteran employees, sometimes accompanied by the hire of lower paid employees, conveys a message of general disdain to most survivors in the organization. Large-scale layoffs and plant closings are given substantial news coverage, increasing fears of layoffs nationally. This may be one reason employees did not take advantage of very low unemployment rates in the years before the recent economic downturn to demand substantial wage increases.

Employers who feel that the large majority of their employees are dime-a-dozen inferiors who should be discarded whenever convenient know better than to state these views publicly, which would undermine morale and generate unflattering publicity. Many managers intuitively recognize that expressions of positive valuation of employees are useful: People who lack power take solace in the kindly words from those in power. It pays to convince as many employees as possible that the company values them: Those who become emotionally attached to their organization accomplish more, are absent less often, and are less likely to quit (Meyer & Allen, 1997). Individuals with strong needs for approval and for whom employment constitutes an important part of their identity will feel better about their jobs and themselves, to some extent, even without favorable treatment.

If, for example, Wal-Mart denies employees a living wage and uses their employees' fear of being let go to enforce acceptance of exhausting workloads and obedience to stringent work rules, its corporate executives nevertheless attempt to convince as many workers as possible that they are valued members of a caring, happy family. According to Wal-Mart's founder, Sam Walton,

> My feeling is that just because we work so hard, we don't have to go around with long faces all the time—while we're doing all of this work, we like to have a good time. It's sort of a "'whistle while you work"' philosophy, and we not only have a heck of a good time with it, we work better because of it. (Silverman, 2004).

Employees are gathered each day for the official cheer: "Give me a *W*, give me an *A*," with a group wriggle for the dash in the company name and topped off with a loud hand clap and an exuberant, "Let's go!" (Piasecki, 2002). Wal-Mart executives understand that subpar pay and medical benefits lead to unstable family life, resulting in increased absenteeism and turnover. To reduce these outcomes, human resource personnel counsel employees on how to apply for public assistance, such as food stamps and health care (Featherstone, 2005; Head, 2004). This facade of a "Wal-Mart Family" does convince a minority of employees that the corporation cares about them, whereas the less satisfied employees are among the half of all Wal-Mart employees who quit each year.

Wal-Mart management's true attitude toward its employees is indicated by the unreasonable work demands that result from purposeful understaffing to reduce costs, by poor pay and fringe benefits, and by extraordinary efforts to block unionization efforts. Wal-Mart is a prime example of the dismissive orientation held by many companies toward their employees: Pay them little and keep them working as hard as possible and as long as possible before they quit or the company decides to replace them with lower paid employees or automated processes.

Demise of the Social Contract

The devaluation of employees by many American corporations differs greatly from employees' treatment during the 2 decades following World War II, a time when paternalistic attitudes among managers were more common, and labor unions represented a quarter of the workforce. Relationships between employee and employer were strongly influenced by an implicit social contract that encouraged employers to provide long-term employment in exchange for diligence and loyalty. Management's enlightened approach was promoted by the knowledge that replacing skilled workers was expensive, especially in times of economic boom, so that the organization's favorable treatment of employees had advantages. Additionally, labor unions secured a balance of power between employees and management. Thus, most skilled employees who worked for large organizations at midcentury could expect to earn a comfortable living working for many years with the same employer if they did their jobs well.

In those days, employees in many organizations could look forward to a long career there, if they wished, with good wages. The relationship might sometimes be stormy, as when union employees engaged in a prolonged strike or when management temporarily laid off workers because of a severe economic downturn. But the prospect of long-term employment with the same organization and steadily increasing wages and benefits led the majority of employees to identify strongly with their organization. It was not unusual for father, son, and grandson to follow one another into employment at General Motors or Bethlehem Steel.

Although unions protected employee rights and brought members considerable economic gain, they also often reduced productivity by insisting on inflexible work rules, better to guard against a faster work pace, a loss of jobs because of automation, and a blurring of the distinction between management and worker functions that might erode union influence. Further, many union contracts required uniformity of pay, regardless of performance, and made the firing of poorly performing workers difficult.

The economic crisis of the early 1970s, when the Japanese seemed destined to overtake the United States as the world's leading economic power, provided a strong impetus for staid American companies to embrace technological change and to alter their traditional long-term relationships with labor. Japan's great economic success came, in part, because its companies were able to produce consumer goods of exceptionally high quality while exploiting employees through required long hours of work, a faster assembly line, and low pay. Japanese employees' tolerance of poor working conditions was encouraged by their strong Confucian work ethic, a history of obedience to authority, and weak union representation (Eisenberger, 1989).

In the United States, global competition became a rationale for moving factories overseas and served as an excuse for low pay, regimentation, and increasing work pace in the manufacturing jobs that this country retained. Union membership declined as manufacturing jobs moved overseas and to anti-union locales in the American South and West. Employers insisted that they needed the flexibility to hire or fire, pay poorly or well, and promote employees slowly or quickly to remain competitive. Management's power was strengthened by the reluctance of the federal government to enforce employees' right to organize and bargain collectively. Also, younger workers with no memory of past union successes failed to see any benefit of joining unions.

Washington's deregulation of the transportation industry and firing of air traffic controllers, who had illegally gone on strike, encouraged a new era in which the power of unions steadily drained away. The reduced enforcement of federal protections for union organization and strikes hastened the decline of union membership. As union influence dwindled, covering far more public than private sector employees, companies felt they had the freedom to impose harsh work demands on employees while limiting pay increases or actually cutting current pay and benefits.

The emphasis on unfettered capitalism and the simultaneous weakening of labor unions in the final decades of the 20th century led to a considerable increase in the power of organizations over employees. The social contract between employer and employee began to fray, especially in large corporations. Here, the business community's former idealization of long-term profitability gave way to the concept of maximizing shareholders' value, which came increasingly to mean simply the short-term price of stocks. Career advancement and rewards for managers in the form of stock options and bonuses were positively related to increased quarterly profits. These changes lead to a lack of concern with the long-term welfare of employees.

Managers were well aware that stock prices were sensitive to short-term cash flow and profit. Short-term profit was often enhanced by layoffs and limitations on wage increases and benefits, including the defunding of reserves for future employee pensions. Although global competition was often used as the reason for holding down wages and benefits, it is notable that foreign competition involves mostly manufacturing, which relates to only one in eight U.S. employees. Yet, wages have also stagnated for the substantial majority of working people who held service jobs (Head, 2005, pp. 4, 188). Thus, the goal of short-term profit, more than foreign competition, is the reason for the stagnation of wages for most Americans. The conglomeration and reorganization of large segments of American business with resultant large numbers of layoffs (of more lasting influence than the recent economic downturn) have created a climate of fear in which employees are reluctant to contest adverse treatment.

These changes are associated with a loss of commitment by many organizations to the welfare of the majority of their employees. As we demonstrate in Chapters 5 through 7 of this volume, such lack of support of employees has had negative consequences for employees' psychological well-being, the favorableness of their orientation toward their organization, and their efforts on behalf of the organization.

The Supportive Organization

Although most American employees no longer have the supportive relationships with their employers of their forebears, many well-known and highly successful organizations strongly encourage employees' contributions to their success. Companies such as Southwest Airlines and Costco insist that they owe a significant portion of their growth and profitability to a workforce that is truly dedicated to helping the organization fulfill its objectives. These organizations communicate through word and deed their positive valuation of employees. As we subsequently document in Chapters 6 and 7, most employees who are treated supportively reciprocate with greater dedication to their work and generally do a better job of contributing to their organization's objectives.

The advantages for organizations of treating employees supportively, including greater employee loyalty, dedication, and effective performance, have received little attention in the popular press beyond stories generated by *FORTUNE*'s annual list of the best 100 U.S. companies for which to work. On the contrary, Wall Street is suspicious of companies that foster long-term employment and organizationwide high wages. Thus, Costco's well-publicized generous wage and benefit policies have been widely cited as one reason such a growing and profitable company was compared unfavorably with Wal-Mart. Indeed, Costco's stock price lagged for years until continued increases in sales and profitability forced analysts and investors to concede that the company could be generous to employees and still be highly profitable.

Wal-Mart's strategy of treating workers poorly to drive down costs appears to work to a company's long-term economic benefit only under special circumstances, in part because the costs of recruiting and training to replace large numbers of disgruntled workers who quit are quite high (Reichfield, 1996). From a purely business perspective, low pay for hard work under poor conditions seems to be an effective strategy only when low job skills are required, when monitoring can readily detect the poor performance of disgruntled workers, and when there is a sufficient pool of labor willing to replace the large numbers of employees who will quit. Employees quit at high rates both because of their unhappiness at the organization and because they do not have the funds and medical insurance to pay their rents and take care of medical bills, so their own and family illnesses push them out of their homes. Customers of such businesses must be willing to tolerate poor service both because employees are poorly trained and staffing is inadequate.

A little-known finding is that during the 1990s, *FORTUNE*'s list of the 100 best U.S. companies for which to work, reflecting supportive treatment of employees, produced substantially greater returns to shareholders than the average returns of the broad stock indexes ("Great workplaces," 2010). Consider, for example, Google, the world's most successful Internet company. Employees receive a wide diversity of free amenities, including day care, meals, a gym, and transportation to and from work. The organization communicates its positive valuation of employee contributions by encouraging them to spend 20% of their time pursuing their own ideas (Auletta, 2009). On Fridays, the cofounders meet with all employees at the main campus and through teleconference to present news about Google, welcome new employees, and engage in a frank question-and-answer period. Numerous internal e-mail lists are used to discuss and elaborate complaints and suggestions, which are given careful consideration by management. New products are often assessed internally, providing employees an opportunity to weigh in with suggestions for improvement (http://www.greatplacetowork.com/best/list-bestusa-2007.htm).

The stories of companies like Costco, Southwest Airlines, Google, and others we discuss in later chapters are inspiring because they suggest that highly successful organizations can be effective because of—not despite—treating employees supportively. However valuable the insights of the founders of such organizations, these insights need to be integrated into a more precise theory.

Chapter 2 describes the development of organizational support theory, designed to explain what exactly constitutes supportive treatment, how it develops, and how it affects employees' beliefs, attitudes, motives, and behaviors at work. In subsequent chapters, we lay out the evidence for the theory and its implications for management practice.

Perceived Organizational Support

2

E mployers would naturally prefer to have employees carry out their job responsibilities earnestly. Employers who take the human capital view believe that the great majority of employees have the potential to contribute to the organization's success and that the organization should help employees realize their potential. Employers who take the marginal capital position hold that most employees are, at best, a limited, short-term benefit to the organization—losers who should be replaced as soon as convenient by such means as efficiencies or the hiring of others who are willing to the do the same job for less pay. But even employers taking the marginal capital view prefer a dedicated workforce, although not one deserving of more than the minimal needed resources to keep voluntary turnover at a level low enough to prevent costly disruptions in normal organizational functions.

Employees, in contrast, are generally concerned with the organization's value for them. Employees believe they are recipients of enduring evaluations by the organization that influence how they are treated. As we discuss, employees' perceptions of positive valuation of the organization are welcomed because they fulfill socioemotional needs (e.g., approval, esteem, affiliation, emotional support), indicate the organization's readiness to provide future resources to help employees do their jobs well, and suggest the organization's willingness to reward increased efforts by employees.

Two decades ago, my students and I began thinking about the relationship between the employee and work organization from the employee's viewpoint. Several early studies had suggested that employees' perception of positive valuation by the organization enhances employees' favorable orientation toward the organization and behaviors helpful to the organization. Buchanan (1974) found, with managers in business and government, that beliefs that the organization recognized their contributions and could be depended on to fulfill promises were related to a positive emotional bond to the organization (*affective organizational commitment*). Steers (1977) reported similar effects of the same beliefs on the affective organizational commitment of hospital staff, engineers, and scientists. Cook and Wall (1980), using a large and diverse sample of British blue-collar workers, found that trust in management to treat employees fairly was positively related to attitudinal measures of employees' identification, involvement, and loyalty. Hrebiniak (1974) found with hospital staff that perceiving the organizational environment as "benign, cooperative, or consistent" increased the rated utility of continued employment in the organization.

It occurred to us that employees might develop a general belief concerning the extent to which the organization values their contributions and cares about their well-being (Eisenberger, Huntington, Hutchison, & Sowa, 1986). We termed this employee belief *perceived organizational support,* and it is now frequently referred to simply as *POS.* We were proposing that beyond beliefs related to the specific benefits provided by the organization, employees generalize about the organization's supportiveness directed toward them. In the years since we proposed this idea, hundreds of scholarly studies have been carried out confirming the view that employees develop a general perception concerning the organization's support. As these studies began to indicate the importance of perceived organizational support for understanding employees' relationship with the work organization, My colleagues and I developed *organizational support theory* to explain and predict the causes of perceived organizational support and the positive consequences of perceived organizational support for employees' psychological well-being, positive orientation toward the organization, and work outcomes favorable to the organization. This book considers these topics and discusses practical steps that managers can take to instill perceived organizational support in employees.

Perceived organizational support, when we first thought about it, was just a concept, an idea. Beyond our intuitive sense that employees formed perceptions about organizational support in their relationships with their organizations and our knowledge of a few preliminary studies that pointed to employees' generalizations about organizational benevolence, we had no real evidence that employees form a general belief that incorporates their positive valuation by the organization as well as the organization's concern for their well-being. To name a new psychological construct does not mean it necessarily does a good job explaining anything.

To find out, we constructed 36 statements representing various possible favorable or unfavorable judgments of employees by the organization and discretionary actions the organization might take in diverse situations to benefit or harm employees. Evidence that employees form global beliefs concerning their valuation by the organization would be indicated by an employee's perception that the organization's various judgments of him or her are consistently favorable or unfavorable to a high or low degree, and the expectancy that the organization would treat the employee beneficially or harmfully, to a consistent degree, in a variety of situations.

We included statements referring to evaluative judgments that the organization might have concerning satisfaction with the employee as a member of the organization and with the employee's performance; anticipation of the employee's future value; appreciation of the employee's extra effort; consideration of the employee's goals and opinions; and the organization's concerns about fair pay, job enrichment, full use of the employee's talents, the employee's satisfaction on the job, and the employee's well-being. Statements referring to actions affecting the employee that the organization would be likely to take in hypothetical situations included willingness to help with job problems; replacing the employee with a lower paid new employee; responses to the employee's possible complaints, mistakes, worsened performance, improved performance, requested change of working conditions, requested special favor, decision to quit, and failure to complete a task on time; rehiring after layoff; and opportunities for promotion.

We asked 361 employees in a variety of occupations (e.g., postal clerks, financial trust company employees, manufacturing white-collar employees, high school teachers) to express their degree of agreement with each of the statements in the just-described Survey of Perceived Organizational Support. Employees' degree of agreement with each of the 36 statements that were designed to assess perceived organizational support was predictive from a moderate to high degree of their agreement with each of the other statements. For example, employees' agreement with the statement "The organization really cares about my well-being" was highly related to their agreement with the statement "The organization takes pride in my accomplishments at work" and was strongly related in the negative direction to the statement "The organization feels that anyone could perform my job as well as I do."[1] These findings

---

[1]Exploratory and confirmatory factor analyses indicate a unitary perception of positive valuation and caring by the organization (Rhoades & Eisenberger, 2002).

suggest that employees think of the organization as having a distinctive view toward them that includes valuing their contributions and caring about their well-being.

Subsequent studies have confirmed that employees show consistently high, medium, or low agreement with a variety of statements concerning the organization's valuation of their contributions and the likelihood that the organization will treat them favorably in various situations (e.g., Eisenberger, Fasolo, & Davis-LaMastro, 1990; Eisenberger et al., 1986; Shore & Tetrick, 1991; Shore & Wayne, 1993). They form a general perception regarding the organization's valuation of their contributions and concern about their well-being.

This result was certainly not preordained. Some of the students working with me raised the possibility that employees' beliefs about the organization's valuation of their contributions might be independent of, or only slightly dependent on, their views regarding the organization's concern about their well-being. However, the data were clear. These two potential aspects of organizational benevolence are merged in the perception of employees. We were surprised that every statement was related to an acceptable degree to every other statement—we had to discard no statements. This is very unusual in the development of a new scale, especially when a large number of items are used. Normally, during scale development clusters of items may be more related to each other than to the original concept the investigators had in mind. This did not happen here.

Because of the simplicity of the concept of perceived organizational support and the excellent way the scale items fit the construct, over 95% of studies on perceived organizational support use the Survey of Perceived Organizational Support. Most of the remaining studies appear to result from consulting arrangements with organizations in which the investigators were constrained to use standardized items not specifically designed to assess perceived organizational support. When interesting findings have resulted from scales that seem to approximate the Survey of Perceived Organizational Support, we discuss them along with the studies using the more standard measurement.

We presented a sample of eight statements from the Survey of Perceived Organizational Support in the Introduction to this book. If you skipped the Introduction, we suggest you take a look at the items now. If you find yourself in slight agreement with most of the positive items and slight disagreement with most of the negative items, you are like most employees. However, there is considerable variation in perceived organizational support from within organizations and from one organization to another. Organizations that view employees as valued human capital and treat them supportively produce high perceived organizational support from most employees. Organizations that treat employees poorly, such as Wal-Mart and U.S. Airways, produce low perceived organizational support. Supportive organizations, such as Google, Whole Foods, and Southwest Airlines, score high on perceived organizational support because they follow the intuitive precepts of their founders who were wise enough and forceful enough to establish a supportive culture. However, as we shall see, even these organizations have much to learn from the theory and scholarly research of hundreds of studies on perceived organizational support that form the basis of this book.

Employees' perceived organizational support changes over time in response to their treatment by the organization. I have found, for example, in most of the organizations I have studied that perceived organizational support initially drops during the first 6 months of employment for the majority of employees as organizations become less attentive to their new employees' needs and concerns. My studies show that many changes in perceived organizational support occur slowly over a period of months and years as employees slowly come to feel more appreciated or less appreciated by the organization.

On the other hand, abrupt events can have great symbolic meaning to employees out of proportion to what one might expect. Sometimes, these events may indicate a callous disregard for employees' welfare, producing a substantial reduction of perceived organizational support. I was once administering an attitude survey to a particular shift of employees and was surprised when seven employees in the same session adamantly refused to take the survey. Asked why, they explained they had recently been docked a day's pay when they had been unable to come to work because of a severe snowstorm. They had been told that they should have gotten to work despite the storm. When the employees complained about this decision, they were told that some others had made it through the storm and they should have as well. Thus, the decision could not be attributed to an oversight or mistake. Several employees angrily vented their frustration and anger. They believed that the company wanted them to greatly endanger their safety to maintain the normal production schedule. There was no way the employees' loss of perceived organizational support, which affected their cooperativeness, in any nonrequired activity such as the survey, was going to be ameliorated any time soon. Further, other employees heard about the treatment of these employees and considered the aversive treatment of their coworkers a callous indifference to the well-being of all, which had missed them by chance. As a result, the perceived organizational support of the entire organization suffered. Other sudden events that cloud one's own future, such as downsizing of fellow employees, can also cause a sudden reduction of perceived organizational support.

Unexpected positive events can also increase perceived organizational support. Once every few weeks, a friend of mine who had retired as head of a university graduate program and was a person who was usually cynical about the motives of others, would repeatedly tell the following story with great enthusiasm:

> Thirty years ago, I was walking to my mail box at school and I noticed a letter from the university president's office. I opened it up and it was a personal letter to me from the president saying he knew of my contributions and thanking me for them. And the letter contained a check for a thousand dollars. Can you imagine? He took the time to find about my work and he showed how much he appreciated it.

At this point, my friend would beam and wait expectantly look for us for affirmation. Though much of our time with our friend was normally spent in a game of friendly insults, neither I nor anyone with me could ever bring ourselves to ruin his pleasure by responding with what normally would have been a sarcastic, if humorous comeback. My friend's general cynicism was countered by the organization's recognition of his work in a way that stood out as something special. The financial reward was small relative to my friend's salary but the favorable recognition of the president's letter and the way the president found to make the recognition seem personal and significant had a strong influence on his perceived organizational support.

In this chapter, we discuss the theoretical framework for understanding how perceived organizational support operates.

Social Exchange: A Major Cause of Work Engagement

Most employees with high perceived organizational support respond with a more favorable orientation toward their organization and greater efforts on its behalf. One important basis for these responses can be usefully understood as what has been termed *social exchange*. For many years, organizational theorists have alluded to employment as the trade of effort and loyalty for material and socioemotional rewards (e.g., Etzioni, 1961; Gould, 1979; Levinson, 1965; March & Simon, 1958; Mowday, Porter, & Steers, 1982; Porter, Steers, Mowday, & Boulian, 1974). These approaches emphasize the gain to organizations produced by the beneficial treatment of employees. Favorable work experiences have, for example, been linked to employees' emotional bond to the organization (Meyer & Allen, 1997; Mowday et al., 1982) and to their willingness to go beyond explicitly required responsibilities in responding flexibly to organizational problems and opportunities (George & Brief, 1992). Social exchange theories advance understanding of why some employees are motivated more than others to help the organization achieve its goals. These theories differ from many traditional accounts of employee motivation by embedding employees' motives to carry out specific activities within the mutual obligations between employees and employers (Aselage & Eisenberger, 2003).

THE NATURE OF SOCIAL EXCHANGE

Social exchange accounts maintain that individuals enter into relationships with others to maximize their gain of resources (P. M. Blau, 1964; Homans, 1974). Social exchange theory first arose to explain the development and maintenance of interpersonal relationships and was later extended to organizations. Social exchange is actually a general view of the basics of social interaction from which specific theories may be developed. Although there are significant differences between individuals' relationships with other persons and their relationship with their work organization, social exchange theory provides a basis for analyzing both.

According to social exchange theory, identifying individuals who are strongly committed to a social relationship allows "individuals to invest their resources in reinforcing those stable dispositions in others which are maximally beneficial to themselves" (M. S. Greenberg, 1980, p. 5; see also Brinberg & Castell, 1982; Heider, 1958; E. E. Jones & Davis, 1965; Organ & Konovsky, 1989; Schopler, 1970). Individuals try to understand why another person has treated them favorably or unfavorably so they will know whether and how to maintain and strengthen the relationship. This allows people to (a) better predict the circumstances under which similar treatment will occur in the future, (b) alter their behavior to increase the likelihood of positive treatment, and (c) evaluate the general effectiveness of their strategies for interacting with the other person.

POSITIVE NORM OF RECIPROCITY

The norm of *reciprocity* (i.e., calling for the return or repayment of favorable treatment) is a key concept in social exchange theory. The reciprocity norm has been termed universal because it has been found to be influential in every culture in which it has been studied, whether primitive or modern. Although some individuals do not repay favorable treatment, the great majority of people do so because they are inculcated with the reciprocity norm as a moral virtue or because they fear retribution or damage to their reputation for violating the norm (Gouldner, 1960). Meeting this obligation helps maintain the self-image of those who repay their debts, avoids the stigma associated with norm violations, and encourages future favorable treatment (Eisenberger, Armeli, Rexwinkel, Lynch, & Rhoades, 2001). Many carefully controlled studies demonstrate that the greater the benefits received when interacting with another person, the higher the benefits generally returned (e.g., Berkowitz & Friedman, 1967; DePaulo, Brittingham, & Kaiser, 1983; M. S. Greenberg & Bar-Tal, 1976; M. S. Greenberg & Frisch, 1972).

The resources people give and receive from others can be impersonal; that is, the value of benefits does not depend on the identity of the sender—for example, providing information or money (U. G. Foa & Foa, 1974). Alternatively, the resources can be socioemotional, such as the communication of caring or respect. According to social exchange theory, individuals, sometimes consciously and sometimes unconsciously, weigh the amount of such resources to be extended to another person against such costs as the physical or mental fatigue incurred in the social relationship, forgone opportunities for interactions with others (Thibaut & Kelley, 1959), lost leisure time (Rachlin, Battalio, Kagel, & Green, 1981), and the temporary satiation that reduces the value of social rewards supplied by a particular partner (P. M. Blau, 1964). A long-term relationship develops if each partner provides a reliable source of desirable resources.

The underlying assumption is that individuals distribute their investments in social relationships to obtain the combination of resources having the greatest expected value. Such calculations rise to the conscious level at times when there is a sudden change in opportunity or cost. For example, one may think, "I really want to get to know this person better." Or, in a less lucky case, "This is the most boring person I have ever met—How can I escape?" However, social exchange theory allows for these calculations to be made at a subconscious level beyond people's understanding. For example, a person may have only a vague understanding of how hard he or she is trying to impress a prospective romantic partner with attractive qualities.

It seems odd and counterintuitive to apply the norm of reciprocity to friendships and romantic relationships. Little children may say, "I will be your friend if you will be mine," but our culture holds that liking, respect, and other valuations of the inner nature of a friend or romantic partner are supposed to be based on the inner qualities of the individual, not the fact that the other individual thinks highly of you. Yet, similar kinds of socioemotional resources do get exchanged. For example, a supervisor may subconsciously feel obligated to care more about a subordinate because this subordinate shows him or her respect. Social exchange theory claims that socioemotional resources are exchanged with similar socioemotional resources. For example, people tend to like those who like them. As we discuss, there is strong evidence that perceived organizational support elicits a positive orientation by employees toward the organization partly on the basis of the norm of reciprocity.

Social exchange relationships differ from more purely economic relationships in their emphasis on longer term outcomes with greater trust by each partner that the other will act in good faith; thus, a careful count of who receives what in the relationship is unnecessary, and the partners rely instead on the expectation that one's investment in the other individual will be fairly rewarded. Applying social exchange theory to the relationship between the employee and the organization, the more the social exchange relationship strengthens, the more employees can focus on acting in ways that benefit the organization, believing that they will be justly rewarded and without worrying that the organization will take advantage of them by failing to reciprocate appropriately. Shore, Tetrick, Lynch, and Barksdale (2006) noted three features of social exchange relationships that contribute make them satisfying to employees. *Trust* in the benevolent intentions of the organization provides assurance that the organization will not violate the reciprocity norm by failing to take into account the employees' efforts on its behalf. Trust encourages the employees' investment of increased resources of time and effort to aid the organization with the expectation that the organization will respond with more favorable treatment of the employee. Finally, employees can take a long-term view of their relationship with the organization so that they can think about benefits of substantial investments of time and effort.

This is not to say that economic benefits are unimportant in social exchange relationships between employee and employer. Social exchange encompasses employees' receipt of pay and fringe benefits no less than socioemotional resources such as approval and esteem. In social exchange relationships, employees tend to be more trusting and have a more long-term outlook concerning their receipt of economic resources.

Coyle-Shapiro and Shore (2007) suggested that other norms besides reciprocity may play an important role in the relationship between employee and employer, and they cited the possible relevance of Clark and Mills's (1979) concept of communal exchange, in which each partner meets the needs of the other without the expectation that the benefits will be reciprocated. Clark and Mills found in experimental situations that when a single college student meets a single attractive individual, the student becomes less concerned with the other's repayment of a small obligation than when the student believes he or she is meeting someone who is married and therefore unavailable. Such findings have been widely interpreted to indicate that a norm of communal exchange replaces the norm of reciprocity when a person desires a strong relationship with another. An alternative explanation is that when a person meets someone new, the possibility of a future strong relationship shifts one's concern with reciprocation from a small repayment to a larger investment. If, for example, one has just met another individual who appears to a possible romantic partner, an insistence on splitting the bill for a meal or the price of gas conveys the message precisely that one is interested more in economic exchange than social exchange.

Consider the difference between students entering a temporary job over a vacation period versus their first long-term job after graduation.

One would expect the students to be more concerned with monitoring their work situation in the temporary situation to ensure that minor obligations on the part of the employer were being met. In contrast, graduating students would generally have a longer term perspective, being more concerned with a balancing of give and take over the long run and with socioemotional benefits than students taking a temporary job.

Applying social exchange theory to employees' relationship with their organization, employees would be expected to reciprocate favorable treatment received from the organization with greater efforts on its behalf and a reduction of such withdrawal behaviors as absenteeism and quitting. Two major theories apply social exchange theory to the employee–organization relationship. Psychological contract theory, discussed in Chapter 3, holds that on the basis of information given them about the organization, employees develop beliefs about their mutual obligations with the organization and react unfavorably when those obligations are not met. Organizational support theory considers employees' favorable reactions to their positive valuations by the organization.

Social exchange theory is often misunderstood as asserting that people engage only in short-term or conscious calculations or are moved primarily by material gain as opposed to socioemotional considerations. This confuses social exchange theory with economic exchange. On the contrary, social exchange involves longer term relationships based on trust. Further, social exchange can involve impersonal resources, socioemotional resources, or both. The inaccurate portrayals of social exchange as economic exchange by many who disagree with social exchange theory have been so persistent over the years that one suspects some individuals prefer willful ignorance on the topic to argue against an easily defeated caricature of the theory rather than its reality. As we discuss, social exchange theory provides key truths about the importance of employees' positive response to perceived organizational support. On the other hand, we also examine certain employee mind-sets, such as identification and commitment, that require new principles that do not readily follow from social exchange theory.

The sociologist Alvin Gouldner (1958) noted that partners in developing social relationships often give each other more help than previously received, which seems to violate social exchange theory's emphasis on maximizing personal gain. He suggested that such overcompensation is an investment based on the belief that one's partner will reciprocate accordingly. Gouldner called the reciprocity norm a *starting mechanism* in the development of interpersonal relationships. By this, he meant that the reciprocity norm encourages people to be helpful by creating the expectancy that when one helps others meet their needs and desires, these others will, in turn, help one achieve his or her own goals. Thus, people are helpful to others partly with the expectation that the favorable treatment will be returned. This is indicated by studies showing that recipients of help return greater aid when they expect to interact with their benefactor in the future (e.g., Danheiser & Graziano, 1982; J. Greenberg, 1979) or when there is evidence that the benefactor's resources will increase in the future (Pruitt, 1968). Both the giver and receiver benefit from the reciprocity norm because each acts to meet the differing needs of the other.

This give and take of favorable treatment allows partners in developing social relationships to investigate the level of benefits each will feel comfortable providing the other, taking into account the costs. In casual relationships, the benefits exchanged tend to focus on less personally revealing communications and gestures of caring, including expressions of interest in one's partner, conversation about topics of common interest, and companionship during leisure activities. In close friendships or romantic relationships, the exchanges include stronger expressions of caring, self-disclosure of personal beliefs or intimate feelings, and attempts to meet the emotional needs of the partner.

The positive reciprocity norm applies to employee–employer relationships as well as interpersonal relationships, obliging employees to recompense favorable or unfavorable treatment. In the case of advantageous treatment received from the organization, employees can reciprocate by helping the organization achieve its objectives. If there is an opportunity, employees may work harder or more carefully in standard job activities. Or they may increase such extrarole or citizenship activities as volunteering for overtime work, making suggestions to improve the functioning of the organization, and protecting the organization when unexpected problems arise. As we discuss later in this chapter, perceived organizational support is valued by employees and therefore creates a felt obligation to repay the organization with greater efforts on its behalf.

Individuals hold beliefs in the ways they should apply the norm of reciprocity in terms of their readiness to invest in others and accept and even encourage the indebtedness of others. M. S. Greenberg and Westcott (1983) proposed that some individuals, termed *creditors*, believe more strongly than others that it is appropriate and efficacious to obligate others by giving rewards of greater value than previously received.

Eisenberger, Cotterell, and Marvel (1987) had college students take part in a bargaining situation with a partner who possessed high resources or low resources and was programmed to act generously or stingily. Partners with a strong creditor belief tended to invest more in two types of partners: a partner with high resources who acted stingily and a partner with low resources who acted generously. Creditors are evidently interested in attracting those with high potential resources or those with lesser resources who can be counted on to be generous with them. Individuals with a strong creditor belief show foresight by using the norm of reciprocity to obligate others. Such a strategy generally benefits a creditor because the majority of people accept the norm and having had their needs met by the creditor, return resources desired by the creditor. Subsequent research (Cotterell, Eisenberger, & Speicher, 1992) found that friends and roommates of high creditors evaluated them as warm and caring individuals, reflecting their favored treatment.

NEGATIVE NORM OF RECIPROCITY

Just as there is a positive norm of reciprocity that calls for the return of favorable treatment, there is a negative norm that invites the reciprocation of mistreatment (Eisenberger, Lynch, Aselage, & Rohdieck, 2004). Harm returned for harm received is a venerable moral precept that is widely accepted because it serves the social purpose of preventing mistreatment and provides a justification for the natural tendency toward revenge. The principle of retaliation (*lex. talionis*) was stated some 3,000 years ago in the Hammurabian code, later in Aristotle's writings, and in the biblical injunction of "A life for life, eye for eye, tooth for tooth . . . bruise for bruise."

In common usage, the term *retribution* emphasizes the return of unfavorable treatment as an appropriate response to a misdeed. The terms *revenge* and *vengeance* give recognition to the anger that generally accompanies an individual's return of unfavorable treatment. According to Aristotle (384–323 B.C.), a conspicuous slight without justification produces anger and an impulse toward revenge, whose fulfillment produces pleasure (Aristotle, 1941, pp. 1380–1381; see Sabini & Silver, 1982).

Justifications for interpersonal retribution have received considerable attention from philosophers, novelists, and playwrights (Henberg, 1990) but surprisingly little analysis by social scientists (see Vidmar, 2002). Gouldner's (1960) seminal explication of the reciprocity norm dealt primarily with the obligation to repay favorable treatment. However, he did briefly discuss a possible negative reciprocity norm, incorporating a retaliation principle in which "the emphasis is placed not on the return of benefits but on the return of injuries" (Gouldner, 1960, p. 172). Other researchers have similarly argued that retribution for physical and symbolic mistreatment is encouraged by a negative reciprocity norm (e.g., Cialdini, Green, & Rusch, 1992; Helm, Bonoma, & Tedeschi, 1972; Tedeschi, 1983; Youngs, 1986).

On the basis of Gouldner's (1960) view, the negative norm of reciprocity would comprise a unitary set of beliefs favoring retribution as the correct and proper way to respond to unfavorable treatment. A person's endorsement of the negative norm of reciprocity might be influenced by enculturation and by rewards or punishments received for retributive behaviors. In addition, individuals with a propensity toward anger might more strongly endorse the negative reciprocity norm as a justification for consummating their anger by punishing the instigator of mistreatment. Gouldner considered the possibilities that positive and negative reciprocity were opposite sides of the same norm or that they were two distinct norms.

My colleagues and I (Eisenberger et al., 2004) investigated the relationship between the positive and negative reciprocity norm in female college students. Students' endorsement of the positive norm was assessed by the extent of their agreement with such statements as "If someone does me a favor, I feel obligated to repay them in some way" and "I feel uncomfortable when someone does me a favor which I know I won't be able to return." The negative reciprocity norm was assessed with such statements as "If someone dislikes you, you should dislike them" and "If someone says something nasty to you, you should say something nasty back."

It was surprising that the students' endorsement of the positive and negative norms showed only a very small relationship. The students' positive reciprocity scores predicted only about 1% of their negative reciprocity scores. Thus, the degree to which individuals feel they should return mistreatment has little to do with the extent to which they feel they should return positive treatment.

We had the students take part in a study in which they expressed their views of the effectiveness of advertisements. They took turns with a confederate of the experimenter, who treated the students in one of two ways: disagreement with most of the students' comments and, on several occasions, insulting comments ("That's ridiculous, what's your problem?" "You're not very good at this") or agreement, with favorable comments. In the just-described negative treatment condition, students who strongly endorsed the negative reciprocity norm reacted with increased disagreement with the partner, greater anger, greater ridicule, less encouragement, and less positive emotional engagement. Thus, the more accepting individuals were of the negative reciprocity norm, the angrier they were at mistreatment and the more they took revenge.

The negative reciprocity norm incites employees to return disadvantageous treatment by harming the company through reduced effort and increased absenteeism or, when the provocation is extreme, by more serious actions such as theft or equipment damage (Robinson & Bennett, 1997). M. S. Mitchell and Ambrose (2007) investigated the relationship between abusive supervision and workplace deviance, involving employee behavior that violates employee norms (Bennett & Robinson, 2003). On the basis of the negative norm of reciprocity, employees may reciprocate against what they consider to be unfair treatment from the supervisor by slowing work or reducing the quality of work. But the concept of workplace deviance goes beyond this to consider violation of commonly accepted practices. When the supervisor is the source of employees' anger, this may involve such activities as making fun of one's supervisor, playing pranks on the supervisor and gossiping about the supervisor (M. S. Mitchell & Ambrose, 2007). When the organization is the source of the employee's wrath, the employee may engage in activities as stealing and withholding effort. Employees are aware that outward displays of deviance may bring sanctions on themselves, so they tend to carry them out stealthily.

Because insults and disrespect are a powerful source of anger and desire for revenge, abusive supervision, involving supervisors' sustained hostile verbal and nonverbal behaviors directed at subordinates (Tepper, 2000), may contribute greatly to negative reciprocity. M. S. Mitchell and Ambrose (2007) found that harmful behaviors directed toward coworkers, supervisors, and the organization increased with abusive mistreatment. Consistent with the view that the reciprocity norm is important in organizational deviance, these investigators found that retribution toward the supervisor for high abuse was enhanced among employees who strongly endorsed the negative reciprocity norm.

Employees' reaction to mistreatment and the role of the negative reciprocity norm in promoting vengeance warrants more attention in the study of organizational behavior. Organizational support theory has focused more on positive reactions to favorable treatment than negative reactions to unfavorable treatment. However, as Aristotle observed more than 1,500 years ago, being belittled can lead to high arousal and anger. For employees, such an attack on self-worth by the organization or its representatives might strongly diminish perceived organizational support. As we subsequently discuss, this may be one reason the organization's fair procedures have a major influence on perceived organizational support.

Social exchange theory provides helpful suggestions concerning why employees might respond positively to high perceived organizational support and negatively to low perceived organizational support. As Gouldner (1960) noted, the norm of reciprocity is a starting mechanism for strengthening social relationships. Perceived organizational support signifies to employees that the organization wants to go beyond a simple economic relationship with them because it values their contributions and cares about their well-being. By initiating such a positive relationship, the organization has invited the employee to reciprocate on the basis of the reciprocity norm. These implications of applying social exchange theory to perceived organizational support have been incorporated into organizational support theory, which seeks to offer an explanation of how perceived organizational support develops and influences employees' psychological well-being, the favorableness of their orientation toward the organization and work, and behavioral outcomes helpful to the organization.

Perceived Organizational Support: Overview of Theory and Findings

Figure 2.1 lists the major antecedents and consequences of perceived organizational support that have been investigated and the processes that organizational support theory uses to explain them. Many antecedents have been found to be positively associated with employees' happiness (subjective well-being), the favorableness of their orientation toward their organization and work, and behavioral outcomes helpful to the organization. Organizational support theory provides explanations for these relationships and predictions concerning the conditions that will be most effective in generating perceived organizational support and its favorable outcomes. The remainder of the chapter examines the key processes in organizational support theory.

Organizational support theory holds that employees personify the organization, viewing it as having a personality with benevolent or malevolent intentions toward them. According to organizational support theory, the degree to which work experiences lead to perceived organizational support depends on employees' perceptions that the organization is providing such treatment voluntarily rather than having been forced by such constraints as government regulations, union contracts, and so on. Expressions of positive regard contribute to perceived organizational support to the degree that they are discriminating and have favorable consequences (*organizational sincerity*). Actions by supervisors and other organizational agents are attributed to the organization to the extent that these individuals are identified with the organization (*organizational embodiment*).

Organizational support theory holds that several features of perceived organizational support contribute to its favorable consequences for employees and their organizations. Perceived organizational support creates felt obligation to the organization, creates an expectation of reward for increased effort, meets socioemotional needs (e.g., approval, esteem, affiliation, emotional support), and produces an expectation that help will be available when needed to perform one's job better.

PERSONIFICATION OF THE ORGANIZATION

Because people frequently describe others in evaluative terms during conversation (Hoffman, Mischel, & Baer, 1984), they recognize that they also are the recipients of numerous evaluations, even when they may not hear them directly. They generalize this experience from everyday life to their experience as employees, believing that they are under the scrutiny

FIGURE 2.1

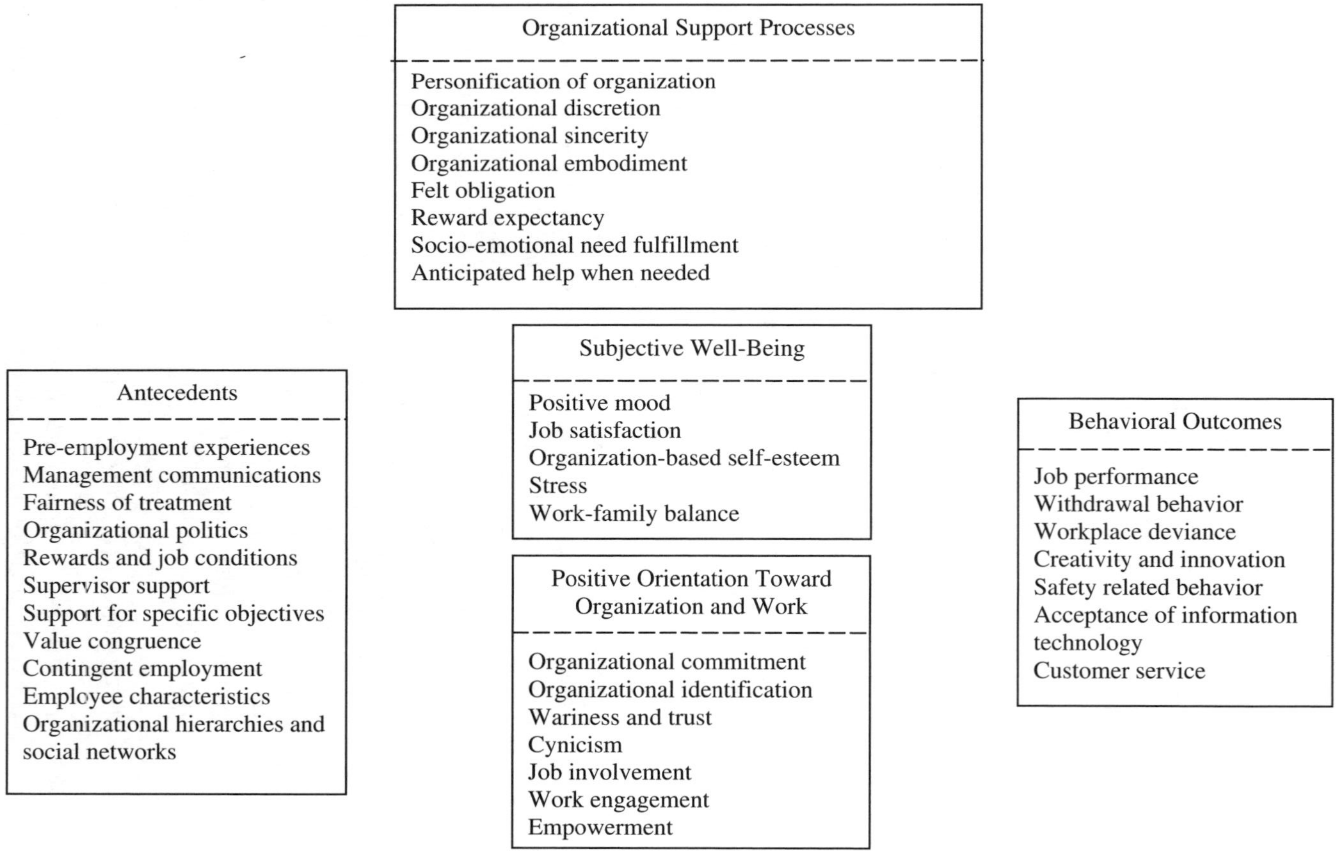

Organizational Support Processes

Personification of organization
Organizational discretion
Organizational sincerity
Organizational embodiment
Felt obligation
Reward expectancy
Socio-emotional need fulfillment
Anticipated help when needed

Subjective Well-Being

Positive mood
Job satisfaction
Organization-based self-esteem
Stress
Work-family balance

Positive Orientation Toward Organization and Work

Organizational commitment
Organizational identification
Wariness and trust
Cynicism
Job involvement
Work engagement
Empowerment

Behavioral Outcomes

Job performance
Withdrawal behavior
Workplace deviance
Creativity and innovation
Safety related behavior
Acceptance of information technology
Customer service

Antecedents

Pre-employment experiences
Management communications
Fairness of treatment
Organizational politics
Rewards and job conditions
Supervisor support
Support for specific objectives
Value congruence
Contingent employment
Employee characteristics
Organizational hierarchies and social networks

Perceived organizational support: Overview of theory and findings.

of organizational representatives. These evaluations not only include the formal reviews employees may receive periodically but also involve being scrutinized in the course of daily activities. Employees recognize that sometimes their individual performance is evaluated and at other times their evaluation is tied to the performance of others, for example, the accomplishments of one's workgroup or department. Organizational support theory assumes that to meet socioemotional needs and to determine the value of increased effort on behalf of the organization, employees form general beliefs concerning the favorableness of their evaluations by the organization as individuals and members of groups.

Employees tend to view their treatment by the organization not as the result of organizational agents acting simply as individuals with their own motives but as strongly influenced by the values and goals perpetuated by upper managers and enacted by their supervisors. Employees at various levels in the organizational hierarchy tend to experience the organization as a unitary force whether benevolent or malevolent. They view the organization as having a personality, using their everyday understanding of personality to try to comprehend why the organization acts as it does, ascribing persisting traits and motives to the organization. This view of the organization as inclined to act consistently to further its goals is enhanced by the following two factors: (a) individuals personify the organization, viewing actions by agents of the organization as actions of the organization itself (Levinson, 1965); and (b) individuals tend to attribute others' behavior to personal dispositions rather than to external pressures on them (E. E. Jones & Nisbett, 1972), especially when making inferences regarding the behavior of powerful individuals (Thibaut & Riecken, 1955).

The formation of perceived organizational support is encouraged by this tendency to ascribe humanlike characteristics to the organization. Employees tend to think of their organization as if it were a powerful individual with a personality and motives that influence the favorableness of its orientation toward them. The employee's experience of the organization as a lifelike being with its own motives is so ubiquitous and powerful that it is immediately recognizable to almost all those who have worked for organizations. Like the tip-of-the-tongue phenomenon, in which one can almost but not quite discern a word one is searching for, or the experience of flow, in which one's consciousness is enveloped in a current absorbing task (Csikszentmihalyi, 1990), the personified organization is a widespread subjective experience.

Personification of the organization, Levinson (1965) suggested, is abetted by the following factors: (a) the organization has legal, moral, and financial responsibility for the action of its agents; (b) organizational precedents, traditions, policies, and norms provide continuity and prescribe role behaviors; and (c) the organization, acting through its agents, exerts power over individual employees. The personification of the organization was assumed to represent an employee's distillation of views concerning all the other members who control the employee's material and socioemotional resources.

In the United States, the personification of the organization has been enhanced by U.S. Supreme Court rulings since 1889 recognizing the corporation as a "person" with the rights of due process and equal protection under the law (Edwards, 2002). Now, frequently, corporations rather than their managers and owners are held responsible for misdeeds. Corporations can also spend money on lobbying and influencing legislation. The U.S. Supreme Court recently loosened restrictions on corporate campaign spending as restrictions on corporate free speech, adding to the tendency to personify the organization.

Of course, organizations are not monoliths but structures operated by individuals and groups whose motives are often not perfectly aligned and sometimes may be in conflict. Yet, organizational culture, strategies, and procedures impose some predictability in the support employees receive and contribute to the formation of perceived organizational support. Moreover, employees' view of the organization as if it were a purposeful being provides the comfort of its apparent predictability. Because they personify the organization, employees view their favorable or unfavorable treatment as an indication that the organization favors or disfavors them as an individual. Even if an employee believes he is too low in the organizational hierarchy to be known personally to higher level managers, he would think of himself as viewed favorably or unfavorably as a member of a class of employees (e.g., a favored or unfavored workgroup, department, or job type) and would thus respond to favorable treatment for himself, or his group, by developing high perceived organizational support. According to organizational support theory (Eisenberger et al., 1986), this attribution of being the target of organizational benevolence meets socioemotional needs (e.g., approval, esteem, and affiliation) and signals the value of increased efforts to help the organization fulfill its objectives.

Coyle-Shapiro and Shore (2007) pointed out that research is needed on the personification process. They asked about how employees integrate sometimes contradictory treatments from different organizational agents in forming a coherent view of the personified organization. In the view of organizational support theory, employees sum up these treatments, giving more weight to those having greater influence and power in determining perceived organizational support. Thus, for example, supervisors contribute more to perceived organizational support than do coworkers. Further, organizational culture and established norms, objectives, rules, and procedures constrain individual managers from deviating too much from how other managers behave toward subordinates. The formation of perceived organizational support and the consistent and strong findings relating various antecedents to perceived organizational support suggest that employees sum up experiences to infer the organization's general orientation toward them. Yet, Coyle-Shapiro and Shore raised the intriguing possibility that organizations that have weak cultures and lack common goals and objectives may deliver mixed messages to employees concerning support to employees, leading employees to be confused about perceived organizational support. In Chapter 4, we address in more detail the ways in which employees integrate information from different organizational representatives and units in the organizational hierarchy (e.g., coworkers, supervisors, and workgroups) to form perceived organizational support. In that chapter, we also examine how employees' social networks within the organization contribute to perceived organizational support.

Coyle-Shapiro and Shore (2007) also suggested that some employees may view their relationship with the organization as involving distinctive units rather than the organization as a whole. Indeed, as we discuss in detail in Chapter 4, some organizational units may have more significance for the employee than the formal organization. In several cases of my study of conglomerates, I used the local company or division title when assessing perceived organizational support because the local entity was more meaningful to employees than the larger organizational unit. Perceived organizational support can be applied to organizational units (e.g., the supervisor, workgroup, department, divisions) as well as the organization as a whole. Moreover, as discussed in Chapter 4, organizational support theory describes how individuals generalize the support they receive from organizational units to the entire organization.

ORGANIZATIONAL DISCRETION

Favorable treatment received from the organization provides important evidence to employees of perceived organizational support. However, employees take into account the context of favorable treatment. A substantial pay raise resulting from a bitterly contested contract dispute that forces the result is attributed by employees to low, not high, perceived organizational support. Similarly, employees understand that improved working conditions may result from new government health and safety regulations rather than the organization's concern for their well-being. Thus, employees use the context in which favorable treatment occurs to infer whether the treatment was motivated by a favorable orientation toward them.

Gouldner (1960, p. 171) reasoned that favorable treatment received from others conveys positive regard to the extent that the treatment indicates a genuine concern for the welfare of the recipient. Support for this view comes from experimental studies in which the recipients of aid received different kinds of information about why the aid was being delivered. Consistent with the view that favorable treatment indicating an interest in the recipient's welfare increases participation in social relationships are findings that, holding the amount of aid constant, recipients express greater liking of the donor and/or engage in greater reciprocation as a function of each of the following factors: (a) the donor contributed a high proportion of his or her resources (Gergen, Ellsworth, Maslach, & Seipel, 1975 ; Pruitt, 1968); (b) help was voluntary as opposed to being accidental (M. S. Greenberg & Frisch, 1972; Gross & Latane, 1974) or required by external constraints (Goranson & Berkowitz, 1966; Gross & Latane, 1974; Kiesler, 1966; Nemeth, 1970); and (c) the donor was not dependent on the recipient for future aid (E. E. Jones & Davis, 1965). Similarly, the recipient's felt gratitude increases with the apparent sincerity of the donor's desire to benefit the recipient and the proportion of the donor's resources involved in the benefit (Tesser, Gatewood, & Driver, 1968).

To employees, and in social relationships generally, the receipt of material and social resources is valued more strongly when it signifies that the donor cares about the well-being of the recipient. Such positive valuation from the organization leads employees to infer that it can be counted on to reward increased participation. Just as people try to understand why other individuals treat them well or poorly in interpersonal relationships, employees attempt to ascertain the organization's reasons for treating them favorably or unfavorably. Koys (1991) compared the influence on employees' affective commitment with the organization of various positive human resource policies (e.g., training, compensation, staffing, employee relations) as a function of whether they were based on legal requirements or a desire to treat employees fairly. The organization's desire for fairness and not the motive to meet legal requirements was related to employees' affective commitment to the organization. Thus, the employees' attributions concerning the organization's intent in providing favorable treatment appear to play a major role in whether employees reciprocate with a positive bond to the organization. From the viewpoint of employees, forced good behavior on the part of the organization creates little positive reaction because it suggests little caring for employees by the organization.

A central tenet of organizational support theory (Eisenberger et al., 1986) is that favorable treatment contributes to perceived organizational support to the extent that it is considered discretionary rather than being impelled by circumstances. Discretionary actions should be a much stronger indication of the organization's favorable or unfavorable orientation toward employees than actions that appear influenced by external constraints such as union contracts or government regulations. Organizational discretion signals that favorable or unfavorable treatment represents the organization's actual regard for the employee rather than external influences over which the organization has little control.

The importance of the discretionary nature of favorable treatment for perceived organizational support was confirmed in a study carried out with college graduates working in a variety of organizations (Eisenberger, Cummings, Armeli, & Lynch, 1997). We asked employees to evaluate the favorableness and the organization's degree of control over 16 diverse job conditions (e.g., opportunity for challenging tasks, physical working conditions, relationship with supervisor, job security). We found that the positive association between the favorableness of a job condition and perceived organizational support was over 6 times greater when the organization was perceived as having high or medium discretion over the job condition than when the organization had little control over the job condition. These findings indicate that favorable treatment by organizations is strongly enhanced if an organization effectively conveys favorable treatment as discretionary.

Employees' views concerning organizational control over job conditions were broken down by the five categories of organizations we studied (private business, education, public sector, hospital, and other nonprofit institutions; Eisenberger et al., 1997). Some job conditions produced substantial disagreement, from one type of organization to another, concerning the discretionary control exerted by the organization. For example, private business employees were twice as likely as teachers to believe that their organization had high control over opportunities for advancement and were 3 times more likely than teachers to believe that their organization highly controlled time for personal life. Teachers were twice as likely as private business employees to believe that their organization highly controlled the employees' relationship with their supervisors. Thus, favorable treatment by supervisors had a relatively greater influence over perceived organizational support for teachers, whereas opportunities for advancement and time for personal life had a relatively greater influence on perceived organizational support for private business employees. Employees in different occupations paid more attention, to some extent, to what kinds of favorable treatment provided by their organization indicated they were positively valued.

Employee attributions concerning employers' voluntary treatment of them play a large role in the development of perceived organizational support. Although high pay and fringe benefits, when supplied voluntarily, are strong indicators of positive valuation, these benefits signify little support when supplied under duress by organizations. Further, organizations can communicate their valuation of employees in a variety of discretionary actions. Consider the markedly different perceived organizational support produced in employees of two large traditional U.S. airlines, United and U.S. Airways, versus newcomer Southwest Airlines. The older lines until recently gave workers high wages and fringe benefits. However, these benefits resulted from difficult, contested negotiations, leading employees to conclude that the favorable benefits were provided involuntarily rather than resulting from the air carriers' high regard for employees. Further, these air carriers provided little evidence of support regarding other kinds of treatment management could readily control, such as the encouragement of employee initiative and innovation. The resulting low perceived organizational support was reciprocated with lackadaisical job performance, including the poor treatment of customers. In contrast, the new, scrappier competitor Southwest Airlines treated its employees favorably in various discretionary ways. For example, Southwest employees were given a high degree of authority to fix unexpected problems, and their creative input was frequently solicited and acted upon. Southwest's discretionary actions indicated a strong positive valuation of employees, leading to high perceived organizational support. Workers reciprocated with excellent treatment of customers, efficient performance, and a low turnover rate (Gittell, 2002).

Google is a good example of a company that conveys positive valuation of employees in ways that are unnecessary simply to recruit and retain a highly talented workforce. In 2007, Google had 472,771 job applications for a company with only 5,000 employees and with a turnover rate of 2.6% (Great Places to Work Institute, Inc., 2007). Working at Google has the attraction of being part of one of the world's most admired and successful companies. Given the supply of prospective employees who would love to work for Google, current employees are aware that management does not feel great pressure to provide such generous on-site benefits, company-matched retirement programs, ample support for advanced education, time allocated to pursue personal ideas, or weekly meetings with top management to promote solidarity. Because these benefits are seen as highly voluntary, they contribute greatly to perceived organizational support.

Beliefs about the organization's discretion also matter strongly in the case of unfavorable treatment of employees. To the extent that aversive treatment of workers is believed to be beyond the organization's control, the negative influence on perceived organizational support will be muted. For example, when employees receive accurate information each year about company profitability, a 1-year reduction in the normal wage increments due to the company's poor earnings should have only a limited detrimental effect on perceived organizational support. By shifting the responsibility for the worsened treatment from the organization to external circumstances over which the organization has little control, the negative consequences for perceived organizational support are reduced. Of course, the employees' acceptance of such explanations will depend on management's past history of openness and honesty with employees.

According to organizational support theory, unfavorable working conditions that appear to be beyond the control of the organization should have little negative influence on perceived organizational support. In a long-term consulting relationship with a chain of retail stores that sold discounted appliances and electronics, I found that most salespeople experienced a high level of stress. This was the result of the financial uncertainties of commission-based income and the necessity to work many weekends, reducing the time the salespeople could spend with family and friends. When I investigated further, I discovered that most salespeople attributed their stress to the requirements of their sales job rather than to policies of management. The employees believed that management had little control over the stressful conditions, did not blame management for them, and retained a generally high level of perceived organizational support. In fact, most of the sales employees preferred to work a considerable number of weekends, despite the stress, because this afforded access to larger numbers of customers.

As a cost savings measure, the company changed from the compensation system of paying commissions as a percentage on sales to a fixed salary. Now salespeople had less control over their income, and the more effective salespeople suffered a financial loss. Sales employees believed they were the targets of a voluntary action that the organization knew would harm them. Perceived organizational support fell, and employee turnover increased. To staunch the flow of its best salespeople to competitors, the company reinstated its commissions on sales, and perceived organizational support began to increase.

In this sales organization, the necessity to work many weekends and the insecurity of sales were blamed on the nature of the job, not on the employer. The favorableness of the compensation system, which was more clearly under the control of the organization, had a stronger influence on perceived organizational support. Thus, some important aspects of the job are considered by employees to be beyond the control of management and to have little association with perceived organizational support. Employees are practical; they are generally concerned with improving those working conditions and benefits that management can readily change. Favorable or unfavorable treatments received from the organization contribute to perceived organizational support to the degree that they are believed to be discretionary.

ORGANIZATION SINCERITY

Expressions of positive regard should contribute more to perceived organizational support when they are used in a discriminating fashion and when they have favorable consequences. Such expressions include praise and approval for good work, and caring and concern when employees experience difficulty. Employees' value expressed positive regard to the extent that they think the organizational representative who provides it is expressing his or her true opinion, as opposed to giving insincere complements. As P. M. Blau (1964) noted, "approval is expected to be governed by internalized normative standards of judgment, and intrinsic attraction, by internal emotional reaction. The simulation of each is condemned" (p. 64). Further, "intrinsic attraction to a person, approval of his opinions, and respect for his [or her] abilities [cannot be openly exchanged] because their significance rests on their being spontaneous reactions rather than calculated" (P. M. Blau, 1964, p. 98).

Insincere expressed positive valuations are given little value beyond politeness because (a) they indicate no true evaluative judgment and so cannot fulfill socioemotional needs that depend on evaluative judgments (e.g., approval, esteem, affiliation, emotional support), and (b) they hold no promise of increased future support in the form of help with one's job or increased benefits. Approval used in a nondiscriminating manner loses its informational value (Cairns, 1970). For example, when a person gives a child random approval, the child no longer pays attention to that person's approval on a future task as a guide to appropriate performance (Eisenberger, Kaplan, & Singer, 1974). A supervisor who presents an easily penetrable facade of disingenuous praise and approval will not instill high perceived organizational support.

Most employees know from everyday experience that favorable personal comments often arise not from sincere belief but from social conventions dictated by the situation or from flattery placed in the service of an ulterior motive. In everyday life, politeness dictates that people take some interest in others and ask about their well-being. Often, this is no more than a greeting. To some extent, individuals may exaggerate their stated positive valuations of a partner with good intentions or flatter someone they would like to know better. However, individuals are also aware that some individuals use stated positive valuations in interpersonal relationships in an entirely guileful way—to mislead others in order to take advantage of them. Professions of love and infatuation by men interested primarily in sex are venerable examples of guileful flattery women are taught to look out for.

Employees generalize from their knowledge of interpersonal relationships when considering the sincerity of favorable comments. Consider the following examples of managers' supportive statements to individual employees that are inconsistent with the managers' other actions, with damaging effects on perceived organizational support:

- The indiscriminate use of compliments, given to most employees regardless of their performance, is a strong indication of insincerity. "Great job," a manager says to everyone, regardless of their performance, so that the recipients learn the manager is being disingenuous.

- Verbal encouragement for undertaking a particular activity is not backed by implied tangible support. An employee may be told that she or he has a great idea and to go ahead developing the idea or project and then have the work ignored. For example, a staff member may spend long hours on a report that he was told was very important only to have the report ignored because the individual's boss had given insufficient thought initially about the importance of the report. Having put a great amount of work into the report and having had it rejected without good reason, the subordinate's perceived organizational support may suffer.

- Expressions of emotional support are not followed by ameliorative action. An employee may describe a difficult problem to a manager who expresses sympathy to the employee but makes no effort to help with the problem. This does not mean that the manager should always make subordinates' problems his or her own. But it does suggest that he or she should take the time to carefully think about why an employee is upset and, if the employee has a legitimate problem, help the employee think through the problem and, where appropriate, provide what resources the manager can muster.

- Feedback concerning poor performance is temporarily masked by compliments to avoid the manager's discomfort in being frank. Here, an employee receives uniformly positive comments during periodic performance evaluations by a supervisor who believes the employee has performed poorly but prefers to avoid the unpleasantness of discussing any of the subordinate's drawbacks. Later, the employee receives the news that she is receiving a low pay raise with no explanation. The incongruity between praise and actions conveys a lack of sincerity, leading the employee to believe that the supervisor and, by extension, the organization not only devalue the employee but are not interested enough in the employee's welfare to discuss how the employee might improve.

Some organizations, as a matter of strategy, attempt to use praise and approval as a facade of support for their employees as substitutes for decent pay, fringe benefits, and good working conditions. Favorable comments by organizational representatives to employees, if not associated with concrete favorable treatment, are judged insincere and do little to enhance perceived organizational support—this is what is meant by the expression "Talk is cheap." If, for example, the organization has frequently broken promises, provided poor pay and fringe benefits, allowed minimal autonomy in carrying out one's job, and frequently increased the pace of required work, favorable comments directed toward the accomplishments of employees will appear hollow.

Wal-Mart's attempt to convey a family atmosphere of fellowship and mirth at the daily morning pep rally is belied by employees' actual experience of enforced uniformity in word and action, continual increases in the required amount of work, and substandard wages and fringe benefits. Under such circumstances, many employees come to view the message of camaraderie and support as a cynical attempt at manipulation.

Of course, companies like Wal-Mart that treat employees poorly have little to lose by presenting a facade of concern and consideration. Why not put the best face on unfavorable treatment and appeal to the gullible minority of employees who will believe them? Some individuals whose job gives them a sense of meaning and purpose want to believe that the organization cares about their well-being, and they therefore accept the organization's propaganda at face value. However, the 50% yearly employee turnover rate at Wal-Mart suggests that the strategy of feigned support and caring has its limits.

Expressions of caring and esteem are more convincing to employees when associated with tangible indications of positive regard. Smucker's, the billion-dollar family-owned producer of jams and sweet fillings, has been repeatedly ranked by *FORTUNE* magazine as among the best U.S. companies for which to work. Employee ratings contribute heavily to these rankings. In 2004, Smucker's made it to Number 1 on *FORTUNE*'s list. The co-chief executives, Tim and Richard Smucker, continually express a desire to listen to employees and to value and express appreciation for their contributions (Boorstin, 2004). Smucker's culture does appear to strongly value its workers' contributions. *Thank you*'s from upper management for high levels of individual performance occur frequently, and workgroups often receive celebratory lunches and gift certificates for making new records. Over 90% of Smucker's employees agree with the statement "Management takes a sincere interest in me as a person, not just as an employee." Employee turnover is less than 4% annually ("The J. M. Smucker company," 2000).

Southwest Airlines, which from its beginning 3 decades ago has grown into the nation's fourth largest and most profitable carrier, is another example of an organization in which praise is used for a job well done and is also backed by specific actions. Founder Herb Kelleher stated, "Who comes first, your employees, your shareholders, or your customers? My mother taught me that your employees come first. If you treat them well, that means your customers will come back and your shareholders are happy" ("The J. M. Smucker company," 2000).

According to Kelleher, accomplishments should receive a "tsunami of gratitude." In his view, "an organization bound by love is more powerful than one bound by fear" (Colvin & Huey, 1999). At Southwest, the sincerity of praise and approval is demonstrated by its conditional nature. Employees are expected to perform well and are praised when they do so. Giving them the ability to make decisions also conveys positive valuation of employees: They are trusted to violate standard operating procedures when reasonable exceptions increase customer satisfaction. All employees' ideas are solicited and considered carefully, such as the adoption of a low-level worker's suggestion for a unit to help employees with their career paths. Thus, the generous praise given to those at Southwest Airlines contributes to perceived organizational support because it is considered genuine: Employees are praised for the actual contributions that they make to the organization.

Verbal praise and awards at Google, such as its Founder's Award, are tied to specific achievements and are associated with rewards, leading employees to believe in their sincerity. Google provides a generous base of benefits for all employees to signify its positive valuation of the group and keep morale high. But the company also uses generous pay-for-performance programs to promote innovation and performance of employees, with lessened pay for underperformance. Performance is rewarded for accomplishments on a sliding scale so that employees are not faced with the nerve-racking alternative of complete success or complete failure. When teams are rewarded, members are frequently compensated in proportion to their judged contributions. Praise, approval, and awards are considered sincere, leading to greater perceived organizational support, when they are associated with superior employee performance and rewards.

ADDITIONAL FEATURES OF TREATMENT CONVEYING POSITIVE REGARD

My colleagues and I (Eisenberger et al., 1986, 2004) have noted several other relevant attributions that employees may use to judge the organizations' regard for them. First, favorable treatment that is costly to the organization would indicate greater positive valuation of employees than favorable treatment requiring few resources (see Gouldner, 1960; Eisenberger et al., 1986). In this view, a program to pay for employees' education would contribute less to perceived organizational support in a highly profitable company than a similar program in an organization with lesser financial resources.

Second, aid helping to meet a strong need would contribute more to perceived organizational support than helping to meet a weaker need (see also Gouldner, 1960). For example, material or socioemotional aid given to an employee with a life-threatening illness or grieving the loss of a family member would contribute substantially to perceived organizational support. Moreover, when the organization responds benevolently to a variety of employees in times of great need and such aid becomes well-known, such acts of kindness become part of the allure of the organization and contribute to perceived organizational support.

Third, organizational support theory similarly holds that treatment specific to an employee's needs should be especially valued and should therefore contribute considerably to perceived organizational support (see also Schopler, 1970). An individual with strong professional goals who receives developmental training opportunities and an individual with an aged, infirm parent who receives a medical support option would be expected to have a greater increase in perceived organizational support than if the benefits were not specific to their needs. This suggests the potential usefulness of cafeteria-designed benefit programs in which employees are given some degree of choice in the kinds of options they choose.

These examples highlight the potential importance of employees' attributional processes in the relationship of favorable treatment with perceived organizational support. On the basis of these processes, the favorableness of treatment might be considerably increased or attenuated as a source of perceived organizational support. Besides the strong relationship found between the voluntariness of the organization's treatment and perceived organizational support (Eisenberger et al., 1997), evidence has yet to be obtained on remaining attributional heuristics described above.

ORGANIZATIONAL EMBODIMENT

Employees are particularly aware of the directive and evaluative nature of their supervisor's job and the fact that the organization assesses employees for various human resource functions (Eisenberger, Stinglhamber, Vandenberghe, Sucharski, & Rhoades, 2002; Levinson, 1965). However, employees view supervisors not simply as organizational agents but also as individuals having values and motivations that differ in similarity to those of the organization. As is discussed in Chapter 4, support received from the supervisor (perceived supervisor support) and a strong exchange relationship between the subordinate and the supervisor (leader–member exchange) are taken as evidence of perceived organizational support by subordinates. Some supervisors strongly endorse the organization's values and objectives, whereas others find less to agree with. Additionally, some supervisors are greatly concerned with the organization's welfare, whereas others primarily promote their own welfare. Thus, subordinates distinguish support from supervisors from perceived organizational support (e.g., Eisenberger et al., 2002; Kottke & Sharafinski, 1988; Stinglhamber & Vandenberghe, 2003, 2004), and differentiate fair treatment received from supervisors from fair treatment by the organization (e.g., Masterson, Lewis, Goldman, & Taylor, 2000; Rupp & Cropanzano, 2002). Further, subordinates' affective commitment (e.g., T. E. Becker, 1992, 2009), trust (e.g., Stinglhamber, De Cremer, & Mercken, 2006; Tan & Tan, 2000), and citizenship behavior

(T. E. Becker & Kernan, 2003) are affected by their relationships with supervisors, over and above relationships with the organization. Finally, some supervisors have little power and influence in the organization, so that their views are considered to provide little evidence of the organization's views (Eisenberger et al., 2002).

Because the organization's favorable or unfavorable orientation toward the employee is important for the employee's future, employees are interested in understanding the extent to which the supervisor's actions represent the organization's orientation. To determine the extent to which support received from the supervisor and a favorable exchange relationship represent a positive valuation by the organization as well as by their supervisor, employees must weigh whether their treatment by the supervisor represents primarily the supervisor's own values, motives, and goals or those of the organization as well.

Employees view the organization as a lifelike entity with benevolent or malevolent intentions toward themselves. They personify the organization, viewing it as a single powerful entity with humanlike characteristics, ascribing to it persisting values, goals, motives, and abilities (Eisenberger et al., 1986; Levinson, 1965). We and our colleagues (Eisenberger, Karagonlar, et al., 2010) suggested that to determine the extent to which their treatment by the supervisor is indicative of the organization's orientation toward them, employees assess the extent to which their supervisor shares the identity with the organization (*supervisor's organizational embodiment;* SOE). Employees compare the prominent characteristics of the organization with those of the supervisor in determining SOE. Notable among these characteristics are power and influence, competence, and values. To the extent that the supervisor overlaps with the perceived characteristics of the organization in these characteristics, he or she will be identified with the organization, and the supervisor's actions will be identified with the organization's actions.

Typically, the organization exerts high power and influence over work life, so supervisors with high influence should tend to be strongly identified with the organization. According to organizational support theory (Eisenberger et al., 2002), organizational CEOs and high-level managers are considered by subordinates to represent the organization because they shape the organization's culture and policies. Supervisors would be identified with the organization to the extent that they were perceived to share some of the high-level managers' power and influence and possess the organization's values.

SOE may be compared and contrasted with organizational identification. Mael and Tetrick (1992) viewed identification with the organization as involving the belief by employees that they share the characteristics of the organization (e.g., values and goals), resulting in the perception of the organization's experiences as their own. SOE is a related concept except that the employee (a) identifies the supervisor with the organization, and

(b) power and influence are key characteristics, in addition to such properties as values and objectives, that employees use in identifying the supervisor with the organization. That is, the supervisors who are strongly identified with the organization are viewed as sharing and exerting the organization's power in furtherance of those values.

SOE may also be compared with the social identity typicality account of the development of leadership. According to Hogg (2001), leaders emerge from groups on the basis of the extent to which they behaviorally and cognitively conform with attributes that distinguish one's own group from other groups. Those who possess the most prototypical position in the group tend to emerge as leaders because normative characteristics bring the group self-esteem. In contrast, SOE refers to subordinates' identification of their supervisors (regardless of their relationship with the supervisor) with a powerful organization that influences them. Moreover, rather than prototypicality, employees identify their supervisors with the organization on the basis of a comparison of the supervisor's and organization's power and established characteristics. Unlike prototypicality, theses characteristics need not be favorable for the supervisor to be strongly identified with the organization. Depending on the organization, the majority of employees may find the personified organization benevolent or malevolent in its relationship with them.

In agreement with this proposal, we found that the relationship between employees' belief that they had a favorable relationship with their supervisor and their emotional bond to the organization was positively related to the extent that they identified the supervisor with the organization (Eisenberger, Karagonlar, et al., 2010). Further, we found that the relationship between employees' belief that they were being supported by their supervisor and perceived organizational support was stronger when employees more strongly identified supervisors with the organization (Stinglhamber, Eisenberger, Aselage, et al., 2010). This strengthened relationship between perceived supervisor support and perceived organizational support carried over to employee performance.

Regarding possible antecedents of SOE, the favorableness of supervisors' comments to subordinates about the organization might serve as an important clue concerning the supervisors' endorsement of the organization's values, goals, objectives, and their power and influence. Subordinates who hear their supervisors expressing positive views about upper management and the organization would infer that the supervisors favor the values, goals, and objectives of the organization or that the supervisors approve of the organization because it has accorded them high power and influence. In contrast, supervisors who complain about the ways of upper management and the organization would be marked by subordinates as lacking the organization's values and goals or being resentful for their low status in the organization. Accordingly, we found with social services employees that SOE was increased by supervisors' expression of favorable attitudes toward the organization (Eisenberger, Karagonlar, et al., 2010).

Moreover, if this were to be the case, this raises the possibility that supervisors' identification with the organization might contribute to SOE through such favorable statements. A recent meta-analysis found that organizational identification, involving a sense of unity with the organization (Ashforth & Mael, 1989), was positively associated with organizational satisfaction and affective organizational commitment (Riketta, 2005). Further, Van Dick, Hirst, Grojean, and Wieseke (2007) suggested that supervisors who identify strongly with their organization are more likely to convey positive information about the organization (e.g., organization's capabilities, reputation, vision). This suggests that supervisors' organizational identification may lead to an increased tendency for them to express attitudes favorable to the organization to subordinates both as a spontaneous expression of their views and as a citizenship behavior carried out to aid the organization (Podsakoff, MacKenzie, Paine, & Bachrach, 2000). Expression of attitudes favorable toward the organization should, in turn, increase SOE among subordinates. Thus, we found that supervisors' identification with the organization was positively related to the expression of favorable attitudes toward the organization, and the latter led to greater SOE among subordinates (Eisenberger, Karagonlar, et al., 2010).

FELT OBLIGATION

Perceived organizational support provides employees with the assurance that the organization is a reliable exchange partner that can be counted on to reward employees' future efforts and provide aid when needed (Aselage & Eisenberger, 2003). Organizational support theory assumes that, on the basis of the norm of reciprocity, employees reciprocate perceived organizational support with a felt obligation to care about the organization's welfare and help reach its goals. Perceived organizational support and felt obligation are causally related yet conceptually distinct (Wayne et al. 2009). Perceived organizational support is an experience-based belief indicating the organization's positive valuation of employees and concern for their welfare. Felt obligation is a morality-based belief regarding whether one should favor the organization.

Because perceived organizational support involves employees' assessment of their history of favorable treatment and the organization's intent to treat them favorably, and most employees accept the norm of reciprocity as applied to organizations, perceived organizational support should increase felt obligation. Eisenberger et al. (2001) found with postal workers that perceived organizational support led to felt obligation, which produced increased organizational spontaneity (George & Brief, 1992), including aiding fellow employees, taking actions that protect the organization from risk, offering constructive suggestions, and gaining knowledge and skills beneficial to the organization.

One type of evidence indicating that the norm of reciprocity contributes to employees' felt obligation to the organization would be to show that the relationship between perceived organizational support and felt obligation is greater for employees who strongly endorse the reciprocity norm as it applies to their relationship with their work organization (Eisenberger et al., 2001). *Exchange ideology* refers to employees' belief that it is appropriate and useful to base their concern with the organization's welfare and work effort on how favorably they have been treated by the organization. A strong employee exchange ideology would result from a personal history of direct experience, observation, and persuasion by others concerning the value of reciprocity in the employee–employer relationship. A strong exchange ideology should increase the relationship between perceived organizational support and felt obligation to help the organization reach its objectives. Accordingly, in our study with postal workers (Eisenberger et al., 2001), we found that the strength of the relationship between perceived organizational support and felt obligation increased with the workers' exchange ideology. This finding supports the view that perceived organizational support contributes to employees' felt obligation to the organization by means of the norm of reciprocity.

Because of a greater experienced obligation to the organization, employees with a high exchange ideology should also show an enhanced relationship between perceived organizational support and outcomes favorable to the organization. Eisenberger et al. (1986) found that the association between perceived organizational support and job attendance was greater among teachers having a strong exchange ideology. The relationship between perceived organizational support and extrarole behaviors helpful to the organization has similarly been found to be greater among employees with a high exchange ideology (Ladd & Henry, 2000; Witt, 1991).

Tsui, Pearce, Porter, and Tripoli (1997) suggested that actions by the organization indicating caring and positive regard for employees act to enhance affective commitment by means of the reciprocity norm. Thus, employees who receive favorable discretionary treatment, resulting in perceived organizational support, should feel an obligation to return the caring suggested by the organization's positive regard. Consistent with this view, Eisenberger et al. (2001) found that the felt obligation resulting from perceived organizational support led to increased affective commitment to the organization.

EXPECTED REWARD FOR HIGH EFFORT

Perceived organizational support results not only in employees' felt obligation, based on the norm of reciprocity, to help the organization reach its objectives, but also in employees' expectation that the organization will reward increased efforts. This is the starting mechanism that Gouldner (1960) wrote about in which the norm of reciprocity provides trust that helping others to meet their needs will be reciprocated at a later time when those others will help meet one's own needs. Applied to organizations, employees increase their efforts to help their organization meet its goals to the extent that they believe it will reciprocate with favorable treatment. Perceived organizational support provides assurance that such investments will be reciprocated by the organization. Accordingly, Eisenberger, Fasolo, and Davis-LaMastro (1990) found a positive relationship between perceived organizational support and performance–reward expectancies. Expected reward for high performance works hand in glove with felt obligation to encourage employees to respond affirmatively to perceived organizational support. Perceived organizational support creates a felt obligation among employees to return past favorable treatment by increased efforts on the organization's behalf while they anticipate being rewarded for these efforts.

SOCIOEMOTIONAL NEED FULFILLMENT

Just as perceived support from friends and relatives fulfills socioemotional needs in interpersonal relationships (S. Cobb, 1976; Cohen & Wills, 1985), perceived organizational support may meet important socioemotional needs in the workplace, such as those for approval, esteem, caring, and affiliation.

Most research concerning individual differences in needs for socioemotional resources has been carried out by personality theorists (e.g., P. M. Blau, 1964; Buss, 1983; Crowne & Marlowe, 1964; E. B. Foa & Foa, 1980; Hill, 1987, 1991; Martin, 1984). Hill (1987) argued that the motivation for social contact has a major influence on human behavior, and he described several such needs, including (a) the need for praise and recognition (more commonly termed *need for esteem*), (b) the need to receive affection and cognitive stimulation (more commonly termed *need for affiliation*), and (c) the need for consolation and sympathy when experiencing distress (more commonly termed *need for emotional support*). As applied to employees' relationship to their organization, the need for affiliation might be better defined as a desire to feel accepted and integrated into social structures. Another relevant socioemotional need involves a desire to act in socially approved ways (need for social approval; Crowne & Marlowe, 1964).

Perceived organizational support may help fulfill these socioemotional needs. Perceived organizational support should convey that the organization judges employees as superior performers and is proud of their accomplishments, which would help satisfy the need for esteem. It may also convey to employees that the organization is committed to them and accepts them as welcomed members, which would help satisfy the need for affiliation. Perceived organizational support should strengthen employees' expectation that the organization would provide sympathetic understanding and material aid to deal with stressful situations at work or home, which would help meet the need for emotional support. Finally, perceived organizational support may strengthen the perception that the organization is satisfied that the employee is acting in accord with established norms and policies, thereby meeting the need for social approval. In sum, perceived organizational support should be especially satisfying for employees with high needs for esteem, affiliation, emotional support, and social approval.

Because perceived organizational support would be more valued by those with high socioemotional needs, they would experience a greater obligation to reciprocate, based on the reciprocity norm, with a high affective commitment to the organization. The fulfillment of these needs should also facilitate the incorporation of employees' organizational membership and role status into their social identity. That is, perceived organizational support should lead employees to feel a sense of unity with the organization and to become emotionally attached to the organization. These topics are discussed in more detail in Chapter 6.

Armeli et al. (1998) provided evidence of the importance of need fulfillment for outcomes of perceived organizational support. Police patrol officers were surveyed to determine the relationship between perceived organizational support and objectively assessed work performance. The association of perceived organizational support with driving-under-the influence arrests and speeding citations generally increased with the strength of the needs for esteem, affiliation, emotional support, and social approval. These findings support the view that fulfillment of socioemotional needs is a basic mechanism contributing to the effects of perceived organizational support on performance.

ANTICIPATED HELP

Perceived organizational support signifies to employees that the organization believes they are making a significant contribution to its objectives. Therefore, from the employee's viewpoint, it is in the organization's interest to provide the resources when needed, to help the employee to continue to perform the job at a high level. Further, because perceived organizational support incorporates the view that the organization cares about one's well-being, employees with high perceived organizational support should believe that the organization would be especially helpful during periods when the employee is placed under high stress owing to such factors as high workloads, projects that carry a high risk of failure, and so on.

George et al. (1993) argued that perceived organizational support indicates the availability of both emotional and tangible support when employees face high work demands. For employees with high perceived organizational support, managers as representatives of the organization, would be expected to show greater empathy and emotional support for employees with difficult work-related problems or life-related difficult family situations. George's and subsequent research suggests the perceived organizational support plays a significant role in reducing stress at work, as we discuss in Chapter 5.

Summary

Employees develop a general perception concerning the extent to which the organization values their contributions and cares about their well-being. Perceived organizational support serves as an important component in the social exchange relationship between employees and the organization by eliciting a felt obligation to return such favorable treatment. The norm of reciprocity dictates the return of favorable or unfavorable treatment to the donor. Employees who are well-treated feel obligated to return the favorable treatment by helping the organization fulfill its objectives, and they develop confidence that their investment of added effort on behalf of the organization will be rewarded. Thus, employees with high perceived organizational support are motivated to be positively oriented toward the organization and to engage in behaviors helpful to it. In contrast, employees with low perceived organizational support feel little obligation to the organization and, to the contrary, may seek vengeance through violation of organization norms to get even for inadequate recompense for their efforts.

To try to make sense of the organization's culture, its values and practices, and the treatment they receive from its representatives, employees personify the organization. They use their everyday understanding of personality to ascribe to the organization humanlike characteristics that will help explain and predict its actions, especially as they affect employees. Employees consider themselves as an object of the organization's motives and goals. Employees believe that the organization views them supportively to a high or low degree, and thus, high or low perceived organizational support develops.

Because perceived organizational support depends on employees' view of their valuation by the organization, it is strongly influenced by attributions concerning the organization's discretion when providing resources. Favorable treatment produced by external constraints has little influence on perceived organizational support. This principle has been demonstrated in a careful research study and is readily observable in everyday life. For example, an increase in pay or safety regulations based on government regulations produces very little increase in perceived organizational support. The sincerity of expressions of favorable organizational valuation from supervisors and other managers, as indicated by their discriminating use of, and follow-up with, implied resources, also contributes substantially to perceived support. In contrast, favorable comments to the same employee or across employees, and encouragement without implied resources, are examples of disingenuous praise that ultimately decrease perceived organizational support.

Because supervisors act as organizational agents in directing, coaching, and evaluating employees, and providing them with resources, employees tend to identify supervisors with the organization. However, employees are also aware that supervisors have characteristics that distinguish them from the organization. To understand the extent to which supervisor support represents organizational support, subordinates form a perception concerning the supervisor's embodiment of the organization. The greater this perception, the more the supervisor's supportive treatment is taken as the organization's favorable treatment as well.

Organizational support theory identifies several processes for the results of perceived organizational support on employees' happiness, favorable orientation toward the organization and work, and behaviors that aid the organization. Perceived organizational support invokes the norm of reciprocity and thus creates a felt obligation among employees to help the organization reach its objectives. Perceived organizational support is valued, in part, for fulfilling socioemotional needs. Being valued by the organization helps fulfill needs for esteem, affiliation, emotional support, and approval. Such need fulfillment should contribute to employees' identification with, and emotional attachment to, the organization. Perceived organizational support also increases employees' expectations that their increased efforts on behalf of the organization will be noticed and rewarded and that the organization will provide material and emotional support when needed.

Although organizational support theory as presented in this chapter explains most of the findings concerning perceived organizational support, in subsequent chapters we consider extensions of the theory proposed by researchers. Of particular interest are the spread of perceived organizational support across organizational hierarchies and networks and the extension of organizational support theory to organizational relationships involving volunteers, unions, and customers.

Antecedents of Perceived Organizational Support 3

Genentech and NetApp are examples of companies that provide employees with a variety of work experiences that enhance perceived organizational support. Headquartered in San Francisco and with 13,000 employees, Genentech pioneered the biotech approaches to the discovery, development, and manufacture of pharmaceuticals to treat serious illnesses. Genentech fosters a sense of fairness in career development, more than many companies, by promoting many current employees through a system in which all qualified employees can apply for, and be given serious consideration for, advertised positions. Upper management engages in considerable two-way communication with employees. Webcasts and an annual conference are used to inform employees of plans and strategy. Each quarter, the CEO e-mails employees about product and financial information and, in turn, responds to employee suggestions and feedback. Additionally, executives meet with employees in small groups to discuss whatever issues the employees would like to bring up. Favorable work–family policies combat the strain that long work hours and immersion in difficult, long-term projects can bring to home life. These policies include opportunities for errands to be carried out on campus (e.g., on-site day care, prescriptions, hair cutting, banking); classes and seminars related to financial, physical, and psychological health; and a paid 6-month sabbatical every 6 years for rejuvenation (Levering & Moskowitz, 2006).

Founded in 1992, with revenues of $3 billion, NetApp is an information technology company specializing in data storage and management. Employees are rewarded for high performance though a patent incentive system, as well as by various other recognition programs that convey NetApp's appreciation of employees' contributions. NetApp's favorable treatment of employees is not confined to the top strata, with nine in 10 employees agreeing that they are treated as full organization citizens regardless of their position and that they feel a sense of pride in their accomplishments. A diversity of internal career development programs and support for external career development further indicate NetApp's positive valuation of employees' contributions as well as a concern with their welfare. Emphasis is placed on data-driven contributions, and employees report that the company is remarkably free of the organizational politics that devastate perceived organizational support (Lyman, 2009).

Employees integrate information concerning organizational support from a variety of work-related experiences. These include preemployment experiences, management communications, fairness, organizational politics, rewards, job conditions, supervisor support, support for specific objectives, value congruence, and contingent employment. Most of these topics are covered in this chapter, as well as personal characteristics of the employee, such as personality.

The reason that the list of antecedents is so long is that there are a variety of ways to indicate positive regard for employees' contributions and caring for their welfare. We discuss the results of meta-analytic reviews of the research findings, involving the quantitative combination of findings, which suggest that some kinds of treatment are especially effective in increasing perceived organizational support (e.g., fairness) or in its destruction (e.g., perceived organizational politics). Beyond these general differences in the effectiveness of different kinds of treatment, the support-related processes discussed in Chapter 2 can have a substantial impact. If, for example, a supervisor rewards a subordinate with praise and approval for high performance, the influence of this treatment will be affected by the extent to which the supervisor is identified with the organization; the perceived sincerity of his or her comments; and the extent to which the supervisor, as an organizational representative, is perceived to be acting voluntarily, as opposed to being driven by external constraints such as the subordinate's knowledge that the organization is trying to head off attempts to unionize by temporarily acting generously to employees.

Our conclusions on antecedents of perceived organizational support are based, in part, on surveys administered to employees. Findings from carefully conducted surveys that assess possible antecedents of perceived organizational support are valuable, especially when confirmed by multiple studies. Repeated findings of the same result make chance-observed relationships less likely. For example, many studies report a positive correlation between employees' perceptions of fairness and perceived organizational support. However, correlational studies are subject to ambiguity concerning causation. Does fairness increase perceived organizational support or the reverse? Additionally, there is the issue of whether some third variable, such as the number of years of employment, is related to both fairness and perceived organizational support and is responsible for some or all of the observed relationship. Most of the studies we discuss controlled statistically for at least one of these third-variable explanations. When multiple studies report the same finding, they are likely to control for an increased number of distinct variables. In this and the following chapters, when multiple studies report a result while assessing a variety of possible variables as explanations, our confidence in a causal relationship is increased. However, the problem of a reverse possible direction of causation remains. We highlight studies that make the reverse causation interpretation less likely by the use of longitudinal designs in which change in time in the outcome variable is measured (panel designs). For example, if fairness at Time 1 is associated with an increase in perceived organizational support from Time 1 to Time 2, we can make a much more convincing case for causality than when fairness and perceived organizational support are simply measured once at the same time.

We also highlight studies that use diverse sources of measurement of the key variables. For example, obtaining separate measures of perceived organizational support from the employee and the employee's performance from the supervisor is preferable to obtaining perceived organizational support and a self-estimate of performance from the employee because some third, unmeasured variable (e.g., the personality trait of Agreeableness) might produce a positive relationship between perceived organizational support and the self-report of performance.

Preemployment Experiences

Preemployment information about the organization begins to influence the extent to which employees view their new organization as likely to provide them with future support. To the extent that prospective or newly hired employees receive information about their employer, they start to form perceived organizational support prior to their first day on the job. Thus, Casper and Buffardi (2004) found that information about a prospective employer's dependent care assistance and schedule flexibility policies influenced the job applicants' anticipated perceived organizational support. Also, applicants for positions to a Belgian bank had greater anticipated perceived organizational support if they believed the selection process was fair and that the interviewer was emotionally supportive of the applicant (Stinglhamber, Eisenberger, Stewart, & Hanin, 2010). The top panel in Figure 3.1 shows these antecedents and consequences of preemployment anticipatory perceived organizational support.

These findings suggest that that perceived organizational support is quite malleable in prospective and new employees. In some cases, employers such as Google and Southwest Airways carry a strong positive reputation, which itself likely evokes high anticipated perceived organizational support, whereas other organizations, such as Wal-Mart, reputed to be unsupportive of employees, likely evoke low perceived organizational support among employees. Most organizations have less well-defined public images so that anticipated perceived organizational support is more strongly determined by the impressions of relatives, friends, or acquaintances who work there, and by the pronouncements of recruiters and interviewers, and information provided by the organization.

Anticipated perceived organizational support has also been studied with reference to future mergers of one's company with another. Using a scenario procedure, Mottola, Bachman, Gaertner, and Dovidio (1997) examined the influence of merger integration patterns on expectations of students who role played employees of a company purchased by a second company. The integration patterns included *absorb,* in which the merged organization closely resembled the acquiring company; *blend,* in which features of both companies were maintained; and *combine,* in which the organization took aspects of both companies to create a new culture. As shown in the bottom panel of Figure 3.1, the researchers found that anticipated perceived organizational support from the newly merged organization increased as the merger pattern varied from absorb to blend to combine. Evidently, the integration of features of both companies provided assurance that the acquiring company valued the contributions of the employees of the acquired company, resulting in high anticipated perceived organizational support.

Although research on anticipated perceived organizational support has only recently begun, studies on perceived organizational support with experienced employees suggest that anticipated perceived organizational support may enhance new employees' psychological well-being, increase their positive orientation toward the organization, and heighten their performance on behalf of the organization. At the same time, one should recognize that anticipated perceived organizational support may also increase perceived obligations on the part of the organization, termed the *psychological contract* (Rousseau, 1989, 1995; Rousseau & McLean Parks, 1993). If the organization does not meet these objectives, employees may become emotionally upset and lessen their favorable orientation toward the organization (Conway & Briner, 2002).

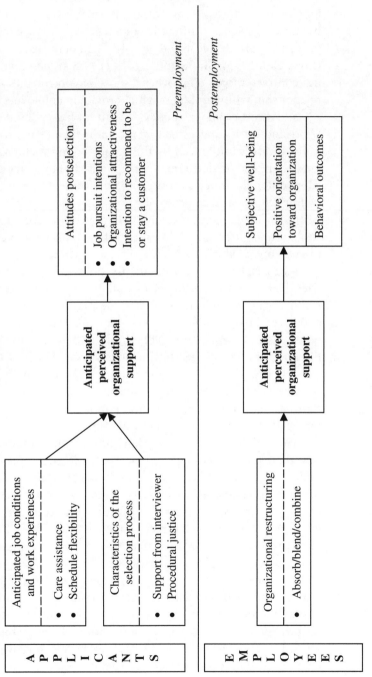

Overview of findings on anticipated perceived organizational support.

Psychological contract theory holds that employees form beliefs concerning the mutual obligations existing between themselves and the organization (Rousseau, 1989, 1995; Rousseau & McLean Parks, 1993). Employment interviews and other information dispensed prior to the 1st work day, as well as during the employee's early work tenure, appear to play an important role in the establishment of the psychological contract (Rousseau, 1995). Shore and Tetrick (1994) argued that the psychological contract affords employees a sense of control and security in their relationship with employers while providing employers a way to manage and direct employee behavior without heavy-handed surveillance. Shore and Tetrick suggested that the nature of an employee's psychological contract is influenced by the organization's inclination to cultivate long-term or short-term relationships with its employees. Organizations adopt different strategies concerning the value of the resources they are willing to invest in their employees (Tsui et al., 1997). Organizations with high-investment strategies would be more likely to convey a psychological contract involving the exchange of highly valued resources than an organization with a low-investment strategy.

As a social exchange account, psychological contract theory emphasizes the importance of the reciprocation of material and socioemotional resources between employee and the organization's representatives, and notes the disruptive emotional and motivational consequences that occur when the organization does not fulfill its obligations. Aselage and Eisenberger (2003) suggested possible ways in which psychological contract theory and organizational support theory might be integrated. Because our focus here is on organizational support theory, we consider those aspects of the psychological contract that have the most direct implications for organizational support theory.

The fulfillment of the psychological contract should increase perceived organizational support, whereas the failure of the organization to fulfill these obligations should result in negative emotional and motivational reactions and reduce perceived organizational support. Unlike commercial contracts, obligations of psychological contracts are frequently overfulfilled, a fact that has received too little attention. Employees commonly receive favorable treatment that exceeds the organization's obligations. For example, in Conway and Briner's (2002) diary study of 45 employees from various organizations, 62% of employees reported that their organization exceeded at least one of its promises during the 10-day period of the study. Organizations adopting policies involving the provision of many valued resources to employees (Shore & Barksdale, 1998; Tsui et al., 1997) might be especially likely to deliver more to their employees than was promised or to deliver resources that were not previously promised, resulting in high perceived organizational support.

Although there has been little research on the relationship between contract fulfillment and perceived organizational support, Coyle-Shapiro and Kessler (2000) and Coyle-Shapiro and Conway (2005) found that employees' perceptions of the organization having fulfilled its contractual obligations were associated with increased perceived organizational support. However, Coyle-Shapiro and Conway had a different explanation for this effect than the fulfillment of obligations. They reported that the effect was eliminated when one took into account the relationship between the current level of the initially promised resources ("inducements") and perceived organizational support. That is, delivered inducements rather than contract fulfillment played the key role.

The reason present treatment (inducements) was found to contribute more to perceived organizational support may be because specific promises concerning economic issues such as salary and benefits are laid out for employees either as a matter of organizational policy or part of a signed contractual agreement and are therefore generally adhered to by the organization. Thus, employees may take adherence to these obligations as a matter of standard practice and not as an indication of their positive valuation by the organization. In contrast, many obligations concerning the favorableness of the organization's treatment of employees, such as scope of responsibility, opportunities for professional training and advancement, and consideration of views, are perhaps a more fundamental part of the psychological contract. When employees are asked about the extent to which the organization has lived up to these obligations, they have a difficult time answering because the promises prior to the start of employment were qualitative and vague. Thus, the employees' understanding of the organization's prior obligations to them from the organization and other sources, such as prior employment and peers and schooling, may be general and hard to measure against what the organization actually provides.

For example, to what extent has the promise inherent in the statement "We have excellent developmental training opportunities" been kept or violated when an employee finds training opportunities to be moderately beneficial to his or her career? In answering questions about psychological contract maintenance or violation, employees may respond more about the favorableness of accumulated experience with a given resource in the organization, such as developmental training opportunities, than about the contract violation. Perhaps, as Coyle-Shapiro and Conway (2005) suggested, employees react more to their accumulated experiences with important resources than to contract violation in the determination of perceived organizational support.

Coyle-Shapiro and Conway (2005) also found that both obligations and perceived organizational support contributed to organizational citizenship behavior. Thus, employees who felt that the organization had high obligations to them were very helpful to the organization. Perhaps these are employees who believe they are involved in strong social relationships with the organization and respond accordingly. Aselage and

Eisenberger (2003) also suggested that perceived organizational support might produce a cognitive revision of the psychological contract based on the norm of reciprocity. Coyle-Shapiro and Conway found that, consistent with this view, perceived organizational support led to reduction by employees of perceived obligations on the part of the organization. Combining these findings, Coyle-Shapiro and Conway concluded that psychological inducements and perceived organizational support, operating together on perceived obligations of the organization, play a greater role on the employee–organization relationship than contract fulfillment.

These findings suggest that employees are very attentive to inducements that influence perceived organizational support. Perceived organizational support, in turn, reduces the extent to which the employee views that the organization is obligated to provide valued resources. It is possible that very often most aspects of the psychological contracts are vague enough to serve as inducements but are hard for employees to pin down as to when specific portions of them are being broken. However, there may be limits to the finding that employees pay attention to inducements and current perceived organizational support to the exclusion of the organization's failure to live up to the psychological contract. Important specific promises typically are not individually assessed with current methodology in the study of psychological contracts, which usually uses an additive summary to assess the whole set of promises made by the organization, many of which are probably vague and general. Perhaps the more emphasis and detail with which the organization describes an obligation to an employee (e.g., developmental training), the more the employee compares what has been provided to what has been promised.

Management Communications

Effective communication from upper management to employees is essential for lessening employees' anxiety and uncertainty about upcoming organizational changes. Further, fostering communication from employees to upper management can provide innovative ideas and lessen closed-minded thinking, termed *groupthink*, when insiders block information that may compete with dominant views (Janis, 1983). In the book *A Colossal Failure of Common Sense* (McDonald & Robinson, 2009), former Lehman Brothers investment bank trader Lawrence McDonald tells of CEO Richard Fuld, who with a small coterie, shut himself off from the rest of the firm while greatly expanding its real estate business, drawing on financial credit of 30 or 40 times the firm's assets, during the final stages of the recent housing bubble. Fuld isolated himself from executives with fresh views, including some who were trying to warn him of the impending danger. Fuld did not communicate future plans for his massive increase in acquisition of real estate, based on credit, nor did he seek others' opinion as to its advisability. He and a small group of devoted senior managers accelerated these investments even as real estate defaults began to escalate and banks started tightening the credit without which Lehman could not maintain its current loan obligations. Perceiving no support from Fuld and the upper echelons of the organization, key managers who were attempting to find ways to mitigate the bank's speculative excesses with hedged investments finally quit, and Lehman went bankrupt. Here was a case of groupthink in which there was deterioration of effective management fostered by a haughty, directive leader who eliminated all outside opinion.

Management's communication of high-quality job information (M. W. Allen, 1992) and comments indicating various kinds of organizational support (M. W. Allen, 1995) were found to contribute to perceived organizational support. These communications were more effective when carried out by managers than coworkers, which is consistent with the assumption of organizational support theory that those who are more influential in shaping the organization's culture, policies, and procedures have a greater influence on perceived organizational support (Eisenberger et al., 1986).

In Chapter 2, we noted the principle of organizational support theory that favorable treatment contributes more strongly to perceived organizational support when it is believed to be voluntary than when due to pressures such as contractual agreements, government regulations or a tight job market. We found that the positive association between the favorableness of job conditions and perceived organizational support was 6 times greater when those conditions were viewed to be discretionary (Eisenberger et al., 1997). Communication can play an important role in employees' interpretation of whether favorable treatment represents such positive intent.

As M. W. Allen's (1992) research suggests, supplying needed information on a timely basis that helps employees carry out their jobs can increase perceived organizational support. The simple act of asking employees whether they have all the information they need to do their job effectively conveys the organization's positive intent. Employees may be asked whether they are getting the specific kinds of information they need to do their jobs well and, if not, what additional kinds of information are needed. Of course, such surveys are pointless unless the organization intends to follow through with real action.

When the organization voluntarily provides favorable changes in job conditions or human resources benefits, it can enhance the effect on perceived organizational support by communicating the discretionary nature of the changes and their benefits for employees. If part of the reason for a change in an accounting system was to simplify its use by employees, employees ought to be told so. If new options have been introduced into a medical or retirement plan to benefit employees, informing employees just how the change is intended to benefit them will convey the employer's favorable intent. Soliciting employee views in large scale upcoming changes, when feasible, is another useful step.

Communication also has an important influence on perceived organizational support with unfavorable treatment (J. R. Jones & Eisenberger, 2004). Social accounts theory (Bies, 1987; Sitkin & Bies, 1993) deals with apologies and explanations for unfavorable treatment in interpersonal relationships. The use of social accounts to justify organizational actions detrimental to employees has been found to lessen employees' negative responses, including anger toward the account giver, feelings of injustice (Bies & Shapiro, 1987), loss of organizational commitment (Brockner, Dewitt, Grover, & Reed, 1990), complaints about the account giver (Bies, Shapiro, & Cummings, 1988), and retaliatory behavior against the organization, such as employee theft (Bies, 1987; J. Greenberg, 1990).

Social accounts may reduce the negative consequences of unfavorable treatment on perceived organizational support. *Mitigating accounts* involve management's attempt to reduce responsibility, as when the lack of a pay raise is explained by poor economic conditions. These accounts involve attribution of the unfavorable treatment to sources outside the organization. The anger of many employees over the past 2 decades at organizations who have met their dedication with stagnant wages or worse, reductions in benefits or even downsizing has been exacerbated by their belief that much of the treatment was voluntary. It is bad enough to have this happen when one is employed by a struggling company whose officers are taking pay cuts. Employees find it far more upsetting to suffer poor treatment by companies making substantial profits or whose top managers obtain record bonuses. When companies have a legitimate case to make about unfavorable treatment of employees, the resulting reduction of perceived organizational support can be lessened by communicating why the organization was forced to act in the way that it did.

In *exonerating social accounts,* managers do not deny they acted voluntarily but assume responsibility by stressing the legitimacy of the decision (Bies, 1987; A. Cobb & Wooten, 1998). For example, if an employee receives a less-than-expected pay increase, the supervisor's careful justification of the reasons for the decision will help lessen the reduction in perceived organizational support. In *reframing accounts,* managers attempt to cast the treatment in a favorable light, as when the employee's small pay raise is compared with the small average pay increase for other employees. In *penitential accounts,* managers apologize and express regret and sorrow, which may reduce employees' tendency to view their treatment as less due to a stable disposition of the manager or organization than as an unusual, isolated event (Weiner, 1985). Moreover, by using penitential accounts, the organization is conveying that in spite of the unfavorable treatment, it cares enough about the employee to lay its pride on the line and express sorrow and regret for harm done. Thus, the deleterious effects of the treatment on perceived organizational support should be lessened.

Much of the research on social accounts has examined the degree to which offering an account reduces the negative consequences of unfavorable treatment in comparison with the complete absence of an account (Sitkin & Bies, 1993). However, it seems highly likely that in everyday life the perceived plausibility of exonerating accounts and the sincerity of penitential accounts matter a great deal. The use of words to lessen the impression of an uncaring or malevolent organization is a helpful tool within a larger context of an organization that genuinely values its employees. Social accounts are used to attempt to place single events in a larger context that employees perceive as an organization that treats its employees fairly. This perception will dissipate unless protestations of organizational fairness are matched by a long-term record of deeds.

Fairness

Shore and Shore (1995) suggested that repeated instances of fairness in decisions concerning resource distribution should have a strong cumulative effect on perceived organizational support by indicating a concern for employees' welfare. *Procedural justice* refers to the fairness of the procedures for outcomes that are important to employees, such as pay, promotions, and job assignments (Byrne & Cropanzano, 2001; J. Greenberg, 1990). Cropanzano and Greenberg (1997) distinguished between structural and social aspects of procedural justice. *Structural* determinants involve formal rules and policies concerning decisions that affect employees, including adequate notice before decisions are implemented, receipt of accurate information, and voice (i.e., employee input in the decision process). *Social* aspects of procedural justice, also known as *interactional justice,* involve the quality of interpersonal treatment in resource allocation. Social aspects include treating employees with dignity and respect (i.e., interpersonal justice) and providing employees with information concerning how outcomes are determined (i.e., informational justice).

Except when an employee fulfils a unique role so that finding a replacement is difficult, an employer usually experiences fewer adverse consequences from losing a good employee than does the employee. In the United States, the decline of union representation and the weakening of cultural norms that provided implicit assurance of long-term employment to well-performing employees have further increased the power differential between management and employees. Most U.S. employees believe themselves to have little ability to resist management's impositions of excessive workloads or inadequate pay and benefits. Because of this power differential, fair treatment is considered by employees an optional behavior by organizations and may be an especially effective way of enhancing employee trust and increasing perceived organizational support (see also Shore & Shore, 1995).

Cropanzano and Byrne (2001) suggested that the organization's use of fair procedures enables employees to better predict what actions will be associated with rewards and punishments, in the long run. The trust developed from fair procedures builds employees' confidence that if they act to further the organization's objectives, they will be rewarded for doing so. Employees with such trust would be more willing to take on assignments that have a limited chance of success, to candidly admit mistakes, and to openly advance innovative views for helping the organization meet its objectives. Because employees recognize the establishment of fair procedures as a discretionary act by the more powerful organization with important implications for protecting their welfare, such procedures convey the organization's concern for employees' well-being, leading to increased perceived organizational support. Accordingly, Rhoades and Eisenberger's (2002) review of the perceived organizational support literature reported a strong positive relationship between procedural justice and perceived organizational support.

A number of studies suggest that perceived organizational support is a major mechanism contributing to the relationship between fairness and positive outcomes for employees and the organization. Perceived organizational support was found partially responsible (Rhoades, Eisenberger, & Armeli, 2001; Moideenkutty, Blau, Kumar, & Nalakath, 2001) or fully responsible (Masterson et al., 2000) for the association between procedural fairness and employees' emotional attachment to the organization. Moorman, Blakely, and Niehoff (1998) reported that perceived organizational support played a key role in the association between procedural justice and three of four forms of extrarole behavior: *interpersonal helping*, which focuses on helping coworkers in their jobs when such help is needed; *personal industry*, which describes the performance of specific tasks above and beyond the call of duty; and *loyal boosterism*, which describes the promotion of the organizational image to outsiders (Graham, 1991). Specifically, Moorman et al. found that employees who felt fairly treated perceived this favorable treatment as an indication of support from their organization, which was in turn reciprocated by demonstrating high extrarole performance.

On the basis of these findings, Moorman et al. (1998) suggested that perceived organizational support serves as a key mechanism by which organizational fairness contributes to employee performance. Similarly, Masterson et al. (2000) found that perceived organizational support was partially responsible for the relationships of fairness with citizenship behavior directed toward helping the organization, as well as job satisfaction. Masterson's (2001) analysis of social exchange in organizations emphasizes the obligation of employees to repay favorable treatment received from the organization.

Fair procedures appear to be especially important in organizations with traditional, mechanistic structures characterized by rigid bureaucratic hierarchies, centralized power, and fixed communication structures, as opposed to organic structures in which administrative direction and work relationships are more fluid. In a study of 68 organizations, Ambrose and Schminke (2003) found that the perceived fairness of rules was more strongly related to perceived organizational support in mechanistic organizations than organic organizations. In mechanistically structured organizations, formal rules and procedures presumably are more important for employees than in organically structured organizations. Therefore, fairness of rules should have a bigger impact on perceived organizational support in mechanistic organizations.

Fair treatment not only for oneself but also for coworkers may influence perceived organizational support. To the extent that employees identify coworkers' favorable treatment from the organization with their own, that favorable treatment would contribute to perceived organizational support. We can advance social exchange theory from its focus on the individual recipient of favorable treatment to a consideration of employees' reactions to the treatment of coworkers. Such identification with coworkers may depend on individual differences in collectivism and competitiveness. Because employees' identification with others differs depending on their collectivism and competiveness, social exchange approaches to employee–employer relationships may be enriched by considering how reciprocation is influenced by these dispositional differences.

Almost all research on work experiences and perceived organizational support has focused on employees' individual relationship to the organization. However, Salancik and Pfeffer (1978) noted that employees' attitudes and beliefs regarding their job are influenced by social information processing of the behaviors and expressed attitudes of fellow employees. Thus, the social environment, including the organization's treatment of coworkers, provides clues that employees would use to form their own views regarding the organization's valuation of themselves.

Accordingly, Knudsen, Johnson, Martin, and Roman (2003) argued that downsizing would cause surviving employees to view their employer as having low concern for their well-being. These researchers found that survivors in downsized firms showed reduced perceived organizational support and affective organizational commitment relative to employees in nondownsized firms.

Similarly, employees' judgments of fairness may be influenced by the treatment of fellow employees. An experiment with college students found that participants' judgments of the fairness of their own treatment were influenced by how well fellow students stated they had been treated (Lind, Kray, & Thompson, 1998). Lind et al. (1998) suggested that these findings have implications for organizations: Employees' perceptions of procedural justice might be affected by how the organization treats one's coworkers.

Examining procedural justice for coworkers in the workplace, Mossholder, Bennett, and Martin (1998) found that procedural justice ratings regarding one's workgroup explained unique variance in one's own job satisfaction beyond perceptions of personal fair treatment. Additionally, Naumann and Bennett (2000) found that procedural justice perceptions for one's workgroup enhanced helping behavior above and beyond justice perceptions for oneself. De Cremer, Stinglhamber, and Eisenberger (2005) showed that procedural justice for fellow employees was associated with the experience of positive emotions. Stinglhamber and De Cremer (2008) found that coworkers' procedural justice judgments were positively related to employees' own procedural justice judgment, which in turn, influenced their affective commitment to the organization. These findings indicate that employees' judgments concerning fairness are influenced not only by what happens to them but also by what they observe happening to coworkers and by coworkers' judgments of fair treatment.

Because employees share membership with coworkers in various organizational collectives (e.g., job types, workgroups, departments), their identification with coworkers may lead them to interpret fair or unfair treatment of coworkers as an indication of the organization's valuation of themselves, with a corresponding influence on perceived organizational support (see also Eisenberger et al., 1986). For example, through social information processing (Salancik & Pfeffer, 1978), observing or hearing accounts of the unfair implementation of a promotion policy with regard to other employees with whom one identifies may lead to reduced perceived organizational support. Eisenberger, Stinglhamber, Shanock, Jones, and Aselage (2009) found with pharmaceutical employees that perceived organizational support increased with procedural justice for coworkers.

Other kinds of fairness have been proposed. *Distributive justice* refers to the fair allocation of organizational resources such as pay and fringe benefits. According the latest meta-analytic review of the literature

(Kurtessis, Ford, Buffardi, & Stewart, 2009), fair procedures and fair pay both had strong relationships with perceived organizational support, procedural fairness having the stronger relationship. Thus, for employees to determine whether the organization values them, employees pay attention to both the fairness of outcomes and the fairness of procedures used to determine those outcomes.

In keeping with the stress on procedural justice by recent theorists, Wayne et al. (2002) found with U.S. fabricating plant employees that procedural fairness had a much stronger influence on perceived organizational support than did distributive justice. In contrast, Moideenkutty et al. (2001) found, using items selected from the same scales, with pharmaceutical sales representatives in India, that distributive justice was more strongly associated with perceived organizational support than was procedural fairness. This raises the possibility that the value of distributive versus procedural fairness may be influenced by culture.

There are now enough findings to compare the results of level of pay versus distributive justice on perceived organizational support. Where distributive justice is strongly related to perceived organizational support, pay is not (Kurtessis et al., 2009). One reason for the lack of such an observed relationship is that pay in many organizations varies primarily with job type, and individuals with higher level jobs do not necessary feel more supported, on average, than those with lower level jobs. Employees tend to compare their pay with that of relevant others, such as others inside and outside the organization holding similar jobs, and this is why distributive fairness makes a more important contribution to perceived organizational support than does amount of pay per se.

Another way of saying this is that relative pay, given one's contributions, makes an important contribution to perceived organizational support. And employees may focus on even a limited portion of total pay when it is provided on a relative basis. Thus, a potential increase in pay beyond the 1% or 2% one is expecting, ascribed to relative merit, may take on substantial symbolic importance. Even when the absolute amounts of differences in bonus awards are small, the knowledge that a colleague down the hall, whom one considers less worthy, is receiving the greater bonus, may elicit jealously and anger at the organization. Conversely, greater pay than one's unworthy colleague can evoke pride and gratitude toward the organization that it has recognized one's potential. Procedural justice is important for limiting reductions of perceived organizational support by those who are not the highest winners in the merit pool.

Bies and Moag (1986) proposed a third category of fairness, *interactional justice*, involving how one is treated by the organization, especially the supervisor. Interactional justice, in turn, has been divided between fairness in the dispensation of information and interpersonal treatment (Colquitt, 2001). These new types of fairness may be difficult to distinguish from current constructs that are embedded in established theory (see Chapter 4). How is interactional justice meaningfully different from leader–member exchange, which involves employees' social exchange relationships with their supervisors, or different from perceived supervisor support, which concerns employees' belief that their supervisor values their contributions and cares about their well-being? What does it add to say that supervisors are fair in their distribution of information as opposed to being open and honest about important matters?

A recent meta-analysis of the research literature reported that informational fairness was positively related to perceived organizational support (Buffardi, Ford, Kurtessis, & Stewart, 2009). Roch and Shanock (2006) reported that both procedural and informational justice led to perceived organizational support but interpersonal fairness did not. However, they included in their analysis both a general measure of interactional fairness and a specific measure of interpersonal fairness, so the effects of one measure may have obscured the effects of the other. A new meta-analysis of 10 studies reports that interactional justice is positively related to perceived organizational support (Buffardi et al., 2009).

One is struck with the basic finding that procedural fairness is closely related to perceived organizational support, in fact, showing one of the strongest antecedent relationships. Employees are highly averse to being treated in a manner they do not deserve, especially slights to their personal worth. Such slights, as we noted in Chapter 2, evoke strong feelings of anger and vengeance, based on the negative norm of reciprocity. Procedural fairness may diminish the interpretation of unfavorable treatment as personal slight, protecting the organization again the elicitation of high anger and negative reciprocity. On the positive side, as previously noted, the organization's added efforts to treat employees fairly convey a concern with the employees' opinions, as well as a view that employees deserve a careful evaluation, which should enhance perceived organizational support.

Organizational Politics

Related to procedural justice is the concept of *perceived organizational politics*, which refers to attempts to influence others in ways that promote self-interest, often at the expense of rewarding individual merit or furthering the interests of the organization (Cropanzano, Howes, Grandey, & Toth, 1997; Kacmar & Carlson, 1997; Nye & Witt, 1993; Randall, Cropanzano, Borman, & Birjulin, 1999). Among the several ways proposed to assess organizational politics is the Perceptions of Politics Scale (Ferris & Kacmar, 1992), which considers views concerning the prevalence of three types of self-oriented political behavior: obtaining valued outcomes by acting in a self-serving manner, going along with ill-advised management decisions to secure valued outcomes, and obtaining pay increases and promotions through favoritism rather than merit (Kacmar & Carlson, 1997). When organizational politics becomes an endemic part of the organizational culture, at the expense of concern for the organization's future or fair treatment of fellow employees, perceived organizational support should plummet. Thus, organizational politics shows the strongest relationship (in the negative direction) of any antecedent of perceived organizational support (Rhoades & Eisenberger, 2002).

Employees appear to discriminate political activity across three hierarchical levels (i.e., at the highest level in the organization, one level up from one's current level, and at one's peer level; Byrne, Kacmar, Stoner, & Hochwarter, 2005; Hochwarter, Kacmar, Perrewé, & Johnson, 2003). Politics perceived at one level up from one's current level and politics at the highest levels in the organization were negatively related to perceived organizational support, whereas politics emanating from one's own level was found unrelated to perceived organizational support (Hochwarter et al., 2003). This makes sense because organizational support theory assumes that individuals identify higher level organizational representatives more strongly than coworkers with the organization. One study also found that employees' perceived organizational support lessened the relationship between perceived politics at one level up and their depressed mood at work (Byrne et al., 2005). But no such effect was found for perceived politics at the highest level of the organization. Perhaps mistreatment by supervisors is strongly associated with negative mood for many employees so that perceived organizational support served as an effective counterweight for this aversive outcome.

Rewards and Job Conditions

Shore and Shore (1995) suggested that human resources practices that recognize employee contributions would be positively related to perceived organizational support. A variety of rewards and job conditions have been studied in relation to perceived organizational support, for example, training and developmental experiences, job security, autonomy, organizational size, role stressors, and work–family policies.

EXPECTED REWARDS

Employees' expectation that the organization will generously reward achievable high levels of performance indicates to employees that the organization values their contributions and thus should increase perceived organizational support. Such rewards would include various kinds of recognition available to the organization, ranging from private awards (e.g., thanks by supervisors) to public awards (e.g., increased pay and promotion). My colleagues and I (Eisenberger, Rhoades, & Cameron, 1999) found a positive relationship between retail employees' expectation of reward for high pay and their perceived organizational support. The expected reward increased perceived organizational support not only directly but also by enhancing the employees' belief that they had increased control over their jobs, or job autonomy.

Rewarding employees for high effort is a hotly debated topic, and we take the affirmative position, with one of its benefits being perceived organizational support. According to cognitive evaluation theory (Deci & Ryan, 1985), individuals view reward as a discomforting attempt to control their behavior. This purported aversive reduction in perceived autonomy reduces task interest (see also Amabile, 1983). Additionally, Amabile and her colleagues (Amabile, 1983; Hennessey & Amabile, 1988) assumed that reward reduces task interest and focuses attention on the reward at the expense of spontaneous task performance.

The view that reward is an unpleasant constraint on behavior, reducing perceived self-determination, seems consistent with empirical findings linking reward to a loss of task interest. Following reward, individuals often spent less time performing an activity and stated they liked the activity less, as compared with a control group that performed the task without reward (Deci, Koestner, & Ryan, 1999). Despite cognitive evaluation theory's role as the most widely accepted explanation for the decremental effects of reward on task interest, few of the more than 100 studies on reward's relationship to task interest assessed the participants' perceived self-determination. However, the great majority of studies demonstrating a decremental effect of reward on task interest used reward in ways seldom used in the workplace: Reward was completely unrelated to performance or contingent on a very low level of performance.

My colleagues and I (Eisenberger, Rhoades, & Cameron, 1999) suggested that use of the reward in everyday life conveys not social control, as supposed by cognitive evaluation theory, but increased self-determination and autonomy. People understand that reward's use in everyday life is utilitarian, involving the reward giver's lack of control over the potential reward recipient; those offering the reward believe that favorable consequences are needed to obtain the cooperation of the person being asked to carry out the task. Specifically, the promise or repeated use of reward communicates that (a) the person, group, or organization giving the reward lacks control over the performance of the potential reward recipient, and (b) the potential reward recipient can, if he or she so desires, decline the reward and not act as requested.

In addition to reward's function of increasing perceived self-determination, we suggested that reward for high performance symbolizes competence beyond that conveyed by favorable performance feedback (Eisenberger, Rhoades, & Cameron, 1999). People recognize that reward for superior performance in everyday life signifies high achievement. Therefore, rewards following high performance magnify the individual's sense of achievement and perception of competence.

We carried out research with college students indicating that a reward contingency requiring a high level of performance increased perceived self-determination and perceived competence, both of which enhanced intrinsic task interest (Eisenberger, Rhoades, & Cameron, 1999). A quantitative review of the small number of studies assessing the effect of reward on perceived self-determination supports the view of a positive relationship (Eisenberger, Pierce, & Cameron, 1999). Moreover, in field studies, employees' expectation of financial rewards for high job performance was associated with perceived self-determination that, in turn, was related to perceived organizational support and performance. Thus, reward for high performance appears to be positively related to perceived organizational support, and this relationship seems to be due partly to employees' perception that they have increased control over their work tasks.

TRAINING AND DEVELOPMENTAL EXPERIENCES

Wayne, Shore, and Liden (1997) suggested that formal training experiences communicate the organization's investment in the employee, leading to an increase in perceived organizational support. The literature review by Rhoades and Eisenberger (2002) reported only a modest relationship between training and perceived organizational support. However, training that develops skills and talents that are helpful to an employee's career should be differentiated from more mundane types of training that simply allow participants to deal with paperwork or routine aspects of work. Training that is narrowly tailored to allow employees to perform their jobs better is probably viewed by employees as undertaken entirely to benefit the organization, with little interest in them. In contrast, training and other developmental experiences that expand employees' knowledge and skills in a meaningful way convey the organization's view of employees as making a valuable contribution to the organization, leading to increased perceived organizational support. Wayne et al. (1997) assessed the influence of challenging assignments and developmental opportunities on perceived organizational support and found a substantially higher relationship than was found when employees were asked simply about training. Tansky and Cohen (2001) found that satisfaction with career development experiences was positively related to perceived organizational support, which in turn, was associated with increased affective commitment to the organization.

Developmental training experiences may be especially important to older employees to revivify jobs marked by a plateauing of opportunities for more interesting job content and promotion. Armstrong-Stassen and Ursel (2009) carried out a pair of studies on this issue with employees over the age of 50 years, with one sample of managerial and professional employees and the other of nurses. The researchers found that promotional plateauing and, even more so, job content plateauing, were negatively related to perceived organizational support. These decremental influences were counteracted to some degree by developmental training practices. Perceived organizational support was positively related to career satisfaction and intention to remain with the organization. It is interesting to note that perceived organizational support had a much greater influence than work centrality (belief in the importance of work in one's life) in influencing intent to remain, and health status had a negligible influence. Because chronic nursing shortages exist in part because of high turnover in a stressful occupation, the retention of older nurses would be a beneficial strategy. By enhancing developmental training practices and reducing job plateauing, retention of older workers in critical jobs could be enhanced.

JOB SECURITY

Researchers lack hard evidence on how employees' views concerning their prospects for job retention have changed over the past several decades. However, anecdotal evidence suggests that even before the recent worldwide economic downturn, U.S. employees were growing more nervous about holding on to their jobs. Large and increasing numbers of Americans face rising financial risks because of high indebtedness, increasing costs for education and medical care, declining insurance coverage by private business. Median U.S. income has shown little gain over the past 2 decades. Workers lack bargaining power, owing to the historic decline in unions' membership and power, and the pressure of worldwide competition. Simultaneously, Americans have faced increasing uncertainty about how they will be able to pay for rising medical costs if they lack or lose the limited insurance provide with their jobs. It has also become much more expensive to pay for advanced schooling for children and, with the widespread curtailment of generous defined benefit retirement plans, Americans must worry about how they will be able to retire. Encouraged by a cultural acceptance of indebtedness to have the manifold products of materialism, employees must worry about meeting substantial debt payments each month if they lose their jobs. Simply put, for most people, it is more risky to lose a job now than in the past decades.

Assurance of continued employment should have a strong positive influence on perceived organizational support (D. G. Allen, Shore, &

Griffeth, 1999). As my colleagues and I found, employees pay considerable attention to the discretionary nature of the favorable or unfavorable treatment they receive from their employer (Eisenberger et al., 1997). My colleagues and I observed that most employees of a diverse sample believed that their organization had substantial control over job security (Eisenberger et al., 1997). Forty-six percent of the participants designated the organization's control over this job condition as high, 31% as medium, and 22% as low. Thus, a majority of employees give credit to the organization for high levels of job security and blame the organization for low job security, with consequences for perceived organizational support. Rhoades and Eisenberger's (2002) meta-analytic review of the literature showed a substantial relationship between job security and perceived organizational support.

Whereas most of the studies on job insecurity have been conducted in the context of organizational crisis or decline, Rosenblatt and Ruvio (1996) suggested that job insecurity can occur and have negative consequences for employee well-being even when the organization has given no indication of imminent layoffs. These researchers found that job insecurity had an adverse effect on perceived organizational support, organizational commitment, perceived performance, intention to quit, and resistance to change. Therefore, if job insecurity has a negative impact on work attitudes in normal times, a considerable adverse impact on organizational effectiveness is expected under the conditions of organizational decline and downsizing, when job insecurity is most conspicuous (Rosenblatt & Ruvio, 1996).

Although perceived organizational support plays a preventative role in reducing the detrimental effects of restructuring on employee turnover, there are limits. Repeated stress-inducing restructuring in which management signifies little concern for employees takes a toll on perceived organizational support. Armstrong-Stassen (1997) conducted an exploratory study on the long-term effects of exposure to repeated organizational downsizings and being designated a surplus employee on survivors' reactions. She found that, compared with managers who had not been declared surplus, managers who had been declared surplus but were still employed by the organization because they were assigned to another temporary position reported they were less likely to engage in active coping, had higher levels of stress and burnout, experienced less perceived organizational support, and were more likely to believe they were remaining with the organization because they had to (i.e., high levels of continuance commitment).

Even though caution is warranted in drawing strong conclusions from these findings because of the small number of participants, the results suggest that companies may need to reexamine the practice of declaring employees surplus, especially if the surplus employees end up remaining with the organization. Evidence provided by this study indicates that those survivors who are personally affected by the downsizing, for example, those who find another position in the organization after having been declared surplus, may have even stronger negative reactions than those survivors who are not directly involved. Perceived support helps prevent aversive reactions to downsizing but is lessened by repeated downsizings or devaluations by employers such as being declared surplus.

AUTONOMY

As we previously discussed, my colleagues and I found a positive relationship between employees' autonomy and perceived organizational support (Eisenberger, Rhoades, & Cameron, 1999), and other studies report large relationships, as well, with perceived organizational support (Rhoades & Eisenberger, 2002). By *autonomy,* we mean employees' perceived control over how they carry out their job, including scheduling, work procedures, and task variety. Autonomy has traditionally been highly valued in Western cultures (Geller, 1982; Hogan, 1975). By indicating the organization's trust in employees to decide wisely how they will carry out their job, high autonomy should increase perceived organizational support (Eisenberger, Rhoades, & Cameron, 1999). Southwest Airlines is a good example of the effective use of job autonomy for lower level employees. They are given decision-making authority to deal effectively with unexpected problems within the scope of their responsibilities and knowledge, and are encouraged to act as effective problem solvers. Equally important, they are given the organizational support they need, such as the access to the latest available needed information and cooperation by other managers and personnel, to help them as they work through a problem, whether it is a group of late-arriving passengers transferring between Southwest flights or a plane that has unexpectedly gone out of service. Autonomy is backed by cooperation and needed resources to create a strong experience of perceived organizational support.

ORGANIZATION SIZE

Dekker and Barling (1995) argued that individuals feel less valued in large organizations, where highly formalized policies and procedures may reduce flexibility in dealing with employees' individual needs. Even though large organizations can show benevolence to groups of employees, as can small ones, the reduced flexibility for meeting the needs of individual employees, imparted by formal rules associated with attempts to regularize procedures in large-scale organizations, could reduce perceived organizational support. Although organizational size might be considered more of an organization-wide characteristic than a job characteristic, this category fits closely with job characteristics and so is discussed here.

The latest meta-analytic examination of 13 studies shows only a slight but statistically significant negative relationship between organizational size and perceived organizational support (Kurtessis et al., 2009). What may be more important for perceived organizational support than the overall size of the organization is the size of the functional units within the organization, the support provided those units by the organization, and the lack of interference by bureaucratic fiefdoms at the organizational level.

At my former university, a moderate-sized organization, a minor fiefdom had been established at one point dealing with hiring. Any variations from established job descriptions or pay schedules could be accomplished only by prostrating oneself before those who ran this office. As they layered rule upon rule and added staff to write and enforce these rules, these managers' power grew, and the staff's capacity to create more and more paperwork grew as well. Some of us who brought research grant funds into the university, from which the university benefited financially by charging overhead, grew ever more frustrated as the simple act of hiring someone with one's grant money became slower and more complicated. Our function seemed to be, in this instance, to service the desire for power of bureaucrats rather than to do a good job, and our perceived organizational support suffered.

In contrast, as discussed in the next chapter, W. L. Gore and Associates, a highly successful manufacturer of synthetic fibers with many employees, keeps its plant sizes and bureaucracy small to encourage flexibility and innovation. As organizations grow larger and increasing layers of formalized procedures distance employees from their earlier relationships with the organization's founders, there may be an increased tendency for lower level employees to view themselves as cogs in an impersonal machine that cares little about their contributions or well-being. Management must be constantly on guard to be sure that the bureaucracy of the organization facilitates the basic goals and objectives of the organization rather than interfering with them.

ROLE STRESSORS

Stressors refer to demands with which individuals feel unable to cope (Lazarus & Folkman, 1984). To the extent that employees attribute job-related stressors to conditions that are controllable by the organization, as opposed to conditions inherent in the job or resulting from outside pressures on the organization, stressors should reduce perceived organizational support. Stressors related to three aspects of employees' role in the organization have been studied as antecedents to lessened perceived organizational support: *work overload*, involving demands that exceed what an employee can reasonably accomplish in a given time;

role ambiguity, involving the absence of clear information about one's job responsibilities; and *role conflict,* involving mutually incompatible job responsibilities. The most recent meta-analytic review of the research literature reported moderate relationships of all three kinds of stressors with perceived organizational support (Kurtessis et al., 2009). It is interesting to note that role conflict seems to be more highly related to perceived organizational support than is work overload, perhaps because conflicting responsibilities are seen as more readily under the control of the organization. As discussed in Chapter 2, I found that sales employees of a retailer with whom I consulted viewed the stress associated with long hours as more a function of the job and an opportunity for greater pay, than as a strategy by management to take advantage of them.

WORK–FAMILY POLICIES

Much of the research on work–family relationships focuses on the interference of work with home life or vice versa. Long hours and emergencies associated with child care, as well as other family difficulties, often interfere with work and enhance negative reactions to problems at work. Thus, elder care responsibility was found to be negatively associated with perceived organizational support and job satisfaction (Buffardi, Smith, O'Brien, & Erdwins, 1999). Specific policies that deal with problems of private life (e.g., day care, maternity leave) add to perceptions that the organization has favorable family policies, contributing to perceived organizational support (Gibson, 2006).

Perceived Support for Specific Organizational Objectives and Employee Needs

Perceived organizational support should be distinguished from what is often termed *perceived organizational support for organizational goals,* such as creativity (Stokols, Clitheroe, & Zmuidzinas, 2002; Zhou & George, 2001). Perceived organizational support for a given goal is not simply a delimited or narrow form of perceived organizational support. In the first place, perceived organizational support for organizational goals does not signify, as does perceived organizational support, that the organization values one's current contributions. Thus, *perceived support for creativity* refers to the encouragement of creativity by such means as supplying needed resources and rewarding desired behavior when it occurs. Perceived organizational support for creativity might contribute to perceived organizational support to the extent that such support is consistent with employees' work values or personal interests and motivations. For example, perceived organizational support for creativity might increase overall perceived organizational support for employees who find personal fulfillment in being creative. In contrast, others who have less creative talent or less interest in being creative might find such an emphasis on creativity a greater source of anxiety than caring on the part of the organization.

Zhou and George (2001) found that creativity increased with job dissatisfaction among employees who perceived high organizational support for creativity. They interpreted the finding to indicate that employees viewed creativity as a way to change their undesirable work situation. This clearly is very different from perceived organizational support, which, by meeting employee socioemotional needs and increasing reward expectancies, increases job satisfaction.

A personal example may be helpful. At my former university, there was a strong emphasis on obtaining grants from scientific agencies. My department fully supported this activity, providing all sorts of budgetary accounting help. The ostensible purpose of the funding was to help professors carry out their research. Professors were evaluated, as at many universities, on the basis of how many grant dollars they obtained. The stated rationale was that obtaining grant funding was an indication of the professor's favorable evaluation by colleagues. I have always disagreed with this philosophy, believing instead that this argument is a fig leaf for the university's monetary motives and that the quality of one's research should be judged by one's publications. Grants certainly do have value, they help get research done—I just think they should be viewed as a means not as an end.

This emphasis on grant getting (perceived organizational support for external funding) no doubt contributed to general perceived organizational support for those faculty members who strongly valued grant getting for themselves. However, I felt it more as pressure from the university than the university's high regard for me. It is true that when I have had grants and received the rewards for them from the university, perceived organizational support for this particular behavior has reduced my negative reactions toward grant getting to some degree. But, overall, perceived organizational support for grants has had a negative impact on my perceived organizational support. The point is, perceived organizational support for meeting organizational goals is not a miniature version of perceived organizational support—it has a qualitatively different meaning. The relationship between perceived support for organizational goals and perceived organizational support is illustrated in Figure 3.2.

Another research category involves organizational support that fulfills specific employee needs. For example, within the context of expatriate

FIGURE 3.2

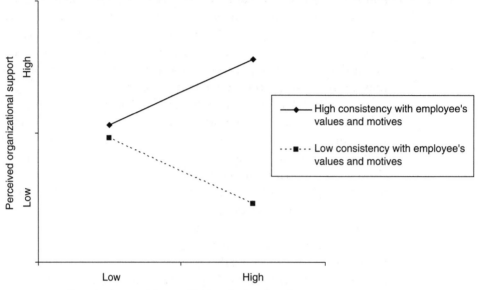

The relationship between perceived support for specific organizational goals and perceived organizational support when inconsistent and when consistent with employees' values and motives. The solid line indicates that perceived support for specific organizational goals is consistent with employees' values and motives. The dashed line indicates that perceived support for specific organizational goals is inconsistent with employees' values and motives.

employee success, Kraimer and Wayne (2004) examined perceived organizational supports for aiding (a) career needs, (b) satisfaction of financial needs in terms of compensation and reward benefits, and (c) expatriates' adjustment following their job transfer. Among the findings of interest were that *career perceived organizational support* increased the expatriates' intention to complete the assignment, *financial perceived organizational support* was positively related to task performance, and *adjustment perceived organizational support* was unexpectedly negatively related to both inrole and extrarole performance and positively related to intention to complete the expatriate assignment. These findings are of considerable interest, and the surprising performance finding concerning expatriates' adjustment certainly warrants replication.

These specific types of support were positively related to perceived organizational support and were viewed as multiple types of perceived organizational support. We certainly agree that the organization's concern with meeting specific employee needs, as perceived by employees, makes an important contribution to perceived organizational support. For the sake of clarity, one should remember that perceived organizational support is not simply an accumulation of the employee's perceptions about the organization's fulfillment of diverse needs. Perceived support incorporates employees' views about the extent to which the organization is concerned about their welfare and the degree to which the organization values their contribution. This valuation of the employees' contributions is omitted if we simply speak of the organization's concern with meeting employees' needs. Further, the organization's concern with meeting employee needs, even multiple needs, does not get at the attribution of an interest by the organization in the employees' total welfare. The difference lies in the employees' expectation that if they have high perceived organizational support, the organization will look beyond established policies and procedures to try to be helpful as new needs and problems arise.

Work Status

The central tenets of organizational support theory have been generally applied to regular employment relationships, wherein employees work for their organizations on a full-time, long-term basis. However, contingent employment relationships, such as part-time and temporary work, are becoming more common (McLean Parks, Kidder, & Gallagher, 1998; Nollen & Axel, 1996; Rousseau, 1997). In today's work environment, organizations frequently use contingent employment with one or more of the following goals: (a) reducing recruitment and selection costs by hiring the temporary workers as needed, (b) increasing staffing level flexibility by providing an efficient way to adjust staffing levels according to current demand, and (c) reducing overall costs in terms of labor and administrative expenses (see also Feldman, Doerpinghaus, & Turnley, 1994). Therefore, many service organizations, such as restaurants, rely heavily on contingent employees (Stamper & Van Dyne, 2001).

Contingent employment raises several issues regarding perceived organizational support. First, management may view contingent employees as less worthy of support than full-time employees, and contingent employees may be less interested in investing their efforts and loyalty on behalf of the organization in return for favorable treatment. Employers provide less training and development for short-term and part-time employees because they view the development of their full-time employees as a better investment (McLean Parks et al., 1998; Tsui, Pearce, Porter, & Hite, 1995), and managers and supervisors may be less likely to develop strong relationships with contingent employees for the same reasons.

Because of management's failure in many organizations to provide a high level of training and development for contingent, as compared with regular, employees, one might expect that perceived organizational support should be higher for regular employees than for contingent employees. However, this result may be far from universal. One would expect these differences to vary substantially from one organization to another. For example, a firm that hires respected contingent employees primarily for specializations it lacks for key roles might treat such employees more supportively than its own permanent employees in comparable positions. In contrast, organizations that hire seasonal contingent employees, such as postal employees during the holidays or farm workers during harvest seasons, may view their temporary workers as less skilled and less worthy of support than their own permanent employees.

Further, in many organizations, the perceived organizational support of regular employees is not particularly high (Eisenberger et al., 1990). Regular employees may expect more from the organization than contingent employees and therefore may be more prone to disappointment. According to psychological contract theory (Rousseau, 1995), regular employees believe that the organization is obliged to provide favorable levels of resources to various kinds to employees. To the extent that these resources are not afforded, employees would believe that their reciprocal exchange relationship with the organization had been violated. Such contract violations may reduce perceived organizational support (Aselage & Eisenberger, 2003). The present authors have commonly observed a considerable decline in perceived organizational support among permanent employees in a variety of organizations during their 1st year of employment. Thus, greater perceived organizational support by regular employees than contingent workers would depend on the organization's fulfillment of its added obligations to them.

An employee working a small number of hours per week or a student taking a summer job may be less responsive to perceived organizational support if the employee is not interested in becoming a future full-time employee with the organization. Nevertheless, organizational support theory suggests that contingent employees should respond with perceived organizational support to being well treated, and perceived organizational support should produce a favorable orientation toward the organization on the basis of the norm or reciprocity and at least some degree of fulfillment of socioemotional needs. For example, college students who are treated supportively at restaurants during summer jobs often return during subsequent summers and speak appreciatively and with fondness of their association with their restaurant. Moorman and Harland (2002) found that temporary employees' perceptions of favorable treatment by the organization were positively related to felt obligation, affective commitment, and extrarole behaviors carried out on behalf of the organization.

Gakovic and Tetrick (2003) compared the perceived organizational support and its consequences for full-time and part-time employees attending college classes. They found that part-time employees reported higher levels of perceived organizational support and no significant differences in the levels of social exchange relationships, the organization's obligations, and the extent to which the obligations had been fulfilled. These findings suggest that the processes studied extensively with full-time employees also apply to part-time employees. Gakovic and Tetrick noted that full-time employees reported higher levels of sacrifice and suggested that they may have higher standards of what constitutes perceived organizational support, leading to lower reported levels of perceived organizational support. These intriguing findings warrant follow-up studies.

The voluntariness of the contingent employees' work status (Feldman, Doerpinghaus, & Turnley, 1995) may influence perceived organizational support. *Voluntary contingent employees* are defined as those who pursue part-time or temporary jobs because they desire these work arrangements. A college student working part-time to earn extra money would be designated a voluntary contingent employee. By contrast, *involuntary contingent employees* work on a part-time or temporary basis but desire regular employment. A new college graduate who takes a part-time job after failing to find regular work would be denoted an involuntary contingent employee. Because attaining regular employment is a salient need for involuntary contingent workers, they may attribute the organization's failure to offer them regular employment to low valuation. This would be more likely if the organization were known to make use of contingent employees on a continuing basis. In such cases, involuntary contingent employees should have lower levels of perceived organizational support than voluntary contingent workers.

The sensitivity of contingent employees to factors that influence organizational support, with consequences for organizational citizenship behavior, suggests that employers should not forgo providing favorable discretionary treatment to these employees. In Chapter 4, we discuss outcomes of perceived organizational support for contingent workers. Having contingent employees who are helpful, committed, and enthusiastic as coworkers can boost morale and productivity, whereas having time servers can have the opposite effect. As Liden et al. (2003) pointed out,

> even though it is relatively easy to dismiss contingent employees who do not perform up to expectation, it may be even more cost effective to bolster commitment and performance through fair treatment and support as opposed to frequently replacing contingent employees. (p. 621)

Value Congruence

In some cases, the organization's values and objectives promote core values of employees. By affirming the employee's self-identity, this alignment between organization and employee should contribute to perceived organizational support. Sometimes individuals join a particular organization precisely so they can have the satisfaction of enacting their values, such as when an individual who loves nature and values its conservation obtains a job related to wilderness conservation.

My colleagues and I carried out a series of studies on dispositional differences in enjoyment of nature, which we termed the *motivation for sensory pleasure* (Eisenberger, Sucharski, et al., 2010), and during the course of which we got to know dedicated managers who worked for the U.S. National Park Service. For many of these managers, the value of preserving and protecting the wilderness was so important that they had refused promotions that would give them greater pay and greater authority but would dilute their opportunity to further these objectives because they would be kept busy by less relevant administrative matters. Over the years I worked with them, their perceived organizational support comported substantially with the extent to which the National Park Service supported their mission.

Organizational behavior that challenges strongly held values can also reduce perceived organizational support. Wendell Porter, the former head of corporate communications at CIGNA, the U.S.'s fourth largest health insurer, reported that he was highly valued and well treated by his organization (http://www.pbs.org/moyers/journal/07102009/transcript4.html). However, when he attended a "health expedition" organized in Tennessee to provide free medical aid to those who could not afford it, he found that

> hundreds of people were standing in line to get free medical care in animal stalls. Some had camped out the night before in the rain. It was like being in a different country. It moved me to tears. Shortly afterward I was flying in a corporate jet and realized someone's insurance premiums were paying for me to fly that way. I knew it wasn't long before I had to leave the industry. (Lieberman, 2009)

Porter felt that as a spokesman for a major health insurance firm he was helping to perpetuate a system in which many individuals went uninsured or underinsured. Among the tactics Porter felt he could not reconcile with his values were substantial increases in the premiums of small businesses that his company imposed when individual employees developed a serious illness so as to make the insurance unaffordable for the businesses, stopping payments for the sick individuals. When he brought such problems to attention to other high-level managers, they quickly dismissed his arguments. Porter felt there was a basic disparity between his fundamental humanity and the values of the organization. The organization refused to recognize the problems he attempted to bring to its attention, and the requirement that he act inconsistently with his values lessened perceived organizational support. Finally, Porter resigned his job and took a position with a public interest group.

Porter stated that he had managed to distance himself from the problems of the U.S. medical care system over many years while working as a high-level manager at the insurance company's corporate headquarters. His work to increase corporate profits, which meant fighting government proposals that would result in greater numbers of Americans being insured, lower rates, and fewer denials of payments for treatment, occurred without any personal or written contract by Porter with the customers of his company. He was used to chauffeured limos and corporate jets—the sick and dying were mere numbers. His original attitude was consistent with classic findings that the more distant individuals are from people physically and psychologically, the greater the willingness to be obedient to instructions to harm them (Milgram, 1974).

There has been little systematic research studying value congruence as an antecedent of perceived organizational support. In an unpublished doctoral dissertation, Ellis (2008) studied the relationship between corporate social responsibility (CSR) and perceived organizational support as a function of the favorableness of employees' attitudes toward CSR. Quoting McWilliams and Siegel (2001, p. 117), Ellis (2008) noted the common definition of CSR as "actions that appear to further some social good, beyond the interest of the firm and that which is required by law" (p. 13). The self-publicity provided by firms engaged in such actions suggests that the motivation behind them is intended partly to promote the organization's positive image. For some companies, such as Ben and Jerry's, Timberland, The Body Shop, Stoneybrook Farms, and Whole Foods, CSR has been used as an integral part of the brand's image to organization's advantage (Ellis, 2008). In some cases, multibillion dollar firms such as McDonald's (think Ronald McDonald House) obtain invaluable publicity by donating a small percentage of profits to highly visible charitable undertakings.

Using employees of a semiconductor manufacturer, Ellis (2008) studied three aspects of CSR policies that might contribute to perceived organizational support. *CSR awareness* referred to employees' knowledge of the organization's ongoing CSR activities. *CSR fit* referred to the consistency of the CSR activities with the firm's primary activities or values. This is an issue of sincerity, according to Ellis. For example, a small amount of funds devoted by a cigarette manufacturer to programs for stopping smoking will be seen as a publicity gimmick. CSR *motivation* concerned the extent to which the company's support for social and charitable causes benefited the cause more than the company. To assess whether value congruence was important, the participants were asked a series of questions about their attitudes toward the company's social responsibilities. The fit and motivation components of CSR were positively related to perceived organizational support, although awareness was not. Further, the relationship between CSR and perceived organizational support tended to become greater for employees with positive attitudes toward the organization, although the relationship was only marginally significant. These results suggest that CSR enhances perceived organizational support. They hint at the possibility that value congruence may increase perceived organizational support. We suggest that this occurs when the organization reflects or negates strongly held employee values and that this is an excellent topic to be followed up.

Employee Characteristics

In the identification of the determinants of perceived organizational support, organizational support theory (e.g., Eisenberger et al., 1986; Shore & Shore, 1995) has primarily focused on actions by the organization that influence perceived organizational support. Persisting individual characteristics have been considered to the extent that they influence consequences of perceived organizational support such as individual differences in endorsement of the reciprocity norm and the strength of socioemotional needs. Dispositional characteristics are beginning to receive more attention as possible antecedents of perceived organizational support.

Dispositional tendencies to experience Positive or Negative Affect, two related but distinct personality dimensions (Watson & Clark, 1984), might influence perceived organizational support by altering whether employees interpret organizational treatment as benevolent or malevolent (Aquino & Griffeth, 1999; Witt & Hellman, 1992). Additionally, personality might influence perceived organizational support by affecting employee behaviors and, consequently, treatment by the organization (Aquino & Griffeth, 1999). Positive Affectivity might lead to expansive and friendly behaviors, which would cause the employee to make a favorable impression on others and would result in more effective working relationships with coworkers and supervisors. Conversely, aggressive or withdrawal behaviors resulting from Negative Affectivity could inhibit the development of favorable working relationships, reducing perceived organizational support. A recent meta-analysis (L. Buffardi, personal communication, September 13, 2009) reported a small positive correlation between perceived organizational support and Positive Affectivity (correlation = .23) and a slightly higher correlation with Negative Affectivity (see, e.g., Byrne et al., 2005; Gosserand, 2003; James, 2005; Konik, 2005; Suazo, 2003).

Some of the Big Five personality dimensions might be related to perceived organizational support. Notably, Conscientiousness might lead to increased job performance, which, in turn, would lead to better treatment by the organization and heightened perceived organizational support. *Conscientiousness*, as defined by Costa and McCrae (1985), is composed of competence, order, dutifulness, achievement, striving, self-discipline, and deliberateness. *Agreeableness*, which might lead to greater collaborative efforts, is composed of trust, straight-forwardness, altruism, compliance, modesty, and tender-mindedness (Costa & McCrae, 1985). A recent meta-analytic review of the literature by Buffardi et al. (2009) reported low but statistically significant relationships of Agreeableness and Conscientiousness with perceived organizational support. The high correlation was .19, between Agreeableness and perceived organizational support, suggesting the possibility that employees with a personality disposition toward friendliness and cooperation are slightly more likely to be supported by the organization. However, the effect is small relative to those related to work experiences.

These results indicate that work experiences of various kinds exert a far greater influence on perceived organizational support than do personality variables. This is consistent with the emphasis of organizational support theory on work experiences as important influences on the development of perceived organizational support. Yet, one little explored possibility is that although dispositional differences may not have an independent influence on perceived organizational support, they may alter the influence of work-related variables on perceived organizational support. We do have evidence of one such effect regarding how employees' individualism and collectivism affect the influence of fair treatment on perceived organizational support.

The effectiveness of antecedents of perceived organizational support might be influenced by various cultural or learned individual differences in reactivity to favorable treatment. We previously noted that the contribution of fairness to perceived organizational support depends on fair treatment for coworkers as well as oneself. The extent to which favorable or unfavorable treatment accorded coworkers influences an employee's perceived organizational support may depend on the employee's collectivist and competitive personal orientations. Collectivism, involving a propensity toward forming strong mutual bonds with others, differs in strength from one culture to another and among the individuals within a culture (Markus & Kitayama, 1991; Oyserman, Coon, & Kemmelmeier, 2002; Rhee, Uleman, & Lee, 1996; Triandis, 1995). Thus, variation in collectivism can be studied either cross-culturally or as an individual propensity. Among those with a collectivist orientation, common goals, values, and shared fate of the ingroup are salient (Oyserman et al.,

2002, p. 8). Collectivists focus on the needs, desires, and goals of group members because the welfare of these others is viewed as necessary to meet personal goals and because the goals of group members tend to be accepted as personal goals.

The orientation toward collectivism might influence employees' reactions toward the favorable treatment of fellow employees. Group membership makes an important contribution to the self-identity for individuals with a strong collectivist orientation. These individuals have an increased tendency to view ingroup outcomes as having personal relevance. Accordingly, we and our colleagues (Eisenberger, Stinglhamber, et al., 2009) found that collectivism increased the relationship between fair treatment for coworkers and perceived organizational support.

Collectivism and individualism have been, in the past, frequently conceptualized as opposite ends on a continuum. More recent theory and empirical evidence indicate that collectivism and individualism form distinct, but related, dimensions (Oyserman et al., 2002; Triandis & Gelfand, 1998). Competitiveness has been conceptualized as a form of individualism that involves a desire to increase status by achieving more than others (Triandis, 1995; Triandis & Gelfand, 1998) and as a basic social value in its own right (Kuhlman & Marshello, 1975; Van Lange, 2000). Triandis and Gelfand (1998) characterized competitors, whom they termed *vertical individualists,* as wanting to gain status through favorable social comparison. Thus, competitors should consider the favorable treatment of others less when inferring their own valuation by the organization.

Although collectivism and competitiveness may appear to be inconsistent orientations, concern with the welfare of the group (i.e., collectivism) and demonstrating success through superior performance (i.e., competitiveness) are not necessarily incompatible (Triandis & Gelfand, 1998). However, competitors view their success primarily in terms of their own personal achievement. Procedural justice for coworkers would thus have reduced relevance for competitors as an indication that the organization values their contributions. Thus, we and our colleagues (Eisenberger, Stinglhamber, et al., 2009) found for competitors that fair treatment for fellow employees had diminished influence on perceived organizational support.

C. Hui, Wong, and Tjosvold (2007) suggested that acceptance of traditional Chinese values should lead to perceived organizational support and provided data consistent with this view. C. Hui et al. suggested that traditional values associated with deference include the expectation that supervisors will use their expertise to solve problems and make decisions that benefit the organization, resulting in high perceived organizational support. This argument assumes that supervisors' view that they should benefit the organization implies that they should be helpful to employees. Chinese employees with traditional values may be more skeptical of their supervisors than this because the finding was not successfully replicated (Farh, Hackett, & Liang, 2007).

Summary and Implications

The diverse ways to increase perceived organizational support provide organizations with many options for showing support for employees, some of which involve little financial cost. One might be tempted to conclude that organizations should set supportive treatment of employees as a general goal, perhaps incorporated in its mission statement, leaving the specifics to individual managers. However, general statements of values and goals are often simply paid lip service. Enron, the Houston, Texas, conglomerate that was bankrupted by its massive illegal financial activities, embraced a code of ethics that strongly emphasized the respectful treatment of all employees and expressed an unequivocal intolerance for abusive treatment. Yet, these guidelines masked a totalitarian atmosphere in which dissent was severely punished. To be effective, the goal of enhancing perceived organizational support must be supported by strategies whose effectiveness is continually monitored.

Prospective and newly hired employees begin to form anticipated perceived organization support prior to organizational entry based on what they hear about the organization from interviewers and other organizational representatives, and from friends and the media. Favorable promises made by the organizational representatives may enhance perceived organizational support. It seems likely that employees' perceptions concerning their reciprocal obligations with their employer (the psychological contract), established early in employees' relationship with the organization, should influence perceived organizational support, and vice versa. Fulfillment of the psychological contract is associated with increased perceived organizational support (Coyle-Shapiro & Kessler, 2000; Coyle-Shapiro & Conway, 2005). However, Coyle-Shapiro and Conway (2005) provided evidence that this effect is actually due to a positive relationship between current resources provided by the organization and perceived organizational support. More work needs to be done on the circumstances under which employees pay attention to the fulfillment of the psychological contract, and not only to current resources provided by the organization, in deciding the organization's support. Perhaps the more important the promise is to a recipient and the more definitively and specifically the promise is stated, the more employees will attend to the promise and not simply to the level of resources currently provided.

Communication of high-quality job information by upper management conveys to employees that the organization, through its representatives, is willing to spend time and effort to keep them well-informed.

Communication also plays an important role in employees' interpretation of the organization's motivation behind the favorable or unfavorable treatment they receive. As previously discussed, employees pay considerable attention to the discretionary nature of their treatment (see Chapter 2). Removal of asbestos or lead from a building as a health hazard generally does little to increase perceived organizational support because it is likely a response to government regulations whose avoidance carries grave risk for organizations. Maternity leave will do little to increase perceived organizational support if required by federal regulations; however, voluntary family-friendly policies such as day care facilities should do a great deal to increase perceived organizational support. A new gym area with exercise equipment will likely to be viewed as voluntary by most employees and thus enhance perceived organizational support. Training procedures that strengthen the employees' skills set and opportunities for advancement should increase perceived organizational support more than training clearly designed to protect the organization legally, such as minimal amounts of diversity or sexual harassment training.

Organizations should not take it for granted that employees will recognize when favorable treatment results from beneficial motivation. For example, the announcement of a cafeteria-style health care or retirement benefit designed to provide a greater fit to individual employee needs may be viewed by many employees as a trick designed by the organization to save money. When organizations act in ways beneficial to employees, but the full benefits and motives behind the change are unclear, the organizations should communicate the benefits and their benevolent intent in a straightforward and transparent manner to enhance perceived organizational support.

When actions by the organization are damaging to employees' interests, such as reductions of fringe benefits, the loss of perceived organizational support might be lessened by offering mitigating social accounts for what has been done, which reduce responsibility; by exonerating accounts, which stress the legitimacy of the decision; by reframing accounts, which cast the decision in a favorable light; or by penitential accounts, which express sorrow and regret. However, excuses for mistreatment can only work as a long-term strategy to the extent that mistreatment is unusual treatment. As discussed in the Chapter 2, judged sincerity has an important effect on acceptance of the veracity of verbal statements of positive regard and valuation. Only when employees are generally treated favorably will they accept the legitimacy of social accounts for occasional mistreatment.

The combination of procedural and distributive fairness in procedures and outcomes is a key determinant of perceived organizational support. Procedural fairness conveys to employees that the organization regards them highly enough to take extra care in meeting its exchange obligations. In contrast, perceptions of self-serving political behavior by managers appears to have strong negative effect on perceived organizational support. A culture of corrupt behavior and favoritism by management at the expense of the organization makes it very difficult for employees to obtain the resources they need to carry out their jobs effectively and to receive the recognition they deserve for doing their job well. Fairness in procedures and perceived organizational politics are the two strongest determinants of perceived organizational support. Fair procedures and low politics convey that the various decisions that affect the employee and the resources that the employee needs to do her job well will be allocated in a reasoned manner.

Not all favorable treatments need to be personally directed to contribute to perceived organizational support. Employees sometimes think of themselves as individuals and at other times as members of groups or organizational units. Thus, the fairness of treatment of coworkers or groups, as well as treatment of oneself, affects perceived organizational support.

Although not as strong determinants of perceived organizational support as fairness, human resource policies related to organizational rewards and job conditions—including expected rewards, training, and developmental experiences; job security; autonomy; small organizations; role stressors; and favorable work–family policies—make a substantial contribution to perceived organizational support.

We noted the difference between what has been called perceived support for specific organizational objectives (e.g., creativity) and employee needs (e.g., career development) versus perceived organizational support. Perceived organizational support for creativity differs from perceived organizational support because it involves an emphasis on a specific objective. Also, perceived organizational support involves a global belief concerning one's positive valuation by the organization rather than simply the promotion of the organization's objectives. Perceived organizational support that fulfills specific needs, such as career development, lacks the organization's concern with the employees' well-being that is an essential component of perceived organizational support.

Preliminary research suggests that agreement between employees' values and those of the organization contributes to perceived organizational support. This is a fertile area for further research. Value congruence may prove particularly important for perceived organizational support when the organization's values and practices are central to the employee's self-concept. This effect would be enhanced to the degree that employees' own jobs further their values and practices. Employees whose values are consistent with jobs in organizations that advocate, for example, environmental or religious causes, would tend to have high perceived organizational support.

Deliverers and Targets of Perceived Organizational Support

4

For most academics, research grants are hard to come by. Some years ago, I, as did many other youthful professors, struggled to obtain a federal grant to support my research. I repeatedly submitted excruciatingly detailed proposals to the National Institutes of Health, each time to be told that I was on the right track but that the proposal needed to be reworked. Finally, after multiple revisions, I received a letter stating the grant was being funded for hundreds of thousands of dollars. Overcome with a mixture of excitement and relief, and wanting to share my good news, I carried the letter into the psychology department's chairperson's office.

I did not know our chairperson well before her hiring a short time previously. During her interviews for the job, I was one of a few professors on our faculty who became concerned about her repeated disparaging comments concerning others. But she came with glowing recommendations, and most of the faculty initially found her bluntness amusing, attributable to a New York City upbringing amusing. But I was born in New York City myself and thought that most New Yorkers had the good sense to be circumspect during job interviews—this suggested poor social skills at the least and possibly a nasty temperament. Few of us felt as I did, though. We hired her.

When I handed the chairperson the letter, she gave it a cursory glance, then tossed it in my general direction and said,

"Humph, this would be something if it involved some real money." She then lowered her eyes to return to what she had been reading. Shocked and dismayed, I scooped up the letter and staggered from her office.

Next came another unsettling incident with the chairperson. I received an angry e-mail over some minor mistake that I literally had nothing to do with. When I e-mailed her to explain in a nice way that I was not involved, she fired back a second e-mail disparaging my inept performance in the matter. Again, I tried to explain my innocence, to which she sent back an even angrier, more insulting e-mail. Drawn into a battle I could not win, I stopped e-mailing her and vowed to have no personal contact with her unless absolutely necessary.

I also began to think about the implications of the chairperson's nastiness. She seemed to want to convey that she thought little of me and my contributions to the department. Clearly, she was in a position to do my career harm. But how much? Was she speaking for herself or for the university that employed me?

If I were to conclude that my supervisor, the chairperson, was speaking for the university, the lessened perceived organizational support would make my job untenable. I could give up any hope of teaching the kind of courses I would prefer, receiving decent pay raises, and being promoted. This was an unpleasant lesson in uncertainty concerning the relationship between treatment by a manager and perceived organizational support.

I soon found out, to my relief, that her negative opinions of me were only her own. She thought of almost everyone as incompetent, and she enjoyed bullying anyone over whom she had power. Soon known as the department's "loose cannon," she was largely ignored and then replaced after several years.

The issue I faced regarding whether my boss spoke for herself or for the organization is also of concern to employees who receive favorable treatment. Does the support they receive from their supervisor or manager indicate the organization's positive valuation, suggesting it will be worthwhile to increase their efforts on behalf of the organization? This question becomes salient for employees who previously worked for a very supportive supervisor and then find themselves with a new supervisor or new job with the organization. Does the organization value them highly, or has it only been their supervisor? Was the fine treatment they received from their former boss indicative of the organizational support, suggesting they should engage in the same high degree of effort and dedication elicited by their prior boss?

This chapter examines organizational support from the standpoint of who provides it and thus considers such topics as leadership, organizational hierarchies, and social networks. The preceding chapter discussed the kinds of treatment that influence perceived organization support. In the present chapter, we begin by considering the organizational representatives whose actions convey organizational support. According to organizational support theory, individuals generalize the favorable treatment they receive from organizational representatives, especially those who strongly symbolize the organization. Thus, top management would exert the most influence, followed in order by supervisors and coworkers. However, as the example with my department chairperson indicates, there is substantial variation in the influence on perceived organizational support, both within and between organizations, of individuals holding a particular position in the organizational hierarchy. Managers' impact on perceived organizational support depends, in part, on their style of leadership, which we examine.

We consider indirect influences by which supportive treatment influences one employee, which influences another, which in turn, influences the perceived organizational support of another. Trickle-down effects involve favorable treatment of managers, leading them to be more supportive of their subordinates, increasing the subordinates' perceived organizational support. We also examine new evidence suggesting that social networks within the organization influence perceived organizational support beyond the influence of one employee communicating directly with another.

Organizational support theory can be applied to individual organizational units, such as workgroups, departments, and overseas facilities, as well as the overall organization. Sometimes it makes more sense to focus on an organizational unit rather than the nominal organization, as in a loosely organized conglomerate in which the employees of a constituent unit have little knowledge or interest in the overall organization. In highly decentralized conglomerates, individual firms may retain their own identity and serve as "the organization" for employees. For example, a small engineering firm we studied had been acquired by Hewlett Packard, yet it retained its original identity and culture except for a few standardized human resources functions. These employees felt little connection to the umbrella organization and considered the original company the organization. In a steel manufacturing plant we studied (Eisenberger et al., 1990, Study 2), because of its substantial autonomy, the particular division to which the plant belonged, rather than the larger company, held the most meaning for employees as the organization.

In other cases we examine, support received from one organizational unit is additionally credited to related organizational units or the entire organization. When workers are obtained from employment agencies, supportive treatment by the employment agency and client agency contributes to the perceived organizational support of each organization, respectively, and generalizes to the other organization. As we also discuss, when expatriate employees begin their work overseas, aid from both the home organization and the overseas facility that enhances adjustment contributes to overall perceived organizational support.

We also consider extensions of organizational support theory to targets of support that do not involve typical employee–employer relationships (members of the military, union members, customers, and volunteers). The uniformed services (e.g., military, police, fire fighters) provide an interesting application of organizational support theory because of continuing difficulties in attracting and retaining motivated and skilled personnel. Many uniformed service occupations involve considerable physical risk for lower pay than may be available in private industry. Further, these personnel are expected to show a high level of dedication involving acceptance of the service ethos and, in the case of the military during times of war, long durations away from family. The application of organizational support theory to police was discussed previously (see Chapter 2). Here we consider the theory's application to the military.

The most fully developed extension of organizational support theory to nontraditional organizational relationships concerns union membership. Shore et al. (1994) argued that the social exchange relationship between union members and their union is similar in fundamental ways to that between employees and their work organization. We examine current theory and research on this application of organizational support theory to union membership, with suggestions for future developments.

Maintaining a high level of attendance and performance in volunteer organizations is an ongoing problem. The sanctions volunteer organizations can apply carry little force because, for most individuals, participation provides limited socioemotional or instrumental benefits. Therefore, we discuss the possible use of organizational support to enhance participation by volunteers (Boezeman & Ellemers, 2007, 2008).

As customers, people like to be treated with respect and have reliable providers of goods and services concerned with meeting their interests and needs. Thus, it seems possible that customers develop general beliefs concerning the extent to which a provider cares about their satisfaction and values them as customers. We discuss the recent application of organizational support theory by Shanock and Eisenberger (2009) to customer–provider relationships.

Support From Organizational Representatives

Levinson (1965) noted that employees "generalize from their feelings about people in the organization who are important to them to the organization as a whole." (p. 377). Because those who influence the organization's course are strongly identified with the organization, individuals with high status and power in the organization would also be strongly identified with the organization (Eisenberger et al., 1986, 2002). The kinds of support provided employees by top management, immediate supervisors, coworkers, and subordinates differ in some ways. Upper level managers influence perceived organizational support through the policies and goals they establish, which are influenced by the extent to which they view employees as valued human capital. Supervisors, invested with the authority to direct, evaluate, and reward performance and provide needed resources, influence perceived organizational support by the favorableness of their treatment of subordinates. Coworkers affect perceived organizational support by aid and cooperation and by conveying their opinions of organizational support provided by the organization. Subordinates influence perceived organizational support on the basis of their cooperativeness in helping their supervisor achieve success. Employees form views concerning the supportiveness of these sources and generalize this perception to the supportiveness of the overall organization.

Because upper level managers are charged with setting the general goals and objectives for the organization, supportive treatment from upper management should be judged by employees as more indicative of organizational support than supportive treatment from other organizational members lower in the organizational hierarchy (see Figure 4.1). Supportive policies of upper management can help establish a general supportive culture of organizational support that permeates the organization. Highly successful companies that value employees' contributions, such as Southwest Airlines, Google, and Costco, had founders who put in place a lasting corporate culture that viewed the workforce as a valued resource deserving of favorable treatment. New managers continued to support the founders' supportive orientation because it had become embedded in the organizational culture and because the managers were

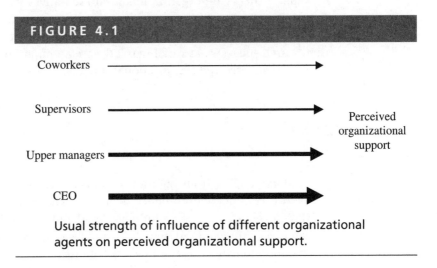

FIGURE 4.1

Coworkers

Supervisors

Upper managers

CEO

Perceived organizational support

Usual strength of influence of different organizational agents on perceived organizational support.

selected and rewarded for sharing this vision. Of course, corporate cultures that devalue their workforce can also become embedded, as in the case of Wal-Mart and U.S. Airways, where command and control became an unquestioned assumption regarding the appropriate way to treat employees.

Although upper level managers often play an important role in the development of perceived organizational support, this is not always the case. High-level managers who are new, have a different vision from the traditional one, and have no established power base may be viewed as usurpers who do not really represent the organization. In contrast to managers, coworkers, particularly among low-ranking employees, would usually have a lessened influence on perceived organizational support because they generally have less influence than management over organizational culture and policies. The relationships just described would be altered in some degree in nations like France and Germany, where worker unions are powerful and the law stipulates union representation in corporate governance.

Because nonmanagerial workers typically do not have delegated authority over coworkers, they have received little attention as possible sources of perceived organizational support. It has even been suggested that support from coworkers may be perceived negatively as politically motivated or implying incompetence on the part of the recipient (Ng & Sorensen, 2008). The fact that such instrumental and emotional support may be less clearly a part of coworkers' jobs further suggests that it might contribute little to perceived organizational support. For these reasons, Ng and Sorensen (2008) predicted and found in a meta-analysis that perceived support from supervisors was more closely related to perceived organizational support than was perceived support from coworkers. These findings support the traditional emphasis by organizational support theory on organizational representatives with power and status in the organization as sources of perceived organizational support (Eisenberger et al., 2002). However, as we subsequently discuss, recent research suggest that social networks are an important supplementary source of perceived organizational support.

Leadership

Leaders, ranging from high-level managers to immediate supervisors, exert a considerable influence over perceived organizational support. High-level managers exert influence by their role in influencing organizational culture and setting policies and procedures for the organization that may convey a high or low level of organizational support. In addition, their high status in the organization adds salience to their communications with lower level employees as indications of the organization's favorable or unfavorable views toward them. Supervisors generally lack the status of high-level managers, but they have the advantage of influencing perceived organizational support by the frequency and immediacy of contract with employees and their delegated authority to direct, evaluate, and coach employees. The relative extent to which supervisors versus upper managers influence perceived organizational support will depend, in part, on the extent to which supervisors are identified with the organization, a factor that we discuss in detail later in the chapter.

SUPPORT FROM SUPERVISORS

Because supervisors act as agents of the organization, having responsibility for directing and evaluating subordinates' performance, employees view their supervisor's favorable or unfavorable orientation toward them as strongly indicative of organizational support (Eisenberger et al., 1986; Levinson, 1965). Additionally, employees understand that supervisors' evaluations of subordinates are often conveyed to upper management, further contributing to employees' association of supervisor support with perceived organizational support. Many studies have found that the perception by employees that their supervisor holds their contributions in high regard and cares about their welfare (perceived supervisor support) is positively associated with perceived organizational support (e.g., Kottke & Sharafinski, 1988; Malatesta, 1995; Rhoades et al., 2001; Shore, Tetrick, Sinclair, & Newton, 1994; Yoon & Lim, 1999). The greater the identification of supervisors with the organization, the stronger would be employees' attribution of treatment received from them to the organization itself. Accordingly, the relationship between the supervisor's support of subordinates and perceived organizational support increases with their informal status within the organization (Eisenberger et al., 2002).

Researchers have usually assessed perceived supervisor support by substituting the word *supervisor* for *organization* in survey items (e.g., "My supervisor really cares about my well-being"; Kottke & Sharafinski, 1988). Various types of support received from the supervisor would be expected to enhance perceived supervisor support and therefore perceived organizational support. Antecedents of perceived supervisor support have received little examination. However, one study found that multiple kinds of supervisor support—emotional support, useful information, and needed supplies and equipment—received by Thai health care workers contributed to perceived organizational support which, in turn, was positively related to employee performance (Bhanthumnavin, 2003).

Findings of a positive relationship has usually been interpreted to indicate that perceived supervisor support leads to perceived organizational support (e.g., Hutchison, 1997; Malatesta, 1995; Rhoades et al., 2001; Yoon, Han, & Seo, 1996; Yoon & Lim, 1999). However, Yoon and Thye (2000) suggested a possible effect in the reverse direction: Employees' perception that the organization values their contribution and cares about their well-being might lead them to believe that supervisors, as agents of the organization, are favorably inclined toward them. Because perceived supervisor support and perceived organizational support were usually assessed simultaneously, the findings left the direction of the relationship uncertain. To help resolve this ambiguity, Eisenberger et al. (2002) measured changes over time in perceived supervisor support and perceived organizational support over a 3-month period. Perceived supervisor support was found to be positively related to a change in time in perceived organizational support, and not the reverse, providing strong evidence that supervisor support contributes to perceived organizational support. However, positive evidence is much more definitive than negative evidence in such "panel" designs. For example, Eisenberger et al. (2002) might have selected too short an interval to observe an effect of perceived organizational support on perceived supervisor support. Thus, the evidence that perceived support from supervisors leads to perceived organizational support is good, whereas the possible occurrence of an effect in the opposite direction is uncertain.

We noted in Chapter 2 that one key feature concerning the extent to which employees generalized support received from their supervisor to the organization was the supervisor's organizational embodiment (SOE). On the basis of the power of the supervisor and the extent to which the supervisor's objectives coincide with those of the organization, employees generalize their support from the supervisor to the organization. Recall my unsupportive treatment by my former department chairperson described at the beginning of the chapter and the question I had asked myself at the time concerning whether the low support was coming from only the chairperson or the organization as a whole. I had been unsure at the time and so had to investigate further. When I did, I found that her power and influence were circumscribed— few would take her evaluations of others seriously because of her emotional outbursts and random animosity. So her low support for me did not markedly reduce my perceived organizational support. At the same time, there was some effect. After all, I thought at the time, she was my boss and did have a degree of power over me, and the university did have the responsibility for appointing her. Thus, SOE influences the magnitude of the relationship between supervisor support and perceived organizational support. But even when SOE is low, the supervisor is seen as a representative of the organization and has some influence over perceived organizational support.

As we have noted, employees interpret support received from the supervisor as indicative of organizational support. However, employees view supervisors not simply as organizational agents but as individuals having their values and motivations that differ in similarity with those of the organization. As discussed in Chapter 2, employees understand that their supervisors are driven by personal values and goals that do not always coincide with those of the organization and that some supervisors may promote their own interests at the expense of the organization. To meet socioemotional needs and to determine the value of increased efforts on behalf of the organization, employees form a perception concerning the extent to which the supervisor shares the identity of the organization. We noted in Chapter 2 that such SOE increased the relationship between perceived support from supervisors and perceived organizational support, with positive consequences for extrarole performance (Eisenberger et al., 2009).

LEADER–MEMBER EXCHANGE

According to leader–member exchange theory, supervisors identify subordinates they consider especially promising and treat them favorably. Subordinates so recognized reciprocate by working harder and providing more help to supervisors, leading to high-quality relationships between supervisors and subordinates (Graen & Scandura, 1987; Liden, Sparrowe, & Wayne, 1997). Leader–member exchange theorists characterize these relationships as involving reciprocation of aid and exchange of expressions of liking, caring, and respect. Consistent with the theory, the strength of leader–member exchange relationships varies within most workgroups (e.g., Liden & Graen, 1980), partly on the basis of the supervisor's liking of individual members (e.g., Wayne & Ferris, 1990), and supervisors' and subordinates' perceptions of their similarity (Liden, Wayne, & Stilwell, 1993; Phillips & Bedeian, 1994). Leader–member exchange has been found to be positively related to increased employee affective commitment to the organization, standard job performance, and various forms of extrarole performance that aid the supervisor and coworkers (Liden et al., 1993). Because supervisors are identified with the organization, organizational support theory suggests that a favorable leader–member exchange relationship should be positively related to perceived organizational support.

One commonly used measure of leader–member exchange, usually assessed from the employee's viewpoint, asks about such aspects of the relationship as how well the subordinate and supervisor work together, how well the supervisor understands the employee's problems and needs, and the supervisor's willingness to defend the employee's decisions (Scandura & Graen, 1984). A more recent leader–member exchange scale (Liden & Maslyn, 1998) assumes leader–member exchange to be composed of several related but separable components. As assessed from the employee's viewpoint, these comprise the employee's liking for the supervisor, public support provided by the supervisor, the employee's willingness to work beyond what is normally required, and the employee's professional respect for the supervisor.

Besides leader–member exchange leading to perceived organizational support, the effect might also occur in the opposite direction: Employees with high perceived organizational support might conclude that their supervisor, as a representative of the organization, has a warm relationship with them. Three studies examined the possibility that the relationship between leader–member exchange and perceived organizational support is bidirectional. One study (Wayne et al., 1997) found support for this view, and two studies found that perceived organizational support led to leader–member exchange but not vice versa (Masterson et al., 2000; Wayne et al., 2002). It does appear, therefore, that leader–member exchange is positively related to perceived organizational support, although the direction of the relationship from the evidence in these studies is uncertain. In these studies, leader–member exchange and perceived organizational support were assessed simultaneously, making it difficult to determine the direction of causality (D. Kaplan, 2000). To determine the direction or directions of causality, it is important to follow up these studies with new research on how leader–member exchange and perceived organizational support change with respect to each other over time.

Uhl-Bien and Maslyn (2003) found that leader–member exchange was positively related to perceived organizational support and examined aspects of the exchange between subordinate and supervisor that might influence perceived organizational support. Employees' agreement with statements that they and their manager are concerned with immediate reciprocation of resources and an equivalent magnitude of resources was related to leader–member exchange and perceived organizational support slightly in the negative direction. According to social exchange theory, these concerns should be indicative of economic relationships with low trust and little exchange of socioemotional resources. Employees' agreement with statements that they and their managers looked out primarily for themselves in their relationship was also associated with a negative relationship with leader–member exchange and perceived organizational support. Here, employees and supervisors appear unconcerned with the other's interests, providing little basis for the exchange of valued resources beyond those absolutely required by their respective roles. In contrast, employees' agreement with statements expressing the mutual interests of employees and supervisors was positively related to leader–member exchange and perceived organizational support. This study suggests that a long-term orientation by subordinates and concern with the mutual interests of their own and the supervisor promote leader–member exchange, leading to greater perceived organizational support.

Previous research has given little attention to how organizations' treatment of managers affects leader–member exchange. According to organizational support theory, when supervisors, as other employees, perceive that the organization values their contributions and cares about their well-being (i.e., high perceived organizational support), they reciprocate by increasing activities helpful to organization (Eisenberger et al., 1986). Because a major part of supervisors' jobs includes directing, evaluating, and coaching subordinates, supervisors would fulfill their reciprocation obligations, in part, with greater support for subordinates. Accordingly, Shanock and Eisenberger (2006) found that supervisors with high perceived organizational support were evaluated as more supportive by subordinates. By providing greater socioemotional support and tangible resources for subordinates, supervisors with high perceived organizational support should establish stronger leader–member exchange relationships with subordinates. Karagonlar, Eisenberger, and Steiger-Mueller (2009) found that supervisors' perceived organizational support enhanced leader–member exchange as rated by subordinates.

Reciprocation wariness, a general fear of exploitation in interpersonal relationships (Cotterell et al., 1992), may lessen the positive influence of supervisors' perceived organizational support on leader–member exchange. Wary individuals treat others well who appear to want little from them but show a reduced positive response to those who are very generous to them or propose mutual projects (Cotterell et al., 1992; Lynch, Eisenberger, & Armeli, 1999). The wariness of the supervisor should lessen the positive influence of supervisors' perceived organizational support on leader–member exchange. Karagonlar et al. (2009) found that supervisors' perceived organizational support enhanced leader–member exchange when supervisors were low in wariness but not when they were high in wariness. Leader–member exchange, in turn, led to increased inrole and extrarole performance.

The overall findings suggest that supervisors who support their subordinates and establish high-quality relationships with them also establish a high level of perceived organizational support. One issue raised by leader–member exchange theorists is that because supervisors have limited time and resources, the establishment of reciprocal relationships with favored subordinates may damage relationships with less favored subordinates. This may be an apt description of what often occurs. Indeed, Jack Welch at General Electric formalized such a procedure by demanding that employees with low ratings be fired no matter how well they might be performing on an absolute rather than a relative level. Yet, research on transformational leadership behavior suggests that although differential treatment of subordinates may be necessary and useful, it is possible to convey caring and support to entire workgroups (Judge & Piccolo, 2004).

TRANSFORMATIONAL LEADERSHIP

In contrast with leader–member exchange theory, which emphasizes the social exchange relationship between leader and subordinate in which each fulfills the needs and desires of the other, transformational leadership focuses on providing followers goals that transcend short-term objectives and meet higher order intrinsic needs (Judge & Piccolo, 2004). Acquiring the affection and loyalty of subordinates requires showing them respect and meeting their socioemotional needs. Transformational leadership theory attempts to understand the excitement that followers feel when their leader instills a belief that subordinates are contributing to an important undertaking, giving followers a strong sensory of purpose. Although meeting employees' intrinsic needs is certainly a part of leader–member exchange theory, as just discussed, leader–member exchange theory lacks the emphasis on inspiring subordinates with a sense of purpose, whereas transformational leadership theory lacks the emphasis of leader–member exchange theory on meeting the mutual motives of supervisor and subordinate.

Bass (1985) articulated four components of transformational leadership behaviors. *Charisma* involves admirable behavior that causes followers to identify with the leader. *Inspirational motivation* concerns articulating an appealing and inspiring vision to followers. *Intellectual stimulation* concerns the leader's challenge to conventional assumptions, taking risks and encouraging followers' creativity. *Individualized consideration* involves attending to each follower's needs by mentoring or coaching and listening to followers' concerns (Judge & Piccolo, 2004, p. 755). Transformational leadership has great appeal to contemporary leadership theorists and businesspeople, probably being the most studied theory of leadership over the past 2 decades. Moreover, the predictive value of the major scales used to assess transformational leadership is impressive (Judge & Piccolo, 2004; Lowe, Kroeck, & Sivasubramaniam, 1996).

The general concept of transformational leadership is intuitively appealing because it gets at the emotional appeal of charismatic leaders, and the construct has substantial empirical support. However, some basic issues remain unresolved. The scales used to assess transformational leadership behavior are typically given to followers whose judgment of certain aspects of inspiring leaders' behavior may reflect a halo effect. The very excitement and dedication created by charismatic leaders may lead followers to ascribe to the leader's behavior an exaggerated set of favorable traits. For example, the most used scale, the Multifactor Leadership Questionnaire (Avolio, Bass, & Jung, 1999), includes an assessment of the degree to which the leader models ethical standards. Devoted followers of transformational leaders may believe their leader to be ethical or moral because of their enthrallment with their leader.

Dynamic leaders of the Enron Corporation in Houston, Texas, who were celebrated by most of the employees turned out to be corrupt and involved in unethical business practices. Most employees may not have known of the arcane bookkeeping being used to create fake profits and undeserved bonuses for many of the stars of the corporation, but they had little evidence on which conclude that their leaders were highly ethical. There are also many charismatic religious leaders who passed themselves off as beacons of piety only to be subsequently discovered to have violated many of their principles advocated in their preaching.

In this, as with other multifaceted theories of leadership, the question arises of whether the theory is actually descriptive as it claims or prescriptive, entailing a style of leadership that proponents of the theory would prefer to see adopted. The idea that successful leaders adopt a complete set of disparate values or behavioral orientations seems unlikely. Rather, it seems more likely that individual leaders differ widely in the individually described dimensions of transformational leadership; that there may be a small, positive correlation among them; and that halo effects are responsible for observed high correlations in employees' responses to questionnaires regarding these dimensions.

One trait argued to characterize transformational leaders involves their quest for diverse views rather than their imposition of their own views on followers. Yet, at Enron, transformational managers repeatedly threatened anyone with firing who disagreed with their own risky and ultimately failing business strategies. A halo effect, coupled with a lack of detailed knowledge about how their leaders operate, may cause subordinates to have a false impression about the openness and other traits of transformational leaders. The supposed distinctive dimensions of transformational leadership behavior are not easily separable and vary across studies, leading some to propose new ways to assess transformational leadership behavior (MacKenzie, Podsakoff, & Rich, 2001).

Howell (1988) drew on McClelland's (1985) distinction between socialized and personalized power motives to suggest that some transformational leaders are motivated primarily by social goals whereas others are motivated by personalized tendencies. Following McClelland, Howell argued that socialized leaders exert their influence primarily through the followers' internalization of the values of the organization, whereas personalized leaders exert their influence mainly through their followers' identification with them, involving an affiliation process. According to Howell, both kinds of leaders would have high expectations for their followers, express confidence in followers' abilities to meet these expectations, exude confidence in themselves, serve as role models, and demonstrate strong communicative skills. However, socialized leaders would empower followers, increasing their self-efficacy, whereas personalized leaders would emphasize unquestioning loyalty and obedience. In this view, socialized leaders espouse values and goals that are mutual and shared, whereas personalized leaders articulate their own motives that they displace onto followers. Socialized leaders use followers' abilities and motivations to benefit the group. Personalized leaders use followers as pawns to be manipulated.

In Howell's (1988) view, socialized leaders inspire followers to greater autonomy and creativity. Personalized leaders demand conformity and produce dependence. Because the socialized leader empowers employees, and provides them with meaningful values not dependent on the identity of the leader, the ideas and actions espoused by the socialized leader outlast the leader's tenure. Because followers of personalized leaders grow dependent on them, and the power of their ideas rests on a satisfying relationship between the leader and the follower, the strength of the personalized leader's ideas and values greatly dissipates after the leader's departure.

Rather than viewing transformational leadership as involving two distinctive styles, Kark, Shamir, and Chen (2003) suggested that individual transformational leaders promote both personal identification and social identification. Kark et al. provided evidence that transformational leadership behavior increased bank employees' identification both with their bank branch and with their bank branch manager. Social identification with the bank branch, in turn, had positive effects on employees' self-efficacy and believed efficacy of the branch as a whole. In contrast to this empowering effect, personal identification led employees to believe that they would be unable to carry out their jobs well without the continual supervision of their bank manager. Thus, the empowering effects of transformational leadership were balanced by greater dependence on the leader.

How, then, can Kark et al.'s (2003) findings be reconciled with Howell's (1988) conceptualization? Kark et al.'s findings suggest that transformational leaders lead employees to identify more with the group, enhancing empowerment yet also increasing personal identification. However, Kark et al. did not deal with individual differences in leaders. As Howell recognized, some leaders may be more concerned with personal control and furthering their own values, whereas other leaders may be more concerned with finding and furthering common values.

Further, leaders may change their orientation from more socialized to more personalized and vice versa. Henry Ford gives us an example of such change. As one of the originators of mass production in the car industry, Ford seems best characterized as a socialized leader in his youth (Eisenberger, 1989). In the Ford Motor Company's first years, Ford saw the automobile as a way to help the common people. He wanted his simply designed, sturdy car to provide the public with cheap, reliable transportation that could be a boon to their lives. And he wanted his workers to be paid well and treated decently.

As a young man, he inspired his employees, from engineers to workmen on the shop floor, with visions of an everyman's car and uncommonly high wages. He inspired others by winning car races and radically simplifying car design that changed the car from an expensive luxury good to a commodity that could be possessed by the average worker. In those first years of the Ford Company, he welcomed methodological innovation from people both within and outside the company, such as Vanadian steel from French inventors or design improvements suggested by his engineers. He and his engineers created the moving assembly line in which each worker stood at a fixed location performing a single task as care components passed by. The lines converged to allow the large pieces to be fitted together.

But the rewards for listening to the advice of others were overwhelmed by the ego-inflating flattery of sycophants. He began to believe the stories of the company's public relations department that he was personally responsible for all the company's innovations. As sales continued to surpass all expectations, he became egotistical and rejected any car improvement in which he had not played a major role. He also became increasingly adamant about deciding the company's policy questions himself. For a time, he remained an inspirational figure to his employees. However, he continued to speed up the assembly line so that any time taken off for lunch, rest, or toilet made it difficult for an employee to catch up. Many Ford workers spent most of their free time sleeping. Ford also made continued employment contingent on maintaining a good home life based on reports from his "Sociological Department." Ford's henchmen used fists and clubs to deal with union organizers. The company floundered financially for several decades until Ford was in his 80s, at which point he was too senile to understand when his wife and son wrenched the company away from him. Ford had started out as a socialized inspirational leader, was for a time a personalized transformational leader, and later in life lost his capacity to lead.

There are, of course, socialized leaders in business who are able to resist the siren call of personal flattery and remain willing to listen to other ideas and take into account their needs and values throughout their careers. For example, Herb Kelleher, the founder of Southwest Airlines, emphasized the importance of employees' morale and innovation to the success of the company to such an extent that he denied the adage that "the customer is always right." Employees at Southwest are asked to go to great lengths to provide excellent customer service but not to grovel to any customers who complain without good reason.

To the extent that transformational leaders are strongly identified by employees with the organization, action by such leaders to fulfill diverse socioemotional needs (e.g., approval, esteem, affiliation, emotional support) should enhance perceived organizational support. Hyatt (2007), in an unpublished doctoral dissertation with MBA students, found positive relationships between dimensions of a transformational leadership scale similar to the Multifactor Leadership Questionnaire and perceived organizational support. These initial findings suggest that transformational leadership contributes to perceived organizational support. Further research needs to be done to establish whether, as would be predicted, transformational leaders' socialized concerns are more closely related to perceived organizational support than their personalized concerns.

SERVANT LEADERSHIP

Servant leadership emphasizes personal integrity and serving others both within and outside the organization (Greenleaf, 1977). Serving others is seen as an end in itself and not simply as a way of furthering the goals of the organization (Liden, Wayne, Zhao, & Henderson, 2008). Among the more unique characteristics of servant leadership, according to Liden et al. (2008), are a strong emphasis on *integrity*, which refers to operating openly, honestly, and dealing fairly with others; *putting subordinates first*, which involves making satisfaction of other's work needs a priority; and a genuine concern for *creating value* for the community. Liden et al. found that servant leadership was positively related to employees' activities carried out on behalf of the community, as well as organizational commitment and standard job performance.

The relationship between servant leadership and perceived organizational support has yet to be examined empirically. But there is good reason to believe that servant leadership should be strongly related to perceived organizational support, with positive consequences for employees' identification with the organization (see Chapter 6) and felt obligation to help fulfill the organization's goals. First, integrity is important to perceived organizational support. Fair treatment indicates the organization's high regard for employees' welfare, whereas perceived organizational politics, involving self-seeking at the cost of the organization's welfare and others' careers, conveys a lack of interest by management in employees' welfare and has a strong decremental influence on perceived organizational support. Satisfying employees' work needs both with respect to resources that help them fulfill their job responsibilities and, where possible, making their jobs more interesting conveys the organization's positive valuation of employees' contributions in addition to a concern with their welfare. Providing value for the community should contribute to perceived organizational support for those employees who share this value and therefore believe their own values are supported by the organization.

Applying Organizational Support Theory to Organizational Units

The decision to focus on the overall organization or on a particular organizational unit with respect to perceived support will depend on the nature of the organization and the purposes of the analysis. Many small organizations are so well integrated that informal and fluctuating work arrangements dominate formal units and lines of authority, allowing little independent identity for workgroups or departments. Here, perceived support from the overall organization is of primary concern to employees (Wayne et al., 2009). In contrast, as previously noted, in loosely integrated conglomerates, divisions or affiliate firms may be given considerable autonomy and therefore be identified by most employees as "the organization."

LOCAL PERCEIVED ORGANIZATIONAL SUPPORT

In decentralized firms, the extent to which managers are supportive of employees may vary considerably by location or division. Gentry, Kuhnert, Mondore, and Page (2007) found with a large global service provider that supervisors were rated by subordinates as showing relatively similar support within districts but dissimilar support from one district to another. These differences in support within versus between districts carried over to employee turnover.

Vardaman, Hancock, Allen, and Shore (2009) found differences in perceived organizational support at the level of the workgroup and examined the influence of workgroup-level perceived organizational support (the average perceived support of the groups) on the relationship of individual employees' perceived organizational support with organizational commitment and turnover. Higher workgroup-level perceived organizational support enhanced the individual-level relationship between perceived organizational support and affective organizational commitment, and reduced the negative relationship between perceived organizational support and turnover. Vardaman et al. suggested that treating workgroups in ways that create shared positive perceptions of support may enhance individuals' perceived organizational support by social influence processes. That is, when support is widespread, employees may convince one another of the organization's support.

CONTINGENT EMPLOYMENT

Some organizational arrangements involve employment by multiple organizations with corresponding distinctive sources of organizational support. Outsourcing has become an increasingly popular business practice, involving an estimated 2 million to 3 million American employees (National Association of Professional Employer Organizations, 2008; as cited by Coyle-Shapiro, Morrow, & Kessler, 2006). Many contingent employees are hired out from an employment agency to a client organization and thus have two employers. According to organizational support theory, employees should form perceptions regarding support to all distinctive organizational units and thus should develop perceived organizational support both to an employment agency and its client organization.

Connelly, Gallagher, and Gilley (2007) found with temporary workers that perceived organizational support from the employment agency was positively related to affective commitment to the client organization, and perceived organizational support from the client organization was positively related to affective commitment to the client organization. Connelly et al. found that perceived organizational support from the employment agency had as substantial an influence on affective commitment to the client organization as on the temporary agency, and there was a more modest effect of perceived organizational support by the client organization on affective commitment to the employment agency. Because employment agencies are responsible for their employment in the client organization, employees may identify the two sources of support and generalize their support from one to the other.

Coyle-Shapiro et al. (2006) found a set of parallel processes for outcomes of perceived organizational support for the employment agency and client organization of long-term public service employees who had been hired to take the place of jobs originally carried out by U.K. city employees. Perceived organizational support from the employment agency led to felt obligation to the employment agency, which in turn, led to affective commitment to the employment agency. Similarly, perceived organizational support from the client organization led to felt obligation to the client organization, which in turn, led to affective commitment to the client organization. Each source of perceived organizational support operated through its own type of felt obligation to increase self-evaluated service oriented citizenship behaviors. Inspection of Coyle-Shapiro et al.'s data indicates that perceived organizational support from the client organization was positively related to affective commitment to the employment agency, whereas perceived organizational support from the employment agency showed a marginally significant relationship with affective commitment to the client organization. These results, like those of Connelly et al. (2007), suggest that employees generalize these experiences from employment agencies to employers and vice versa.

Liden, Wayne, Kraimer, and Sparrowe (2003; see also Camerman, Cropanzano, & Vandenberghe, 2007) found that employee perceptions of fair procedures concerning treatment by their employment agency led to perceived organizational support, which in turn, led to affective commitment. Similarly, procedural justice from the client organization led to client perceived organizational support, which led to client affective commitment. Both agency and client organization perceived organizational support were positively related to the organizational citizenship behavior of altruism or helping others. As in the prior studies, agency-perceived organizational support was positively related to client affective commitment, and client perceived organizational support was positively related to agency affective commitment.

These findings demonstrate that contingent employees, part-time or full-time, short-term or long-term, develop perceived organizational support to their employment agency and to their work organization. Favorable perceived organizational support received from one source influences outcomes for the other source. This suggests that organizations should take care to select hiring agencies that treat their employees supportively. The same may be said for employment agencies. If they refer employees to unsupportive organizations, the employees' loyalty to the agencies will diminish and they may be less responsive to agency calls or simply leave the agency.

OVERSEAS ASSIGNMENTS

Other organizational arrangements may impart substantial importance for employees to particular organizational units. For example, adjustment by employees to overseas assignments has been found to depend strongly on organizational support both from the parent company and the foreign facility, probably because the parent company can help with financial and general logistical support, and the foreign facility affords daily support that increases adjustment in the work setting and local culture (Kraimer, Wayne, & Jaworski, 2001). As a result of a continuing trend toward globalization, organizations increasingly send employees on assignments to other countries. These placements include traditional single 1- to 5-year assignments and sequential assignments received by longer-term expatriates, sometimes called "global nomads."

Perceived organizational support should be welcomed by employees as an indication that the organization will help them, when needed, to adjust to their work situation and their new culture; this expectation, in turn, would lead to greater emotional well-being, affective commitment to the organization, efforts on behalf of the organization, and completion of the tour of duty (Kraimer & Wayne, 2004; Wang & Takeuchi, 2007). In agreement with general findings on perceived organizational support, Guzzo et al. (1994) found that perceived organizational support was positively related to expatriates' affective commitment, which in turn, was linked to reduced intentions to quit the international assignment.

Black and Stephens (1989) defined *expatriate adjustment* as involving psychological comfort with respect to job tasks of the foreign assignment. They suggested such adjustment comprises three relevant facets: work, general, and interaction. *Work adjustment* refers to the expatriate's psychological comfort with respect to the job tasks of the foreign assignment. *General adjustment* involves the general living conditions and culture of the foreign country. *Interaction adjustment* concerns interaction with the host country's nationals.

Using a sample of expatriates in China, Wang and Takeuchi (2007) found that perceived organizational support was positively related to all three facets of expatriate adjustment and to reduced work stress. Work adjustment and general adjustment were related to job performance. Perceived organizational support also operated through general adjustment to reduce premature return intentions. These findings suggest that perceived organizational support increases various aspects of expatriates' adjustment to their overseas assignment and their intention to fulfill their assignment.

In a similar vein, Kraimer et al. (2001) examined organizational support as a source of expatriate adjustment and the impact of the latter on both inrole and extrarole performance. Given the dual employment relationship for expatriates, Kraimer et al. suggested that organizational support can itself be provided from two different subsources: the parent company and the foreign facility (see also Aycan, 1997). The parent company would be the initial source of support and provide benefits and services prior to arriving and, once the employee has entered the foreign country, support from the new facility would be important for continued adjustment on a day-to-day basis. In accord with their expectations, the investigators found that perceived support from the parent company exerted a positive influence on general adjustment, whereas perceived support from the foreign facility had a positive impact on work adjustment, which was positively related to standard job performance, and on interaction adjustment, which was positively related to extrarole performance.

Other research has focused on the roles of the spouse's and family's adjustment in the expatriate's adaptation. Shaffer, Harrison, Gilley, and Luk (2001) noted that spouses have opportunities for learning and psychological growth but that relocation often entails a loss of the normal social support network and institutional affiliations, with resultant loneliness and frustration. Children face the problem of attending a new school, making new friends, and perhaps learning a new language. With expatriates' own psychological resources often challenged by their new work roles, these family issues may create substantial additional burdens. According to Shaffer et al., these challenges create a drain on time and both physical and psychological energy, increasing stress and premature intentions to quit the work assignment. Perceived organizational support provides the assurance that the organization will provide the needed resources to deal with these difficulties. Using a diverse sample of expatriates, Shaffer et al. found that that both work interference with family and family interference with work increased premature return intentions. However, perceived organizational support reduced premature return intentions.

In a similar vein, Grant-Vallone and Ensher (2001) analyzed the effects of work-to-family and family-to-work conflict and perceived organizational support on expatriate employees' mental well-being (i.e., depression, anxiety, and concern for their health). They showed that work-to-family conflict was related to employees' depression and anxiety, whereas family-to-work conflict was related to employees' concern for their health. Organizational support had significant favorable effects on all mental well-being-related variables and work-to-family conflict.

Although organizations are often concerned with work-to-family conflict, that is, the reduction of family interfering with work (e.g., spouse employment, schooling for children), the studies by Shaffer et al. and Grant-Vallone and Ensher suggest that companies should also be concerned with how work interference with family may influence the mental well-being of expatriate employees and their willingness to remain in overseas assignments. Perceived organizational support appears to ameliorate the aversive outcomes associated with both kinds of conflict.

Finally, Lazarova and colleagues (Lazarova & Caligiuri, 2001; Lazarova & Cerdin, 2007) examined factors influencing the retention of returning expatriates. Repatriates have an invaluable role in organizational learning because they can facilitate the transfer of knowledge from host countries to headquarters, and vice versa (Lazarova & Caligiuri, 2001). Repatriates possess firsthand knowledge "about the rules of doing business internationally and the complexities of international operations, the characteristics of national markets, their business climate, cultural patterns, structure of the market system, and, most importantly, knowledge about individual customers and suppliers" (Lazarova & Cerdin, 2007, p. 405). Furthermore, repatriates know how the company is perceived in another country and are part of social networks that can improve the development of the company's business around the world (Downes & Thomas, 1999).

Losing employees with valuable expatriate experience is costly for these reasons and because direct competitors will likely benefit from hiring them (Caligiuri & Lazarova, 2001; Jana, 2000; Lazarova & Tarique, 2005; Poe, 2000). Finally, high turnover rates among repatriates also have a potentially negative influence on the desire of other employees to volunteer for international assignments by signaling that such assignments are unfulfilling (Downes & Thomas, 1999; Tung, 1988).

Lazarova and Caligiuri (2001) found with a sample of expatriates from four North American–based multinational organizations that repatriates who were provided multiple supportive practices such as career planning sessions, mentoring programs while on assignment, continuous communications with the home office, and communications with the home office about the details of the repatriation process and considered them important experienced greater perceived organizational support. Perceived organizational support, in turn, was positively related to intention to remain with the organization. Lazarova and Caligiuri noted that most of the supportive practices were provided before or during, and not after, the expatriate assignment.

Among the various practices examined in this study, repatriates indicated that a key element after repatriation was the creation of a companywide environment that is appreciative of the global experience. This finding suggests that providing repatriates with visible signs that the company values international experience is important for employees and, as such, is probably an important factor for their retention. One caveat about this study is that the investigators' conclusion that supportive practices have positive consequences, including perceived organizational support, was based on a statistical technique in which they multiplied the amount of supportive practice by the employee's weighting of the importance of the practice. That is, the simple frequency of supportive practices was weighted by a psychological factor. So follow-up research should be carried out to investigate whether expatriates generally respond favorably to supportive practices signifying that the organization values international experience.

Hierarchies and Networks of Support

Treating employees supportively may increase the perceived organizational support of other employees. Employees tend to communicate their favorable views to others and reciprocate their favorable treatment by increasing their efforts on behalf of the organization, which may include helping other employees. Thus, management's supportive treatment of one employee may be passed on to other employees. Two cases involve the trickle down of perceived support from supervisors to subordinates and the spread of perceived support across organization's social networks.

TRICKLE-DOWN EFFECTS

According to organizational support theory, perceived organizational support leads to a felt obligation to help the organization reach its objectives, including participation in extrarole or citizenship behaviors such as helping other employees (Eisenberger et al., 2001). Accordingly, Eisenberger et al. (2001) found that postal workers' perceived organizational support was positively associated with a felt obligation to help the organization reach its objectives, which in turn, was related to such extrarole behaviors as helping coworkers and the supervisor. By helping other employees carry out their jobs more effectively, such efforts would aid the organization, as well as other employees, leading to greater productivity (Bell & Menguc, 2002; Lynch et al., 1999; Rhoades & Eisenberger, 2002).

Wayne et al. (1997) found a positive relationship between perceived organizational support and extrarole behavior for managerial-level employees as well as for lower level employees. Managers with high perceived organizational support were more likely to help other employees who had been absent, orient new employees to their jobs, help others when their workload increased, and assist others with their duties. The study by Wayne et al. provides preliminary evidence that managerial-level employees, as well as employees who hold lower level jobs, reciprocate perceived organizational support with extrarole behaviors that benefit the organization by helping others to better carry out their jobs.

Consistent with organizational support theory, Masterson's (2001) analysis of social exchange in organizations emphasizes the obligation of employees to repay favorable treatment received from the organization. Masterson suggested that in the case of service employees, the receipt of favorable treatment would have a trickle-down effect on their treatment of customers. Masterson found that service employees who perceived they were treated fairly responded by treating customers well. Similarly, employees of various service-based organizations who had high perceived organizational support stated a desire to provide good customer service (Susskind, Kacmar, & Borchgrevink, 2003), and service employees with high perceived organizational support were rated by their customers as more attentive, courteous, and concerned about customers' best interest than were employees with low perceived organizational support (Bell & Menguc, 2002).

Tepper and Taylor (2003) extended this approach to the relationship between supervisors and their subordinates. They argued that supervisors who perceived that they were treated fairly by the organization could reciprocate by treating subordinates more favorably. Accordingly, Tepper and Taylor reported that supervisors' perception that they had received fair treatment was positively related to their subordinates' ratings of supportive behaviors, including help with difficult assignments, showing respect, and help in skill building. These results are consistent with the implication of organizational support theory that supervisors who are well-treated will feel an obligation to repay the organization and suggest that such a felt obligation would result in increased support of other employees. Tepper and Taylor's findings suggest that supervisors may view their advantageous position for helping subordinates to better carry out their jobs as an opportunity to repay the organization for its support.

By aiding subordinates in better fulfilling their job responsibilities, supervisors with high perceived organizational support can meet their increased obligation to help the organization reach its objectives. Accordingly, Shanock and Eisenberger (2006) found that supervisors' perceived organizational support was positively related to their subordinates' perceived supervisor support, which in turn, was associated with the subordinates' perceived organizational support and performance.

Erdogan and Enders (2007) argued that supervisors with high perceived organizational support have more benefits from upper management to pass down to favored subordinates. Thus, the association between a favorable relationship of the supervisor and the subordinate (leader–member exchange) with job satisfaction and performance should be greater with supervisors who had high perceived organizational support. Their results supported these predictions. Trickle-down effects through the organizational hierarchy, winding up with favorable treatment of customers, are shown in Figure 4.2.

These findings suggest that top management can influence perceived organizational support not only by general human resource policies but also by treating their subordinates well, leading to trickle-down effects

FIGURE 4.2

Treatment	Recipient	Consequence
Favorable treatment from upper managers and organization	Managers	High perceived organizational support
Favorable treatment from supervisors	Subordinates	High perceived supervisor support and high perceived organizational support
Favorable treatment from subordinates or employees	Customers	Customer satisfaction and loyalty

Trickle-down effects of perceived organizational support.

with lower level employees. Higher level managers who treat subordinates supportively create an obligation to reciprocate favorable treatment, and they model the way such favorable treatment can be repaid through favorable treatment of lower level employees.

SOCIAL NETWORK SUPPORT

Ng and Sorensen (2008) found in their meta-analysis that although, as predicted, supervisors had a greater influence on perceived organizational support than coworkers, contrary to their prediction, coworker support was related to perceived organizational support. Ng and Sorensen suggested that the traditional neglect of coworkers as a possible source of perceived organizational support needed revision and that employees may not draw a clear distinction between coworkers and the concept of organization. In many organizations that stress speed and agility of product innovation, there has been substantial deleveraging of the organizational hierarchy, and ad hoc workgroups are drawn around particular projects. For example, W. L. Gore & Associates in Wilmington, Delaware—the manufacturer of synthetic fibers—keeps its plant sizes small in part to prevent the establishment of a slow moving, multilayered corporate hierarchy. Gore draws project members from around the world as needed. Formal management titles receive little attention or interest and carry little prestige. Evaluations by fellow team members carry substantial weight in an employees' overall evaluation. Under such circumstances, the network of coworkers might play a larger role in employees' concept of the organization than in more traditional, hierarchical organizations.

Zagenczyk, Scott, Gibney, Murrell, and Thatcher (2010) argued that because organizations are complex, employees are motivated to collect information about organizational support from coworkers by asking them or monitoring their behavior. Such social information processing would influence employees' own perceived organizational support (Salancik & Pfeffer, 1978). Zagenczyk et al. examined how employees of an admissions department of a public university and a private manufacturing company might use their social network to obtain information about organizational support. Zaganczyk et al. studied advice ties involving instrumental relationships in which employees shared work-related information and friendship ties based on positive emotional bonds. Further, they considered structural equivalence in which individuals shared the same relationships with others in a social network. Individuals with structurally equivalent ties are likely to receive similar information from others and therefore to develop similar beliefs and attitudes. The researchers suggested that structural equivalence, as advice and friendship ties, should result in similar perceived organizational support across employees.

Zagenczyk et al. (2010) found that employees who had advice ties in the social network had similar perceived organizational support. Further, structural equivalence in the advice and friendship network was also related to perceived organizational support. Shared perceived organizational support was not related to friendship ties. Employees seemed to be convinced less about perceived organizational support by the friendship with coworkers than by high regard for their advice. This important study shows the influence of coworkers on perceived support based on the opinions of coworkers. Further, it represents an important advance by suggesting that one's pattern of relationships (structural equivalence) contributes to perceived organizational support.

Hayton, Carnabuci, and Eisenberger (2009) suggested that trends in organizational structure that reduce the number of organizational hierarchical levels and provide more decision-making responsibilities to lower level employees (e.g., Kochan & Weinstein, 1994; Osterman, 1994; O'Toole & Lawler, 2006) may increase the extent to which actions by coworkers are identified with the organization itself. Additionally, employees recognize that instrumental and socioemotional support among coworkers is encouraged by organizations that value human capital. Therefore, employees who receive support from multiple coworkers would experience increased perceived organizational support (Hayton et al., 2009).

Hayton et al. (2009) investigated the relationship between the support received from the organization's social network and perceived organizational support. They examined both instrumental and expressive ties among coworkers of managerial and staff employees of a large Greek manufacturing firm. Instrumental ties involve the receipt of resources needed to complete work-related tasks. Expressive ties afford socioemotional support (Podolny & Baron, 1997). Controlling for supervisor support, perceived organizational support was positively related to the size, density and quality of employees' networks involving these social ties. The findings suggest that social networks, as well as the traditional organizational hierarchy, contribute to perceived organizational support. Zagenczyk et al.'s (2010) findings suggest that the social network provides respected judgments about the supportiveness of the organization, whereas Hayton et al.'s results indicate that support from the network influences perceived organizational support.

Just as the social network may influence an individual's perceived organizational support, the individual employee may influence the perceived organizational support of group. Earlier in this chapter, we discussed trickle-down effects in which the favorable treatment received by the supervisor is passed down to subordinates, increasing their perceived organizational support. Recent research suggests that a single employee with high perceived organizational support may influence an entire group to perform well. Shore, Ehrhart, and Coyle-Shapiro (2009) found that teams reciprocated exceptionally high perceived support for a single one of its members and that this effect was enhanced by group cohesion and a helping norm. Employees who value their membership or who believe in aiding other group members should be especially gratified and ready to reciprocate the organization for the favorable treatment of coworkers.

The findings that coworkers as individuals and members of social networks influence perceived organizational support suggest that coworkers make a larger contribution to perceived organizational support than I contemplated when introducing the concept (Eisenberger et al., 1986). Yet, it remains the case that the employees' identification of organizational representatives with the organization is strongly related to their power and influence on organizational values and strategies. Thus, Ng and Sorensen's (2008) literature review indicates that managers' influences on perceived organizational support are substantially stronger than those of coworkers.

Extensions of Organizational Support Theory

Perceived support has been found to have positive outcomes for individuals and organizations beyond those in traditional employee–employer relationships. As shown in Table 4.1, perceived support has been found to have important outcomes for military employees, union members, volunteers, and customers.

TABLE 4.1

Extensions of Organizational Support Theory to Other Organization Relationships

Deliverers of support	Targets of support	Distinct outcomes
Military organizations	Military employees	Intention to remain in the military Military ethos
Unions	Union members	Union loyalty Union participation
Volunteer organizations	Volunteers	Perceived respect in the organization Volunteers' performance Volunteers' attendance
Providers of goods and services	Customers	Customer loyalty Customer satisfaction

MILITARY SUPPORT

Since the cold war ended in the early 1990s, military organizations in Western democracies that do not use compulsory service have struggled to maintain needed staffing levels (Capon, Chernyshenko, & Stark, 2007). The military faces the difficult problem of maintaining sufficient levels of recruitment, performance, and retention to fight protracted insurgencies with volunteer recruits. Military life often requires long periods away from family, prolonged exposure to stressful environments, and short recuperation periods. Further, because of policy decisions that are often beyond the military's control, high demands on personnel may result in training opportunities and assignments that compare unfavorably with what has been explicitly promised or expected based on the military's traditions. Furthermore, the military is increasingly forced to compete with civilian employers that offer higher pay and more favorable working conditions.

Although loss of talented employees is harmful for various kinds of organizations, it is especially difficult for the military. Unlike organizations that can hire away skilled employees from other organizations, the military depends heavily on specialized training and promotion from within. Training following enlistment and at service academies provides a basic level of knowledge, but there is no substitute for the experience to be gained in actual operations. The ongoing training needed to become proficient in specialized tasks requires years (Mason, 2002). Thus, when many military personnel leave service, they cannot be easily replaced, and too few qualified individuals may be available for important missions (Gibson & Tremble, 2006).

The military finds it especially difficult to recruit during periods of low civilian unemployment. At these times, educational standards have been lowered. A more satisfactory approach has been to offer substantial enlistment and retention bonuses. Although monetary inducements are very useful, difficulties in meeting these goals remain and suggest that additional strategies are needed. Pay is only one component of a multifaceted approach that will be necessary to enhance military ethos and retention as voluntary military service competes against the private job market during good economic times. Consequently, researchers have begun examining various factors contributing to the retention and attrition of military personnel. As Capon et al. (2007) pointed out, many published studies on military retention have focused on employees' demographic variables (e.g., gender, marital status) and features of military jobs that cannot readily be changed (e.g., length of overseas assignment, male:female ratio), with little attention to the possible contributions of employees' personal characteristics or human resources practices.

In contrast, research on civilian retention has treated turnover as an instance of motivated personal choice that is influenced by employees' personal characteristics (employees' personality traits and attitudes in the workplace) and organizations' human resources management practices (e.g., personnel support programs, recruitment techniques). Assessing the applicability of civilian retention findings to the military, researchers on military retention found that work attitudes such as organizational commitment and job satisfaction are relevant to military settings and are beginning to receive deserved attention (see also D. G. Allen, Shore, & Griffeth, 2003).

As a well-known determinant of both affective organizational commitment and job satisfaction, perceived organizational support (i.e., perceived support from the military organization) has been integrated into some of these studies. This research has shown that the general pattern of relationships found in the civilian literature applies to the military context. For instance, Capon et al. (2007) found that perceived organizational support increased affective organizational commitment among New Zealand army personnel, which in turn, decreased intention to quit. Perceived organizational support had a positive influence on the job satisfaction of Canadian military personnel, leading to better health and to reduced turnover intentions (Dupré & Day, 2007). Dobreva-Martinova, Villeneuve, Strickland, and Matheson (2002) reported that perceived organizational support was related to reduced stress and increased job satisfaction and organizational commitment among Canadian Regular Forces personnel. Gibson and Tremble (2006) showed that an awareness of available benefits fostered perceived organizational support among U.S. Army captains, which had a positive influence on affective organizational commitment.

Bradley (1997) found that prospects for promotion and coworker support among Canadian military personnel were positively related to perceived organizational support, which in turn, was associated with increased affective organizational commitment and increased intent to remain in the military. Bradley also suggested that perceived organizational support would increase the military ethos of military personnel. Bradley used Cotton's (1982) scale to assess the distinction between the military as just a job versus a more encompassing mind-set that embodied the norms and values of the military. According to Cotton, military ethos involves putting the needs of the military ahead of self when necessary, as characteristic of the difference between a vocational orientation (suggesting an important purpose) and an occupational orientation (suggesting time serving). Perceived organizational support showed a modest positive relationship with military ethos.

This is a promising start in the study of the relationship between perceived organizational support and military ethos. One area for future research involves refinement of the measurement of military ethos and, more generally, military culture, to see how endorsement of military ethos and culture by military personnel is influenced by perceived organizational support. Half of the six items in Cotton's (1982) scale concern the relevance of the individual's off-duty life for the military, and the internal reliability of the scale is low, suggesting that there is limited agreement by personnel that the assessed values fully portray Canada's military ethos. Thus, it would be worthwhile to examine a more diverse sample of values. Further, the values constituting the military ethos may vary across cultures, so that transnational studies would be very helpful.

PERCEIVED UNION SUPPORT

Shore et al. (1994) found that union members formed general beliefs concerning the extent to which the union valued their contributions and cared about their well-being. Such perceived union support was positively related to affective commitment to the union and participation in union activities. Tetrick, Shore, McClurg, and Vandenberg (2007) found that union instrumentality, involving a cognitive assessment of the net rewards of union representation, led to perceived union support, which increased union loyalty and union participation.

Of course, some notable distinctions exist between unions versus employers that may be relevant to how social exchange works (Tetrick et al., 2007; Wayne et al., 2009). Although employees receive compensation from their employers for their contributions, members pay their unions for services and benefits received through their union dues (Tetrick, 1995). In addition, the union represents all individuals in the bargaining unit whether or not they are members of the union, and all members of the bargaining unit enjoy the rewards and favorable working conditions attained without differentiation among the members based on their contributions. Thus, as Tetrick et al. (2007) noted, organizational discretionary treatment, which plays an important role in employer–employee relations, may not be as important in union–member relationship.

Although these characteristics of employee–union relationships may differ from most employee–organization relationships, a wide variety of employee–organization relationships exist, some of which are rather similar to those of employees with their union. Consider first the proposition that unions generally represent group interests rather than individual interests. This differs from employee–employer relationships to the extent that employees are treated individually and thus think of themselves in a one-to-one relationship in the organization. Yet, whether or not employees are unionized, they are sometimes treated by their employer as undifferentiated group members rather than individually. For example, some general human resources policies apply to all employees in a given group. Also, in some cases, union membership can provide attention to individual needs, such as when it negotiates a package that provides a choice among fringe benefits.

According to organizational support theory (Eisenberger et al., 1986), a person does not have to be identified as an individual to believe she is a valued member of an organization, but simply as a member of a well-treated group. As we discuss in Chapter 5, for employees high in collectivism, the benefits received by coworkers had an important influence on perceived organizational support. For employees high in competitiveness, the benefits received by coworkers had a reduced impact. Thus, the importance of individual recognition for perceived organizational support may depend on the social values of the individual. Actions taken by the union to support the entire group membership may contribute most to the perceived support of collectivists, whereas actions that personally affect individuals may contribute most to the perceived support of competitors.

Regarding the influence of union discretion in perceived union support, it is true that the union has no choice over its membership and that all members enjoy the fruits of its labors, reducing the latitude of union action. Thus, union discretion probably does have less influence over perceived union support than does organizational discretion in most organizations, as Tetrick et al. (2007) suggested. Yet, the union does have discretion over other possible antecedents of perceived union support, such as those associated with extensiveness of communication with union members, opportunities of union members to participate in decision making, pursuit of grievances on behalf of coworkers, and so on. To the extent that these kinds of activity are viewed as discretionary, as opposed to being forced on the union by regulations or activists, perceived union support should be enhanced.

The conceptualization and research findings concerning perceived union support suggest that employees understand how they are valued by their union in a way similar to how they are valued by their organization. The findings open the possibility that individuals may attempt to understand their relationship with various kinds of organizations by forming a generalization concerning their valuation by these organizations.

PERCEIVED PROVIDER SUPPORT

In the United States, as of this writing, Apple's customer support has maintained its traditional high ratings, helping to retain a loyal customer base (Oliver, 2010). In contrast, Dell has dropped below Apple and upstart Lenovo on time waiting on the phone, knowledgeability of support staff, and finding a problem solution. Dell previously ranked much higher on customer support but let its support suffer as a way to reduce costs. Dell's staff is stretched very thin, and many service personnel lack adequate training. Phone calls are not returned. Problems that should be fixed quickly require hours. Some service representatives, unequipped to handle difficult problems, use the old trick of putting customers on hold and then hanging up. This lack of concern with customers' needs appears to have reached higher levels of the organization. According to internal documents uncovered in a pending lawsuit, Dell shipped at least 11.8 million computers from 2003 to 2005 that were at risk of failure because of flawed components, and Dell employees concealed the problems from customers who experienced computer failures (Vance, 2010). Dell thus became a company viewed as caring little for its clients. In an industry in which low-end products, which Dell produces, are becoming more similar so as to be considered almost a commodity, this is not a winning strategy.

Shanock and Eisenberger (2009) extended organizational support theory to the relationship between customers and organizations that provide services or products. Customer loyalty has been described as an individual's bond with a product or provider, leading the customers to engage in repeat business, offer favorable recommendations to other potential customers, and provide suggestions for improvements and evaluations when asked (Anderson, Fornell, & Lehmann, 1994; Buttle & Burton, 2002; A. Dean, 2007; Szymanski & Henard, 2001). To maintain such loyalty, providers have traditionally sought to enhance general customers' satisfaction, involving their global favorable judgment of the product or service. Although customer satisfaction clearly contributes to loyalty (Anderson et al., 1994; Gustafsson, Johnson, & Roos, 2005), maintaining loyalty solely through satisfaction has been increasingly difficult for many businesses in recent years as greater deregulation, access to the Internet, and international trade increase competition (Caceres & Paparoidamis, 2007; Schneider, White, & Paul, 1997).

Because such competition limits the durability of price or quality advantages (Arnett, German, & Hunt, 2003; Eiriz & Wilson, 2006; Ford, 2003; Schneider, Holcombe et al., 1997), researchers in marketing and organizational psychology have recently begun to consider socioemotional factors as an additional source of customer loyalty, an approach often called *relationship marketing* (Schneider, Holcombe et al., 1997; see Eiriz & Wilson, 2006, for a review). Gustafsson et al. (2005) argued that building long-term relationships with customers requires "a 'stickiness' that keeps customers loyal even when satisfaction is low" (p. 211). Many researchers maintain that providers should focus on fulfilling customers' needs and desires to establish long-term relationships (e.g., Caceres & Paparoidamis, 2007; Ford, 2003; Gustafsson et al., 2005; Schneider, Holcombe et al., 1997).

Eiriz and Wilson (2006) and Arnett et al. (2003) suggested that social exchange theory can aid the understanding of socioemotional relationships between customers and providers. As we discussed in

Chapter 2, social exchange theory applies the norm of reciprocity to diverse benefits exchanged among individuals or groups (P. M. Blau, 1964; Shore et al., 2006). The reciprocity norm obligates the recipient of favorable treatment to compensate the donor (Gouldner, 1958). With continuing reciprocal exchanges of valued resources, the partners become more assured that by meeting the other's needs, their own needs will be met in the future. Thus, as relationships become stronger, partners come to trust each other more and become less concerned with short-term outcomes and more willing to invest resources for long-term benefits (P. M. Blau, 1964; Shore et al., 2006).

Organizational support theory seems well-suited to adapt to customer–provider relationships because it deals, in part, with one party's development of loyalty (the employee) based on the provision of socioemotional and tangible resources of a second party (the organization). Customers might react to favorable treatment in ways that parallel those of employees as described by organizational support theory. Marketing researchers such as Buttle and Burton (2002), Gustafsson et al. (2005), and Narayandas (1998) have argued that to maintain a loyal customer base, providers should make customers feel valued and important. Just as employees value perceived organizational support partly to meet socioemotional needs for approval, esteem, and affiliation (Eisenberger et al., 2001), customers may welcome treatment that conveys approval, esteem, and affiliation. Additionally, customers may react positively to signs that the provider cares about their satisfaction as an indication that the provider can be counted on in the future to fashion products and services to meet customers' wants and needs.

Shanock and Eisenberger (2009) suggested that to meet socioemotional needs and determine the likelihood that the provider will act in their interests, customers develop general beliefs concerning the extent to which the provider cares about their satisfaction and values them as customers (i.e., *perceived provider support*). As shown in Figure 4.3, customers would infer perceived support by examining providers' favorable actions that appear intended to fulfill the customers' motivations and needs and by providers' helpful responses to suggestions or complaints. Also, as shown in Figure 4.3, on the basis of the norm of reciprocity, perceived provider support would create a felt obligation to be loyal to the provider. Additionally, by fulfilling socioemotional needs (e.g., esteem, affiliation), perceived provider support would enhance the customers' social identity as valued customers. Such identification would increase customers' affective commitment to the provider, also resulting in increased loyalty. Thus, both felt obligation and affective commitment would increase customer loyalty as indicated by repeat business, recommendations to other potential customers, and provision of advice and help to the provider when asked. Finally, perceived provider

FIGURE 4.3

Antecedents and consequences of perceived provider support. PPS = perceived provider support; SAT = customer satisfaction.

support would increase loyalty by contributing to customers' overall feelings of satisfaction with the provider.

Consider Southwest Airlines' treatment of its customers. During a recent flight on Southwest Airlines, I was waiting to take off in the crowded cabin. All but three seats were taken. Suddenly, a late passenger dashed on board, out of breath and lugging a suitcase. In similar situations, I have seen attendants on traditional air carriers act with annoyance and tell the customer to quickly take a seat so we would not be held up. Instead, on Southwest, a flight attendant good-naturedly presented the three remaining seats as options and helped the late arrival find a rack for his suitcase. After we had taken off, another attendant walked over the late comer and said "We are so glad to have you with us," and listened and nodded sympathetically as the passenger told his story of woe for being late. After all this attention, the passenger had a broad smile on his face and, one suspects, Southwest had a customer for life.

This treatment is consistent with Southwest's training of employees that emphasizes efficiency and customer satisfaction over adherence to rules. Despite being a no-frills airline that serves no onboard meals and provides no seat assignments, Southwest is highly popular with fliers. Southwest employees are encouraged to solve problems to enhance customer service. They are given the latitude to alter certain standard procedures when this would aid fliers, such as delaying a flight a short time to meet a late incoming flight.

Southwest wants their passengers to have fun on flights. Pilots and attendants are encouraged to work from the Southwest activity book, which contains jokes and songs, but the staff generally prefers to ad lib. On another recent flight, the chief attendant ended a song with the words "and if you're good, you can marry me." I could not believe the song was in the Southwest activities book. It was not, but the attendant thought this innovation would be more mirthful. As flying has gotten more aggravating in recent years owing to severe crowding and a decline in customer service, it is all the more amazing when flight after flight of Southwest ends in laughter and, often, good-natured cheers.

Just as Southwest does an excellent job of instilling perceived organizational support in its employees, the airline provides exceptional service that conveys to customers that it cares about their satisfaction and values their business. Thus, customers develop general perceptions concerning their support by providers of goods and services (Shanock & Eisenberger, 2009).

Shanock and Eisenberger (2009) carried out three studies to examine the contribution of perceived provider support to customer loyalty. The first two studies examined the customer–provider relationship between college students and their university. Universities have increasingly marketed themselves to prospective students as providers of opportunities for personal growth, favorable campus life, and sellable educational skills (Bok, 2004; Clay, 2008; McHenry, 2007). Assessed loyalty behaviors included volunteering of slogans to aid admissions and recommendation of the university to others. The third study extended their findings to customer service with a different type of provider, a health care information service having corporate clients. Loyalty behaviors included anticipated repeated business and recommending the organization to others. The results indicated that the college students and customers of the information service formed a general belief concerning their valuation by their providing organization, the strength of which depended on the extent to which the favorableness of treatment appeared to the customers to be based on the providers' voluntary choice. Perceived provider support, in turn, was positively related to felt obligation and affective commitment to the provider, with positive consequences for loyalty behaviors. Perceived provider support also enhanced loyalty behaviors by increasing customer satisfaction.

Perceived provider support was influenced far more by the favorableness of treatment over which students believed that their university had medium or high discretion than by the favorableness of treatment perceived to involve low discretion. This is exactly the same pattern of results found for discretionary treatment with employees (Eisenberger et al., 1997; Stinglhamber & Vandenberghe, 2004). Evidently, the receipt of favorable treatment from a provider contributes to perceived provider support to the extent that the treatment is viewed as voluntary and therefore indicative of the provider's positive valuation of the customer. This powerful effect is readily observed in everyday life. For example, a provider that personally contacts a recent customer with the only stated purpose of seeing how well a recent product or service is operating is engaged in a voluntary act that tends to strongly promote perceived provider support.

These results suggest that customers respond positively to perceived support from organizational providers, similar to how employees respond positively to support by the organization. When providing support to customers, organizations conveyed that they cared about customer satisfaction and valued individuals as customers. Customers responded with greater loyalty. As competitive forces make maintaining customer loyalty increasingly difficult, perceived provider support provides an understanding of how organizations can cope with this new reality.

PERCEIVED ORGANIZATIONAL SUPPORT FOR VOLUNTEERS

I served as an evaluation consultant for a couple of years for the Healthy Heart Program of Salem County, New Jersey, the southernmost county in the state. The program was designed to provide a comprehensive approach to reducing cardiovascular disease among residents whose rate was the highest among all the state counties owing to industrial pollution, high intake of fatty foods, heavy consumption of alcohol, and lack of physical exercise. The program had a small number of paid staff, but the majority of participants were volunteers with varied motives for participation. Some were retired nurses and doctors who enjoyed practicing their profession and helping others at a more leisurely pace than when they had been employed. Some came from organizations that expected them to provide community service and were there as time servers. Some volunteers were spouses who had never worked outside the home and found fulfillment in the program. In many cases, a motivation to help the community was accompanied by a desire to meet and get to know other volunteers. This was particularly true of retirees who no longer had the social contact supplied by their former jobs.

Commitment to the program fell along a broad range. Some volunteers remained for years and happily tackled any task given to them. Others simply dropped out as soon as they found their time occupied by activities of greater interest or urgency. Maintaining the motivation of such volunteers is a general problem for organizations that depend on volunteer workers. How can the loyalty and investment of time and effort be increased for individuals with such diverse motivations for volunteering?

Paid employees know that their pay and continued employment depend on meeting minimum standards concerning attendance, performance, and following organizational norms and rules. In contrast, volunteer organizations have less power. The threat to terminate volunteers carries little cost to them beyond the severance of social and business contacts at the organization and the lessening of good feelings associated with any community service. Further, volunteers know they can subsequently volunteer for other organizations if they desire. Therefore, organizations relying on volunteer labor are often confronted with low performance and low attendance of volunteers, referred to as the *reliability problem* (J. L. Pearce, 1993).

Socioemotional benefits, as opposed to the material, calculative, or instrumental reasons for participation in volunteer activities, may be key for long-term involvement among volunteers in many kinds of organizations. On the basis of a social identity theory (Tajfel & Turner, 1979), Boezeman and Ellemers (2007, 2008) argued that pride and respect are important bases for volunteers' continued affiliation with charitable organizations. In this view, a group's favorable status increases pride, and a group member's favorable status in the organization increases the perception of the receipt of respect, both of which contribute to the member's self-image and incorporation of role status into the individual's social identity. These investigators found with charitable fundraising volunteers that pride and respect were positively related to normative and affective organizational commitment, with normative commitment associated with intent to remain with the organization.

In a second study with fundraising volunteers, Boezeman and Ellemers (2007) found that the perceived importance of the volunteer work was positively related to pride in being a member of the organization. Also, two kinds of specific perceived organizational support, emotion-oriented support and task-oriented support, were positively related to the respect that the volunteers experienced in the organization, leading to affective organizational commitment. The items used to assess perceived emotion-oriented support suggest that what was being measured came close to the positive valuation component of perceived organizational support, except that volunteers responded regarding the organization's orientation toward volunteers generally rather than for the individual volunteer. This is a significant difference because volunteers may feel that their appreciation by the organization differs in the positive or negative direction from how the organization views volunteers generally. The items used to assess perceived task-oriented support pertained to how the organization valued the volunteers' contributions and cared about their well-being as related to work as opposed to the interest in employees' well-being generally supposed by perceived organizational support. Although these two kinds of specific organizational support lack some features of the general perception of organizational support, taken together, they come close. Further, the two kinds of support show a substantial positive relationship. Thus, it appears that perceived organizational support from the volunteer organization leads to greater experienced respect and organizational commitment.

These findings indicate that volunteer organizations should develop policies and practices that induce pride, self-respect, and perceived organizational support as means to reinforce volunteers' commitment to the organization and to reduce their withdrawal behaviors. For example, organizations might ensure that supervisors convey their appreciation for volunteers' efforts and that volunteers are provided with help when needed to carry out their jobs effectively.

Summary and Implications

Considerable research has confirmed supervisors' substantial contribution to perceived organizational support. However, organizational support theory holds that employees derive the greatest organizational support from high-level managers, viewing them as important for promulgating organizational values and strategies. Unfortunately, research is lacking concerning the relative influence of upper level managers and supervisors on perceived organizational support. We can say for now that those aspects of organizational culture that are promulgated by high-level managers and are related to fair treatment and perceived organizational politics make a major contribution to perceived organizational support.

The influence of supervisors on perceived organizational support comes partly through employees' identification of them with the organization through their assigned roles of directing, evaluating, and coaching subordinates. Employees differ in the power and influence they attribute to supervisors partly because supervisors differ in the impressions they give of wielding power and adhering to organizational values. The resulting SOE influences the strength of the relationship between support received from supervisors and perceived organizational support.

Style of leadership also affects perceived organizational support. Leaders who establish strong exchange relationships with followers tend to produce high perceived organizational support because their supportive treatment is attributed partly to the organization. For the same reason, transformational leadership, in which the leader inspires followers with a strong sense of purpose and meets individual needs, contributes to perceived organizational support. Servant leadership, emphasizing attention to integrity and the work needs of employees, also appears likely to be related to perceived organizational support.

Arguments favoring one theory of leadership over the other often ignore benefits found in the others and the fact that some different leadership styles are not mutually exclusive. For example, although transformational leadership has often been considered the province of higher level leaders, such as CEOs and statesmen, and leader–member exchange has been applied typically to lower level managers, a quantitative analysis of the research literature found transformational leadership to be equally effective for lower level employees (Lowe et al., 1996) and studies of leader–member exchange often incorporate employees at multiple levels in the organizational hierarchy.

Leaders vary in the extent to which they enact the various performance elements considered by the leader–member exchange, transformational, and servant theories of leadership. Elements emphasized in one theory are unrepresented in the other theories. But as has been demonstrated with leader–member exchange and transformational leadership and is likely for servant leadership, the distinctive supportive behaviors suggested by these theories contribute to perceived organizational support. There is no reason, for example, why a leader cannot establish a strong social exchange relationship with a subordinate, as described by leader–member exchange theory, and inspire that subordinate to greater objectives, as described by transformational leadership theory. In fact, many successful leaders use a combination of elements described by the two theories. Beloved leaders are especially good at offering a vision to sweep up followers while enhancing the bonds of trust and mutual benefit through social exchange. A careful study of Julius Caesar's favorite, 10th legion (Dando-Collins, 2002) indicates that Caesar was a highly effective transformational leader, instilling a vision of being part of a great epic, the making of an indomitable Rome master of the known world. Ordinary soldiers became a core unit of a famous army on a grand and successful quest, giving their lives purpose and meaning, and enhancing their self-esteem. At a more mundane level, Caesar encouraged trust and loyalty through leader–member exchange by taking care that his men were well-fed and quartered and enjoyed their share of the riches gained through their conquests.

One of the newer and more exciting areas of research on perceived organizational support involves *multiplier effects,* in which supportive treatment received by one employee spreads to a second, then a third, and so on, down through the formal organizational hierarchy or through social networks within the organization. One type of multiplier effect involves perceived organizational support of supervisors, which influences their treatment of subordinates, increasing perceived organizational support and performance. Research is needed on how organizational strategies related to human capital influence affect the strength of such trickle-down effects. A second type of multiplier effect works through the social network in which favorable or unfavorable opinions concerning the organization's supportiveness spread among employees. Also, perceived organizational support is related to the size and density of employees' social networks involving expressive and instrumental relationships. In dynamic organizations in which power and decision making have been placed in the hands of lower level employees, and groups form readily to deal with projects as needed, one would expect coworkers would be considered more central than in more traditional organizational structures such that social networks would contribute more strongly to perceived organizational support.

For organizational support theory, the entity that constitutes "the organization" for the purpose of analysis is a matter of convenience dependent on the issues to be addressed. Employees have a strong tendency to personify organized units, as well as the entire organization, and they are most concerned with the favorable or unfavorable orientation toward them of the units with the greatest apparent impact on their working lives. Depending on the organization, this may be the department, local facility, division, or affiliate of a conglomerate.

Support may generalize from embedded organizational units to the entire organization. For example, support received both from home and the overseas branches of organizations increases expatriate employees' perceived support from the overall organization. Sometimes support from two related organizations for which an employee works may have mutual influence, for example, when support from the employment agency and the client organization enhances perceived organizational support for both parties.

Although the organizational unit to which perceived organizational unit is applied depends on its relevance for analytic reasons, the nature of perceived organizational support remains the same. Employees create an overall perception concerning the extent to which the organization, however defined, values their contributions and cares about their well-being.

In recent years, organizational support theory has been expanded beyond traditional employee–employer associations. Perceived organizational support has been found to apply to unusual employment relationships (the military), to employees' relationship with their unions, and to nonemployment relationships with organizations (customers, volunteers). These results suggest that when individuals form consequential relationships with organizations, they are motivated to determine their valuation by those organizations to meet socioemotional needs and to assess the benefits of sustained or increased involvement. Servicemembers' relationships with the military have been found to involve many of the same processes regarding perceived organizational support and affective commitment as found with civilian employment.

Yet, there are elements concerning the nature of work in uniformed jobs (e.g., military, police, fire fighters) that differ from most civilian jobs. These include the immersion in the military ethos of high dedication; the frequent danger and stress involved in deployments during wartime; and the dependence on a small, enduring group of comrades for physical protection and emotional sustenance. Research has only just begun to examine the ways in which this environment may influence the operation of perceived organizational support.

Employees develop a general perception concerning the extent to which their union values their contributions and cares about their well-being. Such perceived union support has been found to be positively related to employees' affective commitment to the union and their participation in union activities. Researchers need to know more about antecedents of perceived union support. As with perceived organizational support, we suggest that discretionary action by union leaders and representatives may be important. For example, to what degree are union leaders seen to be advancing the interests of the membership as opposed to their own benefits and lifestyle? How available are union representatives to discuss the problems and needs of individual union members and to follow up persistently and competently?

Customers form general beliefs concerning their valuation by organizations that provide them with services and products. Perceived provider support enhances the understanding of customer loyalty beyond the more temporary influence of customer satisfaction. The best of providers cannot always satisfy customers because providers are dependent on their own vendors for their goods or services. Also, providers must compete with other providers who may offer the same or similar products at temporarily reduced prices to attract new customers. Perceived provider support fulfills socioemotional needs and creates a felt obligation to the provider, leading customers to believe that they will be better off remaining with the provider than jumping to another provider when a short-term favorable opportunity presents itself. Discretionary behaviors by the provider were found to play a key role in the development of such perceived provider support, resulting in enhanced loyalty behaviors. This initial research needs to be extended to broader array of customer–provider relationships and loyalty behaviors.

There is preliminary evidence that perceived organizational support is related to volunteers' affective commitment to a charitable organization. The two scales used by Boezeman and Ellemers (2007, 2008) to measure organizational support, taken together, come close to assessing the extent to which the organization values volunteers' contributions and cares about their well-being. More evidence is needed specifically on the formation of global perceptions of perceived organizational support and its influence on volunteer behavior.

As we can see from the extensions of organizational support theory to military personnel, union members, customers, and volunteers, individuals form general perceptions concerning their valuation in diverse kinds of organizations. Socioemotional needs (e.g., esteem, affiliation, emotional support) and the norm of reciprocity are salient in a variety of contexts, making perceived support by the organization important to the individual. Although organizational support theory was developed to explain employee–employer relationships, the processes described by the theory apply to other kinds of relationships that people have with organizations.

Employees' Subjective Well-Being 5

E very time I fly Southwest Airlines, I hear boisterous flight attendants telling jokes over the intercom to the passengers. Near the end of my last flight on Southwest, the head attendant announces, "We have someone very special on board. He is 79 years old. It's his birthday and he's taking his first flight. Let's give him a cheer." CHEERS, CHEERS, CHEERS. "It's the pilot." Raucous laughter. As I am exiting the plane, I overhear another flight attendant say to the head flight attendant, "They loved your jokes—You made this flight so much fun." "No," she replies, "We all did it. We are a great team." By contrast, more often than not when I fly U.S. Airways, I see sullen attendants ignoring passengers' call buttons or gruffly ordering them to conform to rules. Southwest employees, as we have stressed throughout this book, feel supported; more, they are happy with their jobs and working life. U.S. Airways employees believe the company cares nothing for them, has been double-crossing them for years, and is waiting for them to make mistakes to fire them. Thus, they have little reason to be happy with their jobs or to pretend to be happy for the sake of their passengers.

Many factors besides perceived organizational support, of course, contribute to employees' happiness and satisfaction at work, from personality to home life. Yet, perceived organizational support matters greatly for most employees. One of the ways that organizational support theory is distinct in its approach to employee–organization relationships is its emphasis on the centrality of the employee's viewpoint. Employees spend half their waking hours at work, so how the organization treats them and how it appears to view them have considerable influence on subjective well-being at work, with a spillover to home life as well. Employees' personification of the organization causes them to focus on it as if it were a powerful living being with considerable power to influence their welfare. The organization is viewed as having a persisting positive or negative orientation toward the employee involving its valuation of the employee's contributions and its concern with the employee's well-being.

Perceived organizational support enhances the emotional tone of an employee's workday. Supported employees are in a better mood, experience greater work satisfaction and less stress. They feel they make a greater impact in the organization and have a better adjusted home life. *Subjective well-being*, which we discuss in the present chapter, concerns employees' moods, emotions, and evaluation of their satisfaction (Diener, Scollon, & Lucas, 2004; Diener, Suh, Lucas, & Smith, 1999). As shown in Figure 5.1, four mechanisms have been proposed for the effects of perceived organizational support on different types of subjective well-being. The organization's positive valuation of employees' contributions may increase self-efficacy (Bandura, 1986), involving the belief that they can muster the skill or motivation to carry out their jobs well. Such positive valuation and care about employees' well-being may also increase (a) anticipated help when needed, (b) expected reward for high effort, and (c) fulfillment of socioemotional needs.

Positive Mood

Mood refers to a general directional dimension of emotionality. Watson, Clark, and Tellegen (1988) described *positive mood* as involving feelings of enthusiasm, excitement, and alertness. Larsen and Diener (1992, p. 28) noted that Watson et al.'s construct of positive mood primarily involves a state of high activation with pleasant hedonic tone. Mood has been proposed as the state or nonheritable component of affectivity, influenced by environment (George & Brief, 1992). Dependent on the situation, positive mood can be distinguished from a predisposition toward positive emotional experience (Watson et al., 1988). Furthermore, it differs conceptually from job satisfaction in that it involves a general emotional state without a specific object (George, 1989). Positive mood has been found to be positively related to helping others and thinking creatively, both of which are included in George and Brief's (1992) concept of organizational spontaneity. George and Brief noted

FIGURE 5.1

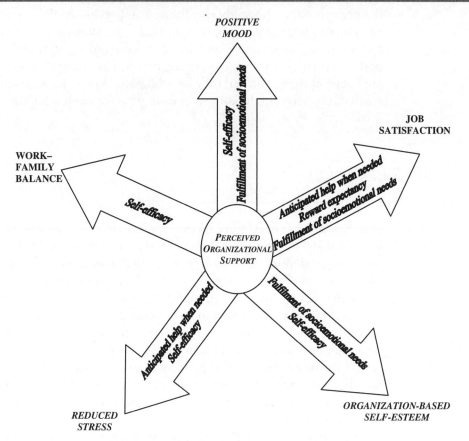

Effects of perceived organizational support on subjective well-being and proposed underlying mechanisms.

that positive mood may prime employees to think about favorable characteristics of coworkers, leading to helping behavior. They also noted that positive mood appears to increase creative thinking, which would increase employee innovation.

George and Brief (1992) proposed that events at work signifying an employee's competence, worth, or achievement enhance positive mood. Accordingly, Eisenberger et al. (2001) and Rhoades and Eisenberger (2002) have suggested that perceived organizational support may increase employees' positive mood by enhancing perceived competence (self-efficacy) and fulfilling socioemotional needs. In support of their view, Eisenberger et al. (2001) found with postal employees that perceived organizational support contributed to positive mood, which in turn led to increased extrarole performance, including aiding fellow employees, taking actions that protect the organization from risk, offering constructive suggestions, and gaining knowledge and skills beneficial to the organization. This study also showed, as previously discussed, that perceived organizational support led to felt organizational and affective commitment. Thus, employees with high perceived organizational support find themselves bound to the organization in a pleasant way. They are happy at work. Further, they feel obligated to help the organization reach its objectives in the context of having a positive emotional attachment to the organization.

Job Satisfaction

Overall job satisfaction refers to employees' affect-laden attitude toward their job (Witt, 1991). Shore and Tetrick (1991) noted that, in contrast, perceived organizational support is an affect-free assessment by employees of their valuation by the organization, which has positive emotional consequences. Shore and Tetrick (1991) also argued that overall job satisfaction was more subject to recent changes in job conditions than was perceived organizational support, which was assumed to be more dependent on accumulated experience. For example, job satisfaction would fluctuate more on a short-term basis, responding to such factors as workload and treatment by one's supervisor; the accumulation of these experiences would signify the organization's valuation of the employee.

Despite these theoretical distinctions between perceived organizational support and overall job satisfaction, Shore and Tetrick (1991) were unable to find a clear distinction between the constructs. Eisenberger et al. (1997) suggested that a lack of variability of perceived organizational support and overall job satisfaction among employees in the same organization might explain these findings. They surveyed employees from a variety of organizations to obtain empirical evidence for the distinction between perceived organizational support and overall job satisfaction. Their results showed that perceived organizational support and overall job satisfaction were better represented by two distinct constructs than by a single common construct.

Based on organizational support theory, an additional important distinction between perceived organizational support and job satisfaction concerns their relationship to discretionary treatment by the organization. As noted in Chapter 2, perceived organizational support should be strongly dependent on employees' attributions concerning the organization's discretion in providing favorable treatment (e.g., high wages, fringe benefits) as opposed to being forced to do so by such external influences as contractual obligations, government regulations, or a competitive job market. In contrast, favorable treatment should influence job satisfaction relatively independently of employee beliefs concerning the organization's discretion. For instance, employees' enjoyment of a pay raise should be affected relatively little by whether this action was voluntary or forced on the organization. My colleagues and I (Eisenberger et al., 1997) conducted a study with employees from a variety of organizations that confirmed these predictions. Perceived organizational support increased with the degree of perceived discretion of favorable treatment. Job satisfaction had no systematic relationship with the perceived discretion of favorable treatment.

An employee may believe that the organization strongly values his or her contributions and cares about his or her well-being yet have little overall job satisfaction because the employer does not have the resources to prevent unfavorable treatment. For example, poor economic conditions may reduce sales of products or services and thereby lessen a company's ability to give substantial pay raises or improve physical working conditions. The employee's recognition of these financial restrictions may prevent a decline in perceived organizational support but not stop a loss of overall job satisfaction. Conversely, favorable job conditions over which the organization has little discretionary control may lead to an increase in overall job satisfaction without an accompanying increase in perceived organizational support. For example, favorable pay and physical working conditions resulting from a union strike would be more likely to increase job satisfaction than to increase perceived organizational support.

Yet, perceived organizational support should generally make employees more satisfied with their jobs, and many studies report such a relationship. Organizational support theory suggests three possible ways perceived organization support affects job satisfaction. First, it should signal the availability of needed resources (Rhoades & Eisenberger, 2002). Perceived support indicates that help will be available when needed to help the employee to carry out his or her job more effectively. Second, such support has been found to increase employees' expectation that increased effort on the organization's behalf will be followed by greater material and socioemotional rewards (Eisenberger et al., 1990). These favorable outcomes and anticipation of favorable future outcomes should make employees happier with their jobs. Third, perceived organizational support may contribute to job satisfaction by fulfilling employees' socioemotional needs (Eisenberger et al., 1986). This conclusion is supported by findings, discussed in Chapter 2, that the relationship between perceived organizational support and police performance was greater for employees with high needs for esteem, affiliation, approval, and emotional support. Also, as is discussed in more detail in the section on stress, a number of studies have indicated that perceived organizational support serves to reduce stress in the workplace. Employees who have their socioemotional needs met and are helped by the organization to cope with stressors should be happier in their jobs.

In sum, the evidence clearly shows that perceived organizational support and overall job satisfaction are distinct, but positively related, constructs. The findings are consistent with the view that perceived organizational support increases overall job satisfaction (see also Rhoades & Eisenberger, 2002). However, because employees' perceived organizational support and satisfaction were measured simultaneously in these studies, the direction of causality in this relationship remains uncertain. Indeed, one might hypothesize that individuals perceive their organization as supportive because they are satisfied with their work situation (Shore & Tetrick, 1991). Future research should thus provide more direct evidence on the direction of the link between perceived organizational support and job satisfaction.

In addition to contributing to overall job satisfaction, perceived organizational support might increase *career satisfaction,* which refers to the fulfillment employees derive from intrinsic and extrinsic aspects of their careers, including pay, advancement, and developmental opportunities (Greenhaus, Parasuraman, & Wormley, 1990; Judge, Cable, Boudreau, & Bretz, 1995). Erdogan, Kraimer, and Liden (2004) examined the extent to which congruence between Turkish high school teachers' values and their school's values contributed to career satisfaction. Work value congruence contributed to career satisfaction when either perceived organizational support or the exchange relationship with the supervisor was low but not when perceived organizational support or the relationship with the supervisor was high. These authors suggested that perceived organizational support and the exchange relationship with the supervisor played compensatory roles, increasing the employees' career satisfaction when their values did not provide a good fit with those of the organization.

Organization-Based Self-Esteem

Organization-based self-esteem refers to employees' belief that they can fulfill their socioemotional needs through participation in their organizational roles. Individuals high in organizational-based self-esteem are said to have a sense of personal adequacy arising from fulfilling their needs and thus perceiving themselves as "important, meaningful, effectual, and worthwhile within their employing organization" (Pierce, Gardner, Cummings, & Dunham, 1989, p. 625). Some of the items in the

10-item scale usually used to assess organization-based self-esteem are similar to those used to assess the organization's positive valuation of the employee's contributions in the assessment of perceived organizational support (e.g., "I am trusted" and "There is faith in me"); others appear to get mainly at the employees' self-efficacy and impact on the organization (e.g., "I am important," "I can make a difference," "I am valuable," and "I am helpful"); and a few may cover both bases (e.g., "I am taken seriously").

Z. X. Chen, Aryee, and Lee (2005) and Lee and Pecce (2007) have suggested that perceived organizational support would lead to organization-based self-esteem by meeting socioemotional needs, which in turn would lead to affective organizational commitment. Both studies found support for their view. These findings are intriguing. Perhaps perceived organizational support leads employees to feel more important and self-efficacious in their organizational roles. Note, however, that the relationship between perceived organizational support and organization-based self-esteem might hold even without needs fulfillment. Positive valuation by the organization could simply signal that one is competent and influential in one's role. Thus, future research could provide additional evidence on the role of socioemotional needs. For example, one might assess whether the relationship between perceived organizational support and organization-based self-esteem is greater among individuals with high socioemotional needs.

Future research could also examine whether the assessment of organization-based self-esteem is suitable in its present form because some items tap appreciation of the employee by the organization, similar to the positive valuation of the employee inherent in the construct of perceived organizational support. The assessed impact and self-efficacy aspects of the construct seem to better distinguish it from perceived organizational support.

Lee and Pecce (2007) reported a positive relationship between perceived organizational support and organization-based self-esteem, whose strength was reduced by job insecurity. The study was conducted in two banks that experienced significant turbulence and uncertainty as a result of the 1997 Korean financial crisis and instituted programs of downsizing. The authors suggested that employees who were unsure of their future in the organization may have found it more difficult to form a clear view concerning the extent to which the organization cares about their well-being, the reasons they may be receiving such favorable treatment, and whether this treatment was likely to continue in the future. In contrast, job insecurity increased the positive relationship between perceived organizational support and affective commitment. Because of their weak position vis-à-vis the organization, employees whose jobs were more insecure may have attributed greater importance to any signs of support they received from the organization than were employees who experienced greater employment security. As a result, they may also have been more ready to reciprocate any act of goodwill from the organization to improve their employment chances and reduce their uncertainty. In other words, a given level of organizational support may be likely to produce a stronger sense of felt obligation among individuals who experience job insecurity than among those who perceive their job to be more secure. These intriguing results certainly warrant replication.

Reactions to Stress

Occupational stress has been demonstrated to have highly deleterious effects on employee burnout and health, costing U.S. business and industry an estimated $150 billion a year (Spielberger, Vagg, & Wasala, 2003). Stressors produce various aversive psychological consequences, termed *strains,* including anxiety and psychosomatic illness (Cropanzano et al., 1997). Large, long-term studies indicate that over 60% of all absenteeism and visits to health care providers are caused by stress-related disorders (Quillian-Wolever & Wolever, 2003). The major contemporary theories of occupational stress deal in one way or another with employees' perceived inability to deal with job demands placed on them. Of particular interest is Lazarus's cognitive appraisal approach (Folkman & Lazarus, 1991), which emphasizes the employees' assessment of their ability to deal successfully with stressors.

It is helpful to compare and contrast social support and organizational support theory analyses of employees' reactions to stress. *Social support* involves "the availability of helping relationships and the quality of those relationships" (Leavy, 1983, p. 5). As applied to employees at work, social support refers to "the availability and quality of an employee's relationship with supervisors, coworkers, family, and friends and the amount of positive consideration and task assistance received from them" (Spielberger et al., 2003, p. 192). Cohen and Wills (1985, p. 313) provided a comprehensive typology of support functions that could be provided by various sources. *Esteem support* refers to the availability of "information that a person is esteemed and accepted." *Informational support* involves "help in defining, understanding, and coping with problematic events." *Social companionship* concerns "spending time with others in leisure and recreational activities." Finally, *instrumental support* involves "provision of financial aid, material resources, and needed services." Distinctions are also frequently made between different sources of organizational support (e.g., friends, family, community, coworkers, supervisors).

Using Lazarus's appraisal model of stress (e.g., Folkman & Lazarus, 1991), Cohen and Wills (1985) suggested that social support might reduce stress initially by lessening the appraisal of a stressor as a threat to control. Once a stressor was interpreted as a threat, social support might lessen its influence by reappraisal of the threat, inhibition of maladaptive responses to it, or facilitation of adjustive counter responses to the threat. Organization theorists have suggested various ways in which the organization and employees may lessen stress (Quillian-Wolever & Wolever, 2003). The organization may reduce stress through such changes as job redesign, thereby eliminating its causes. Employees themselves may be taught to reinterpret short-term stressors as not so challenging to control. Employees may alter changeable stressors by solution-focused coping. In the case of unchangeable long-term stressors, they may engage in a variety of techniques to reduce strain, including finding social support and enacting relaxation techniques and cognitive reframing to frame the stressor in a less harmful light.

Some studies have reported that social support results in a reduction in aversive reaction at all levels of intensity of the stressor, and other studies have reported a buffering effect in which the lessening of the aversive reaction is greatest at high levels of the stressor. Cohen and Wills (1985) suggested that buffering effects will be observed when there is a "reasonable match" between the stressful event and the coping resource. Thus, in examples provided by Cohen and Wills, broad stress scales that measured cumulative stress in one's life or measures that included a large number of social relationships were considered too insensitive to observe buffering effects of social support.

Although the social support viewpoint provides valuable insights for organizational support theory, there are distinct differences between the approaches. Esteem, helpful information, and instrumental resources received from the organization may be viewed as antecedents of perceived organizational support. Perceived organizational support is not simply an accumulation of these kinds of support. Remember that perceived organizational support is a global attribution by employees concerning the extent to which the organization values their contributions and cares about their well-being, and is not a particular kind or class of support.

Perceived organizational support differs from social support in other ways. For example, perceived organizational support depends strongly on information concerning the cause of treatment received by employees. Favorable treatment that is considered highly discretionary on the part of the organization contributed more to perceived organizational support than did treatment over which the organization had little control (Eisenberger et al., 1997; Stinglhamber & Vandenberghe, 2004). Thus, the contribution of resources to perceived organizational support is transformed by the organization's discretion over their provision. Further, the consequences of perceived organizational support are derived from organizational support theory, whose principles make unique predictions (e.g., felt obligation, socioemotional needs) not found in social support theory.

As this discussion suggests, perceived organizational support is not a form of social support. Perceived organizational support should nevertheless reduce psychological strain by signaling to employees that emotional and tangible support is available when needed (George, Reed, Ballard, Colin, & Fielding, 1993; Robblee, 1998). Further, the positive valuation by the organization conveyed by perceived organizational support should reduce strain by bolstering employees' self-esteem. Also, perceived organizational support should encourage proactive problem-solving behavior to deal with stressors by providing assurance that the organization will provide assistance.

Based on Cohen and Wills's (1985) reasoning, whether perceived organizational support is observed to result in a reduction in aversive reactions at all levels of intensity of the stressor or shows its greatest effect at high levels of the stressor (buffering effect) will depend on whether the organization's global esteem and caring, and the organizational support they imply, are specific to the stressor. For example, perceived organizational support by a well-respected organization might have a substantial buffering effect on strain associated with a threat to one's self-esteem in one's professional career, whereas perceived organizational support from a poorly respected organization might have a lesser effect. As another example, if one had a long-term computer problem at work, perceived organizational support might produce a stronger buffering effect if one's company had a good information technology department than if no such department was available to provide aid.

Several studies have reported buffering effects of perceived organizational support on stress. George et al. (1993) surveyed nurses who were exposed to patients with AIDS as part of their work role. They found that the extent of exposure was positively associated with distress, as indexed by negative mood at work, and this relationship was lessened for nurses who perceived a high organizational support. George suggested that perceptions of organizational support led nurses to believe that their organization was providing them with all the relevant information for dealing with patients wth AIDS and the material resources to cope with this potential stressor. More generally, this research suggests that perceived organizational support indicates the availability of emotional and tangible support when needed to face high demands at work (George et al., 1993).

In a similar vein, Byrne et al. (2005) examined the buffering effect of perceived organizational support in the relationship between organizational politics perceived at the next level up and depressed mood. Considering perceived politics as a stressor that leads to strains such as job distress and tension (e.g., Cropanzano et al., 1997), Byrne et al. suggested that perceived organizational support indicates the availability of physical and emotional sustenance (see also George et al., 1993). As a consequence, perceived organizational support was expected to reduce reactions to stressors, that is, to minimize the magnitude of their effects. In support of their hypothesis, Byrne et al. found that when individuals perceived little organizational support and their perception of politics at the next level up from their peer level in the organization was high, they reported higher levels of depressed mood compared with individuals who perceived high levels of support.

Perceived organizational support also tempered the negative relationship between British pub workers' experiences of threats and violence and their work-related well-being (Leather, Lawrence, Beale, Cox, & Dickson, 1998). Perceived organizational support reduced the relationship between work–reward imbalance (considered a source of stress) and turnover intention (Kinnunen, Feldt, & Makikangas, 2008). In contrast, sometimes perceived organizational support is found to produce equivalent reductions in strain at both low and high levels of stress, including such outcomes as fatigue (Cropanzano et al., 1997), burnout (Cropanzano et al., 1997; Jawahar, Stone, & Kisamore, 2007), anxiety (Robblee, 1998; Venkatachalam, 1995), and headaches (Robblee, 1998). Overall, regardless of whether perceived support has a buffering effect on strain or reduces strain at both low and high levels of stressors, it appears that perceived organizational support is beneficial for lessening the effects of stress on employees' subjective well-being. Because perceived organizational support is a perception specifically about the employee's organization, it may be more effective in reducing workplace stress than sources of stress outside the workplace as, for example, friends and relatives.

The positive psychology movement emphasizes favorable subjective experience and adaptive individual traits (Seligman & Csikszentmihalyi, 2000), suggesting the value of taking a closer look at the traditional view of workplace stress as a completely detrimental experience. Many employees report positive aspects of common stressors (Nelson & Simmons, 2003). Nelson and Simmons (2003) defined *eustress* as a positive psychological response to a stressor that results when a "cognitive appraisal of a situation or event is seen to either benefit an individual or enhance his or her well-being" (p. 104). Work situations that involve complex learning, autonomy in choosing how to complete work responsibilities, or creative goals often entail risks of failure that increase stress. Yet, to the extent that the employee welcomes these opportunities for grown, he or she may find the overall experience positive despite the increased strain.

Cavanaugh, Boswell, Roehling, and Boudreau (2000) found with a large sample of U.S. managers that some stressors were viewed more as positive challenges to work goals, whereas others were viewed primarily as hindrances. The extent of stress associated with the hindrance-related stressors (organizational politics, role ambiguity, red tape, job insecurity, stalled career) was strongly associated with job satisfaction in the negative direction whereas challenge stressors (number of projects, time at work, volume of work, time pressures, amount and scope of responsibility) was slightly related to job satisfaction in the positive direction.

LePine, Podsakoff, and LePine (2005) suggested that challenge stressors are appraised as having the potential for personal gain and growth and therefore trigger problem-focused coping behavior. Hindrance stressors, in contrast, are appraised as harmful to the individual and therefore produce negative emotions and passive coping, such as withdrawal behavior. According to LePine et al. (2005), the effects of challenge stressors would not be entirely positive because the emotional and cognitive effort associated with appraisal and coping produce fatigue and exhaustion. In a study with college students, LePine, LePine, and Jackson (2004) provided evidence that both challenge stressors and hindrance stressors contribute to emotional exhaustion but that challenge stressors increase motivation to learn and academic performance of college students. LePine et al. (2005) carried out a meta-analytic review of the literature on employees, dividing up stressors into those related to challenge and those related to hindrance, and obtained results similar to those obtained with college students. One caution about these results is that challenge-related stressors tend to be rated as less severe than hindrance stressors, which could be responsible for the findings.

Wallace, Edwards, Arnold, Frazier, and Finch (2009) examined the possibility that perceived organizational support could reduce employees' aversive reaction to hindrance stressors and enhance their favorable reaction to challenge stressors, thereby influencing performance. Wallace et al. found that perceived organizational support increased the positive effect of challenge stressors on performance. That is, perceived organizational support had its strongest effect at the highest levels of challenge stressors. Perceived organizational support may increase the positive effects of challenge stressors on performance by signaling that the organization is prepared to provide various kinds of resources when needed and by communicating to employees the organization's favorable evaluation of their competence, thereby enhancing their self-efficacy, with positive consequences for motivation. In contrast, perceived organizational support had an equally large incremental effect on performance at all levels of hindrance stressors. It is currently unclear why perceived support had its greatest effects on challenge stressors at their highest levels and operated equally at all levels of hindrance stressors. The overall pattern suggests that perceived organizational support is influential in reducing the effects of various kinds of stressors, including those containing primarily negative elements and those involving opportunities for personal growth or achieving goals.

In addition to helping employees cope with the stress produced by their particular job conditions, perceived organizational support may aid employees who are subjected to disruptive large-scale organizational change. To survive and prosper in increasingly competitive markets, many companies are attempting a variety of large-scale strategies, including mergers and acquisitions, downsizing, restructuring, and reengineering. Yet, the anticipated economic and organizational benefits of these changes (e.g., higher profits, increased competitiveness) often do not materialize (e.g., Cascio, 1993). This low success rate has prompted considerable research focusing on strategic, financial, and operational factors that might lead to greater success (Mottola et al., 1997). There has been a growing recognition of the roles of organizational culture and of the individual factors such as difficulties of employee adjustment in the lack of success of many restructuring efforts.

Some of this research considers the protective role of perceived organizational support in coping with stress produced by major organizational changes. Armstrong-Stassen et al. (2001) assessed the reactions of nurses to a hospital amalgamation over a 5-year period. Using Lazarus and Folkman's (1984) stress and coping model as theoretical basis, the researchers found that nurses with higher perceived organizational support at the beginning of the amalgamation expressed less job insecurity; engaged in more control-oriented coping (i.e., actions and cognitive reappraisals that have a proactive, take-charge in nature); reported significantly higher job satisfaction, organizational commitment, and organizational trust; and had less intention to quit their job during the amalgamation period 2 years later. The findings suggest that managers can help reduce the emotional strain associated with mergers and other disruptive large-scale organizational changes by signaling to employees that the organization will help provide the resources needed to deal with the new environment and will continue to value their contributions.

Work–Family Balance

Changes in societal demographics, technological developments, increasing globalization, and international business competitiveness have challenged employers, employees, and policymakers to develop strategies and tactics to balance competing demands of work and family life (Brough, O'Driscoll, & Kalliath, 2005; Kossek & Lambert, 2005; O'Driscoll, 1996; Thompson & Prottas, 2005). For example, the greater proportion of women entering the workforce, along with the higher percentages of dual-earner and dual-career couples and single-parent households, implies that responsibilities for work, housework, and child care are no longer confined to traditional gender roles (T. D. Allen, Herst, Bruck, & Sutton, 2000; Byron, 2005; Kinnunen, Geurts, & Mauno, 2004). Thus, a strong case can be made that economic and technological developments and deregulation have led to more competition for individuals' time and energy between work and home (Brough et al., 2005).

The problems and issues related to work–family balance encountered by employees facing these societal and business-related changes have prompted considerable research and theory on how the work and family domains affect one another (e.g., Kossek, Noe, & DeMarr, 1999; Perrewé & Hochwarter, 2001). *Work–family conflict* refers either to work interfering with family life or vice versa. Effects in one direction are termed *work-to-family conflict* or *family-to-work conflict.*

Work–family conflict has been found to decrease psychological well-being (e.g., increased stress, psychosomatic symptoms) and adjustment and involvement in the workplace (e.g., higher turnover and absenteeism, lower commitment, job satisfaction, and job performance; T. D. Allen et al., 2000). R. Kahn, Wolfe, Quinn, Snoek, and Rosenthal (1964) viewed work–family conflict in terms of the incompatible demands required by different roles. For example, the normative expectation of frequently working overtime and weekends, present at a particular job position, would interfere with the expectation of family members to be fully engaged as a parent (Greenhaus & Beutell, 1985; Kopelman, Greenhaus, & Connolly, 1983). Although early studies treated work as primarily interfering with family life, more recent research (Frone, Russell, & Cooper, 1992; Netemeyer, Boles, & McMurrian, 1996) has also suggested that family life can also interfere with work.

Researchers have also begun to investigate the possibility of positive relationships between work and family experiences. As described by Wadsworth and Owens (2007), "success at work may 'spill over' into the home, benefiting family relationships and influencing an individual's general attitudes about life" (p. 76). And as is the case for work–family conflict, work–family enrichment can occur in both directions: work-to-family and family-to-work (Frone, 2003). Buffardi (2007) pointed out that some workplace factors that have been studied as possible ways of providing reduced interference with home life (e.g., supervisor support, flexible schedules, dependent care services) are the same or similar to conditions found to enhance perceived organizational support (e.g., supervisor support, favorable job conditions and fringe benefits). He suggested that various workplace treatments favorable to home life adjustment may operate through perceived organizational support.

Several studies have examined the influence that perceived organizational support may have on work–family relationships. Although most have considered the general potential benefits of perceived organizational support on family life, a few have examined how perceived organizational support may reduce the influence of stressful effects of work or family life on the other. Wadsworth and Owens (2007) conducted a study in the public sector on the influences of both perceived organizational support and social support on work–family relationships. The authors suggested that perceived organizational support may be influenced by the family-friendly benefits or policies offered by the organization and by a family-supportive culture within the organization. They suggested that by providing employees with these policies to assist them in managing their family responsibilities, organizations might lead their personnel to feel that they value them as workers who have important individual needs outside the workplace (Wadsworth & Owens, 2007). Furthermore, they assumed that perceived organizational support should be negatively related to work-to-family and family-to-work conflicts, whereas it should be positively related to work-to-family and family-to-work enhancements.

Their results showed that, above and beyond the social support received from work (coworkers and supervisor) and nonwork (friends, spouse and children) sources, perceived organizational support was related to better adjustment at home: lower work-to-family conflict and higher work-to-family enhancement. In contrast, perceived organizational support did not enhance transfer of experiences from home to work: There was no effect on family-to-work conflict and family-to-work enhancement. These results are consistent with Byron's (2005) meta-analytic findings that showed that work support (which includes supervisor, coworkers, organization, and mentor supports) is more strongly related with work interference with family than with family interference with work. These results make sense because perceived organizational support should have its primary positive effects on employee attitudes and affect in the workplace, which would carry over to family life.

As Wadsworth and Owens (2007) pointed out, these findings may appear to be of little interest to organizations because one might assume that organizations are more interested in workplace satisfaction and motivation than adjustment at home. However, research has consistently shown the negative impact of work–family conflict on employees' job satisfaction, organizational commitment, productivity, or withdrawal behaviors (see T. D. Allen et al., 2000). Therefore, the positive role of perceived organizational support on home life subjective well-being could feed back into the workplace.

In Chapter 3, we distinguished between perceived support by the organization to meet particular employee needs and perceived organizational support. Perceived organizational support is qualitatively different because it incorporates employees' attributions concerning their general valuation by organization, including employees' contributions as well as their well-being. Thus, perceived organizational support implies a willingness to deal with new employee needs as they arise. We noted that specific favorable family policies that deal with the problems of private life (e.g., day care, maternity leave) contribute to perceived organizational support.

On the one hand, one might think that family-oriented values and policies within the organization would be more effective in reducing work-to-family conflict because they imply a specific concern with home life issues. On the other hand, perceived organizational support may have a positive effect on subjective well-being over and beyond specific arrangements at work to reduce interference with home life.

Behson (2002) made use of two employee assessments of a pro-family orientation by the organization. First, he used Thompson et al.'s (1999) measure of work–family culture, involving "the shared assumptions, beliefs, and values regarding the extent to which an organization supports and values the integration of employees' work and family lives" (p. 394). Second, he used T. D. Allen's (2001) measure of family-supportive organization perceptions, involving "global perceptions that employees form regarding the extent the organization is family-supportive" (p. 414). With a sample of employed students, he found that perceived organizational support and these two work–family specific constructs reduced work–family conflict, although the specific measures showed a stronger relationship than perceived organizational support. However, in contrast with these findings, Buffardi (2007) reported results by Gibson (2006), who found that perceived organizational support was more strongly negatively related than family-supportive organization perceptions to work interference with family.

We would like to make several points about the relative contributions of a specific family-friendly orientation versus perceived organizational support on work-to-family conflict. First, family-friendly orientation by the organization lessens work-to family conflict in part by contributing to perceived organizational support. Second, perceived organizational support makes a contribution to reducing family-to-work conflict distinct from family-friendly policies. Third, the apparent relative contributions of these influences are probably strongly dependent on how work-to-family conflict is measured. To the extent that such conflict is measured by asking employees about specific kinds of interference (e.g., too much time taken at work), assessments of family-friendly orientations related to such conflict would tend to have a larger effect. To the extent that such conflict is measured by asking about employees' strain owing to difficulties at work, the ameliorative influence of perceived organizational support on strain would tend to produce a larger effect on work-to-family conflict. In the study by Behson (2002), the majority of items used to assess work-to-family conflict appear to assess time or scheduling issues at work, for which a specific family-friendly orientation would be particularly important.

Erdwins, Buffardi, Casper, and O'Brien (2001) examined the processes underlying the relationship between perceived organizational support and work–family conflict in a sample of working women. They assumed that support received from various sources enhances a woman's sense of being able to cope effectively with the demands of her various life roles, which in turn would ultimately reduce her experience of work–family conflict. Specifically, they found that a woman's perception that her organization was supportive enhanced her feelings of competency and effectiveness in her job, which in turn reduced conflict between her work and family roles. Thus, perceived organizational support operated through self-efficacy to reduce perceptions of work–family conflict.

Witt and Carlson (2006) suggested that perceived organizational support might help employees cope with the depleted psychological resources resulting from stressors experienced at home. Perceived organizational support would signify the availability of material resources on which to draw and provide socioemotional support to reduce the effects of stress. The resources will be especially helpful for employees who come to the workplace with resources depleted from pressures at home. Thus, as predicted, the negative relationship between family-to-work conflict and performance decreased markedly with high perceived organizational support.

In sum, family supportive practices and perceived organizational support reduce work-to-family conflict and family-to-work conflict partly independently and partly by the influence of family-supportive practices on perceived organizational support. Family-supportive practices are taken as an indication of more general support by the organization. Perceived organizational support has stress-reducing properties that are important for ameliorating conflicts between work and home and to some extent between home and work.

Summary and Implications

Perceived organizational support has very positive outcomes for employees' subjective well-being. The workplace becomes much more pleasant. As with the Southwest Airlines attendants we discussed at the start of the chapter, employees with high perceived organizational support smile more, joke more, and even sing more. The cluster of favorable experiences incorporated into positive well-being includes positive mood, satisfaction, organization-based self-esteem, reduced stress, and enhanced work–family balance.

Employees with high perceived organizational support generally have an enhanced positive mood at work. They are more enthusiastic, alert, and happy. George and Brief (1992) suggested that events at work indicating employees' high competence, worth, or achievement make them happier. Perceived organizational support may contribute to positive mood by meeting socioemotional needs for approval, esteem, emotional support, and belonging and by incorporating employees' organizational membership and work roles into social identity, providing a sense of purpose. Employees with high perceived organizational support also make a more positive overall judgment about their job: They are more satisfied. Again, we noted evidence in Chapter 2 that perceived support is more important for employees with high needs for esteem, affiliation, approval, and emotional support. Meeting these needs might contribute to such satisfaction. However, the instrumental value of perceived organizational support should not be forgotten. Perceived organizational support conveys to employees the availability of information and other basic organizational resources that make work run more smoothly and prevent frustration when employees are constrained from carrying out their jobs skillfully.

Perceived organizational support leads to organization-based self-esteem, a construct that incorporates employees' view that they are appreciated by the organization and that they can have an impact on it. Because the first part of the construct's definition is similar to perceived organizational support, it would be helpful to understand the extent to which perceived organizational support is related to the second part, involving the employees' view that they can make a significant contribution to the organization. This possible added outcome of perceived organizational support seems likely in view of findings that perceived organizational politics, involving managers' self-seeking behavior, which would interfere with organization-based self-esteem, is negatively related to perceived organizational support.

Perceived organizational support has been found to reduce strain at both low and high levels of stressors, resulting in decreased fatigue, burnout, and headaches. Sometimes perceived organizational support is associated with reduced strain primarily at high levels of a stressor, such as contagious illness, organizational politics, and threatened violence. Sometimes it is equally effective at all levels of the stressor. Evidence is needed on the suggestion that buffering effects, involving increased effectiveness of perceived organizational support at high levels of the stressor, take place mainly when perceived organizational support involves potential resources for effectively dealing with the stressor in question. In this view, perceived organizational support would be effective in reducing the anxiety of hospital nurses because of a work overload if the nurses believed the organization had the resources to help valued employees.

The positive psychology movement has begun to examine favorable aspects of stress, including challenge stressors that constrain performance but are viewed as opportunities for personal growth and rewards. Wallace et al. (2009) found that perceived organizational support increased performance at higher levels of challenge stressors (number of projects, time at work, volume of work, time pressures, amount and scope of responsibility). This finding suggests that the extent to which employees view many organizational events as opportunities versus constraints depends on perceived organizational support. In a study with postal employees, my colleagues and I (Eisenberger et al., 2001) found that a significant number of excellent employees had refused promotion to supervisor. Those approached for promotion told me the promotion would bring them a stressful lack of control. Observing how current supervisors were treated, they believed that higher level managers would ask much of them but not trust them with the authority to accomplish what was asked. Perceived organizational support was low, making the proffered promotion appear stressful with no redeeming outcomes.

In contrast, at Google, where employees have input on the new projects the organization will undertake, and where prudent risk taking is encouraged and rewarded, such opportunities cause employees to view stress in a more positive light. Perceived organizational support helps provide confidence that material and emotional support will be available as needed and that management can be trusted to patiently await the positive outcomes of diligent effort.

Positive Orientation Toward the Organization and Work $\Big|\; 6$

A chemical engineer friend of mine we will call Bill recently retired from DuPont, the chemical and agricultural conglomerate. A veteran of multiyear stints at two other chemical companies, he was lured to DuPont by offers of better pay and more interesting work. During his career there, Bill was given a variety of long-term projects that made good use of his skills, and he became known as an excellent problem solver. Consecutive managers praised his work, and he received several companywide awards. Work assignments that made full use of his talents and continued demonstrations of appreciation for his contributions produced a high level of perceived organizational support. He came to identify himself strongly with DuPont and often brought up his experiences there in casual conversation, smiling with pleasure as he discussed a current or upcoming project. DuPont's corporate partners and customers came to recognize my friend's abilities and tried to lure him away with offers of a higher salary and more prestigious position. My friend was tempted, but he wound up turning the offers down. Being appreciated by DuPont meant a great deal to him—it contributed greatly to his sense of identity. He continues to consult with DuPont from time to time because he takes pride in continuing to feel valued and appreciated by the company.

According to recent research, because Bill's achievements at work were an important component of his esteem, his perceived organizational support led him to identify himself strongly as a "DuPont Man" and develop a high degree of affective commitment to the company. Perceived organizational support led to greater engagement in his work by meeting his need for esteem, by creating the expectation that the company would provide him with resources when needed to do his job better, and by leading to expectation of reward for high performance.

The positive valuation of employees, communicated by perceived organizational support, leads employees to take a more positive orientation toward work and the organization. Figure 6.1 presents seven such outcomes that have been found by researchers, together with mechanisms they have suggested for these outcomes. In this chapter, we examine the various ways in which perceived organizational support increases employees' enjoyment of their work (empowerment, engagement, and involvement) and develop a more positive orientation toward the organization (commitment, identification, trust, and reduced cynicism).

Organizational Commitment

Employers and theorists alike have long tried to understand why some employees show a long-term dedication to their work organization while others care little about the organization for which they happen to work. The term *commitment* is commonly used in everyday language to refer to the sense of being bound to a course of action, which may include a person's relationship with another individual, group, or organization. Commitment involves activities that are maintained despite the availability of attractive alternatives or a diminution of the incentives that contributed to their establishment. If individuals acted in what was simply in their short-term best interest, there would be no need for a concept of commitment.

A traditional marriage vow asks the couple to commit to stay together in sickness and in health when leaving a partner who has a terminal illness makes cold-blooded sense. Yet, as the religious and legal bounds holding married couples together in Western societies have weakened and divorce rates have increased, it is nevertheless the case that many couples stay together when their partner is providing them with less fulfillment than expected. Even when one partner has developed a wasting illness and is unable to help meet the physical and psychological needs of the other, it is common for love and commitment to keep many partners together. Many of the same processes involved in commitment to friends and romantic partners may be involved in employees' commitment to organizations.

FIGURE 6.1

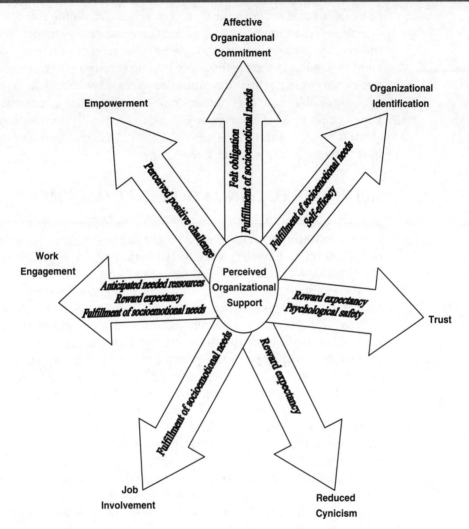

Effects of perceived organizational support on employees' positive orientation toward the organization and proposed underlying mechanisms.

Employees with strong bonds to their organization remain with it during periods when tangible rewards are less than might be obtained elsewhere. Such employees are less likely to quit when they have a new boss with whom they do not get along or during times when the company's financial future is in jeopardy. The comparison between the strong possible bonds in marriage and organization may appear exaggerated. But there is a broad distribution of commitment by different individuals in both cases.

It has long been recognized that commitment to an organization may have multiple motivational bases. Meyer and Allen (1991, 1997) helped bring clarity and order to the divergent views concerning the different varieties of commitment by proposing a three-component model. In their memorable phraseology, *affective commitment* refers to the employees' emotional bond to the organization, leading employees to want to continue employment with the organization. *Normative commitment* involves a feeling of obligation to continue employment with the organization in which employees believe they ought to remain. Finally, *continuance commitment* refers to a consideration of the costs of leaving the organization in which employees feel they need to stay.

AFFECTIVE ORGANIZATIONAL COMMITMENT

Employees' emotional bond to their organization (affective organizational commitment) has been considered an important determinant of dedication and loyalty. Affectively committed employees show an increased involvement in their organization's activities, a greater willingness to pursue the organization's goals, and a greater desire to remain with the organization (Klein, Becker, & Meyer, 2009; Meyer & Allen, 1991; Mowday et al., 1982). Notice that these views of affective commitment go beyond Meyer and Allen's (1991, 1997) formulation of wanting to remain with one's work organization. The concept of an emotional bond to the organization also implies a desire to be helpful to the organization, to help it meet its objectives and goals. Accordingly, affective commitment has been found to be positively related to employees' performance as well as job retention (Mathieu & Zajac, 1990; Meyer & Allen, 1997; Mowday et al., 1982), although the relationship is strongest with job retention (Meyer & Allen, 1997).

The contribution of perceived organizational support to affective commitment is supported by studies that link the two, and more complete studies show a three-way association of favorable work conditions leading to perceived organizational support, which, in turn, leads to affective commitment (e.g., Eisenberger et al., 1990; Guzzo et al., 1994; Hutchison, 1997; Hutchison & Garstka, 1996; B. Jones, Flynn, & Kelloway, 1995; Settoon, Bennett, & Liden, 1996; Shore & Tetrick, 1991; Shore & Wayne, 1993; Wayne et al., 1997). These results indicate that the more employees feel supported by the organization, the more they feel emotionally attached to it.

Because perceived organizational support and affective commitment are strongly related, distinctions between the two should be clarified. Wayne et al. (2009) noted that perceived organizational support is an affect-free cognition whose consequences depend on the operation of the reciprocity norm and the satisfaction of socioemotional needs. In contrast, affect directed at the organization is an essential part of the affective commitment, as conceived by Meyer and Herscovitch (2001). Perceived organizational support involves the employee's perceptions of the benevolent intentions on the basis of the organization's discretionary acts. Employees' affective commitment involves their favorable intentions toward the organization, which should be strongly dependent on perceived organizational support.

To assess the causal direction of the relationship between perceived organizational support and affective commitment, Rhoades et al. (2001) took repeated measurements of perceived organizational support and affective commitment over time in two samples of employees working for a large electronics and appliance sales organization. Using such a panel design, they showed that perceived organizational support was positively related to temporal changes in affective commitment in both samples. These findings indicate that perceived organizational support leads to affective commitment, which is consistent with a causal relationship. In sum, we can conclude from this study that, when employees feel supported by their organization, they are more likely to develop a subsequent affective bond with the organization.

Three major categories of work experiences—organizational rewards, procedural justice, and supervisor support—have been found to be positively related to affective commitment (Meyer & Allen, 1997). Tsui et al. (1997) argued that organizational actions indicating caring and positive regard increase affective commitment. Similarly, Meyer and Allen (1997) and D. G. Allen et al. (1999) suggested that perceived organizational support is partly responsible for the association between favorable work experiences and affective commitment. A meta-analytic review of the literature (Meyer et al., 2002) found that perceived organizational support has a stronger relationship with affective organizational commitment than favorable job experiences, such as leadership and procedural and distributive justice. Because these favorable job experiences partly increase affective commitment through their common influence on perceived organizational support (e.g., Rhoades et al., 2001; Wayne et al., 1997), it is not surprising that perceived organizational support is more strongly related to affective commitment than any of the factors considered alone. Meyer et al. (2002) suggested that perceived organization support might help bring order and understanding to the growing list of variables that have been linked to affective organizational commitment. They further suggested that this understanding would provide a way to search more systematically for variables influencing affective organizational commitment.

Organizational support theory helps explain the role perceived organizational support plays in the relationship between favorable work experiences and employees' emotional attachment to the organization. On the basis of the reciprocity norm, perceived organizational support creates a felt obligation to care about the organization's welfare and help it reach its objectives. That is, on the basis of the reciprocity norm, employees seek a balance in their exchange relationships with the organization by developing attitudes and behaviors commensurate with their favorable treatment by the organization. Because perceived organizational support indicates that the organization values and cares about employees, they should feel an obligation to return such caring (see also Tsui et al., 1997). Thus, favorable treatment of employees of a large mail-processing facility was found to lead to perceived organizational support, which in turn, led to affective commitment (Eisenberger et al., 2001). Further supporting a reciprocity interpretation, the relationship between perceived organizational support and felt obligation was stronger among those employees who strongly endorsed the reciprocity norm as applied to work.

As discussed in Chapter 2, perceived organizational support would also increase affective commitment by fulfilling needs for esteem, approval, emotional support, and affiliation, leading to the incorporation of organizational membership and role status into social identity. The fulfillment of socioemotional needs by perceived organizational support is suggested by the previously discussed finding that the association between police officers' perceived organizational support and their job performance was greater among police having high socioemotional needs (Armeli et al., 1998).

Shore et al. (2006) developed a scale to assess the strength of the employee–employer social exchange relationship from the vantage point of the employee on the basis of the perceived trust between the two, the investment each has made in the relationship, the involvement of long-term obligations, and the emphasis on exchange of socioemotional resources. Shore et al. (2006) reported that perceived organizational support led to affective commitment, which led to increased social exchange which finally led to greater employee performance. The authors' new scale is a particularly useful tool for assessing changes in the strength of the social exchange relationship.

One issue for future research is the temporal order of the relationship between affective organizational commitment and the strength of the employee–employer social exchange relationship. Shore et al. (2006) proposed that affective organizational commitment leads to a strengthening of the social exchange. According to organizational support theory, perceived organizational support operates through felt obligation (the social exchange relationship) and fulfillment of socioemotional needs to increase affective commitment. Shore et al. (2006) used a cross-sectional design. Thus, it is uncertain whether affective commitment is an outcome or the cause of the social exchange processes. It is also possible that perceived organizational support strengthens the exchange relationship, leading to affective commitment, and as proposed by Shore et al. (2006), this leads to a further strengthening of the exchange relationship with positive consequences for performance.

NORMATIVE COMMITMENT

Numerous studies show a relationship between perceived organizational support and employees' perceived obligation to remain with their organization, or normative commitment (Rhoades & Eisenberger, 2002). Meyer and Allen (1997) suggested that normative commitment might be attributable to internalization of socialization experiences regarding loyalty to one's organization in everyday life and, in the current organizational context, a sense of obligation based on the norm of reciprocity for having received favorable treatment. More recently, Meyer and Herscovitch (2001) reformulated normative commitment, so that this concept has moved away from the heavy emphasis on obligation to remain with the organization to a more diverse set of obligations to the organization. As Wayne et al. (2009) pointed out, a consequence of the current conceptualization of normative commitment is that this construct is now very similar to the felt obligation concept of organizational support theory. Thus, findings of a positive relationship between perceived organizational support and normative commitment are similar to findings relating perceived organizational support to felt obligation. Meyer and Allen's (1997) suggestion that the reciprocity norm may contribute to the formation of normative commitment is consistent with findings that the relationship between perceived organizational support and felt obligation was greater among employees who strongly endorsed the reciprocity norm.

A recent meta-analytic review of the research literature (Kurtessis et al., 2009) found that the relationship of perceived organizational support with affective organizational commitment was somewhat greater than with normative commitment. The scales used by Meyer and Allen (1997) to assess the two types of commitment have approximately the same levels of internal reliability, so this finding does not appear to be a measurement issue. According to organizational support theory (Eisenberger et al., 1986; Rhoades et al., 2001), perceived organizational support should work through both felt obligation (i.e., normative commitment) and the fulfillment of socioemotional needs to increase affective organizational commitment. Thus, perceived support would be expected to have a stronger relationship with affective organizational commitment than normative commitment.

CONTINUANCE COMMITMENT

Continuance commitment refers to employees' perceptions of the costs of leaving their work organization. According to Meyer and Allen (1997), employees bound to the organizations in this way remain because of necessity. This view is based partly on H. S. Becker's (1960) analysis of the ways in which employees' sustained employment in an organization results from the high costs of leaving or the lack of employment alternatives. Tenure in a job often carries various implicit or explicit benefits that an employee would lose if he or she left. For example, retirement benefits may not be fully recoverable and the power and influence over matters such as choice over tasks and schedule, which often increases with tenure, may not be fully replaced in a new job. Further, many of the employee's skills may have become specific to needs of the current organization so that new skills would have to be acquired with a change in employers. Leaving may involve one's romantic partner having to leave his or her job, and children leaving their friends. And with age comes rampant discrimination in hiring.

The identification of high costs of leaving an organization as a form of commitment has always seemed an odd conceptualization. In the cases of affective and normative commitment, the constructs are designed to answer questions regarding employees' dedication to the organization despite short-term losses of incentives that make it inviting to work less hard or join another organization. In the case of continuance commitment, incentives that are often implicit, or the lack of alternative job opportunities, keep the employees from quitting their jobs. However, unlike the other two forms of commitment, there is no sense of dedication that keeps the employee loyal, just the incentive structure. To view continuance commitment as a singular mind-set implies that employees combine in their thinking the disparate incentives, implicit and explicit, keeping them at the same job. One wonders whether this actually occurs except at times when alternatives to one's current job do present themselves, such as contemplating a switch to a new job, or when contemplating retirement. In any case, continuance commitment would seem likely to have differing properties than the two other kinds of commitment.

Shore and Tetrick (1991) suggested that perceived organizational support might reduce feelings of entrapment that occur when employees are forced to stay with an organization because of the high cost of leaving. Accordingly, a meta-analytic review of the research literature by Rhoades and Eisenberger (2002) found a small negative correlation between perceived organizational support and continuance commitment. However, a more recent meta-analysis (L. Buffardi, personal communication, November 10, 2010) with 6 times the number of studies reports a negligible correlation between perceived organizational support and continuance commitment.

Although the results indicate that perceived organizational support has little or no influence on continuance commitment alone, it may influence continuance commitment in combination with affective and normative commitment. Recently, Gellatly, Hunter, Luchak, and Meyer (2007) examined the influence of perceived organizational support on different combinations of commitment (commitment profiles) among academic physicians. Their results showed that perceived organizational support was related positively to the high-affective-commitment–high-normative-commitment profile and negatively to the low-affective-commitment–low-normative-commitment profile. Moreover, these two relationships were enhanced by positive and negative continuance commitment, respectively (Wayne et al., 2009).

Wayne et al. (2009) suggested the following explanation for these results. Organizational support theory holds, as supported by evidence, that perceived organizational support enhances reward expectancies (Eisenberger et al., 1986; Rhoades & Eisenberger, 2002). On the one hand, for employees experiencing high affective commitment and normative commitment, continuance commitment might be experienced positively. For these employees, perceived organizational support might indeed enhance the favorableness of perceived entitlements and opportunities that are specific to the organization and would thus be difficult to find elsewhere. On the other hand, without the positive context of affective commitment and normative commitment, continuance commitment might be experienced negatively. For many employees, continuance commitment may be related to the perception of "being trapped" in the organization and a loss of self-determination, which might be reduced by the feeling of being supported and valued by the organization. In accord with this view, Gellatly et al. (2007) showed that perceived organizational support was positively related to perceived job autonomy and that job autonomy was negatively related to continuance commitment.

In sum, the findings suggest that perceived organizational support is positively related to both affective commitment and normative commitment. The evidence indicates little relationship with continuance commitment, except for one new study (Gellatly et al., 2007) suggesting that perceived organizational support may have a positive influence in the context of high affective and normative commitment.

Organizational Identification

Buchanan (1974, 1975), Levinson (1965), Mowday et al. (1982), and Porter et al. (1974) viewed identification as involving employees' incorporation of their membership in the organization and participation in various organizational roles into their self-identity together with the affective bond to the organization. To distinguish organizational identification from affective organizational commitment, employees' identification has, more recently, been conceptualized as primarily cognitive in nature, often described as a sense of unity with the organization in which employees experience the organization's outcomes as their own. According to social identity theory (Tajfel, 1978; Turner, 1984), individuals incorporate valued group memberships into their self-concept and adopt the group's values and norms as their own. This approach has been extended to employee–organization relationships (Ashforth & Mael, 1989; Dutton, Dukerich, & Harquail, 1994; Mael & Ashforth, 1992; Mael & Tetrick, 1992).

Several factors may contribute to employees' incorporation of their organizational membership and role status into their self identity, including (a) the provision of stable and elaborated role behaviors that provide sustaining purpose and a sense of direction (Buchanan, 1974), (b) the experience of striving to achieve common goals or shared values (Etzioni, 1961; Gould, 1979; Kelman, 1961), (c) approval and praise by powerful individuals to whom one can feel closer by identifying with the organization (Mowday et al., 1982), (d) pride in being connected with a prestigious enterprise (Tajfel, 1978; Turner, 1984), and (e) the satisfaction of socioemotional needs (e.g., esteem, affiliation) that lend a comfort with being affiliated with the organization (Eisenberger et al., 1986).

Mael and Ashforth (1992) held that to the extent employees take pride in the organization, they enhance their self-esteem by viewing the prototypical characteristics of the personified organization as their own, thereby increasing organizational identification. Having high organizational identification, employees view the organization's characteristics as their characteristics and would see their experiences and organization's as shared, experiencing the organization's gains and losses as their own. In this view, such communality of interests increases employees' concern for the organization's welfare. As van Knippenberg, van Dick, and Tavares (2007) noted, "the more people identify with a group or organization, the more the group's or organization's interests are incorporated in the self-concept, and the more likely the individual is to act with the organization's best interest in mind" (p. 461).

The study of organizational identification has faced the problem of conceptual overlap with one of the major early accounts of affective commitment to the organization (Mowday et al., 1982), which incorporated identification. Meyer and Allen (1997) attempted to distinguish affective commitment from identification by confining the latter to an emotional bond reflecting a mindset in which the employee wants to remain with the organization. Organizational identification has been found to be highly correlated with affective commitment to the organization (see the review by Riketta, 2005). As suggested by social identity theory, shared identity with a valued group may meet important socioemotional needs and therefore lead to a positive emotional bond to the organization. Some theorists have returned to the earlier view that affect is engrained in, rather than being the consequence of, organizational identification. It is easy to see how these constructs might be closely related, and Mael's (1988) doctoral research devoted considerable attention to distinguishing them in the face of high correlations between them. Subsequent research in these two areas has proceeded largely independently, with only recent attention turning again to their possible relationships (see also Meyer, Becker, & Van Dick, 2006; Riketta, 2005).

Further, there is a methodological problem because some items included in the scale generally used to measure affective organizational commitment—the Affective Commitment Scale (Meyer & Allen, 1997)—are similar to those used in organizational identification scales (e.g., "I feel as if this organization's problems are my own"). Thus, the overlap between the constructs may be somewhat overstated. In his meta-analytic review of the literature, Riketta (2005) reported that even with this overlap in wording, the correlation between Mael and Tetrick's (1992) scale of organizational identification and Meyer and Allen's (1997) Affective Commitment Scale was .71, which leaves about half the variance left to be explained (see also Edwards, 2005). Riketta found some small but reliable differences in outcomes for organizational identification and affective commitment. Organizational commitment was more closely related to job satisfaction and intent to stay with the organization, whereas organizational identification was more closely related to extrarole performance. This suggests that affective commitment may be somewhat more associated with emotional bonding than organizational identification, whereas organizational identification may produce somewhat greater intrinsic job interest (Riketta, 2005) or a redefinition of one's role to incorporate a greater span of activities.

In meeting socioemotional needs, perceived organizational support increases the attractiveness of the organization, resulting in greater organizational identification. Thus, employees with high perceived organizational support experience a sense of unity with the organization and are more likely to increase their view of the personified organization's characteristics as their characteristics and to consider their outcomes and the organization's outcomes as related. Consequently, employees who identify strongly with the organization would be more likely to act in ways beneficial to it that do not present a clear personal gain. To the extent that the employee identifies himself or herself with the organization and thinks of "us" instead of "I," he or she may engage in behaviors that focus more on aiding the organization rather than himself or herself, such as mentoring new employees, helping coworkers, becoming more engaged in organizational social activities, and representing the organization to the community through volunteer activities.

Although perceived organizational support enhances employees' concern with the welfare of the organization, the "we" of identification never completely subsumes the "I" of self-interest. One constraint involves the personality dimension of individualism, which competes with collectivism for dominance in individuals. Individualism is valued by most employees, at least to some extent, and prevents the employee from being swallowed up by complete identification with the organization. A second constraint is that part of the motivation elicited by perceived organizational support involves an increased reward expectancy, which is self-oriented. Thus, employees' relationship with their work organization, based on perceived organizational support, represents a combination of self-oriented motivation, based on social exchange, and group-orientated motivation, based on identification. As the previous and the following chapters show, this combination of motives generally results in happier and more productive employees.

Van Knippenberg and Sleebos (2006) hypothesized that perceived organizational support leads to affective commitment but not organizational identification. In support of their proposition, they found that, when controlling for affective commitment, the relationship between perceived organizational support and organizational identification was no longer significant. They concluded that perceived organizational support does not contribute to organizational identification. They further suggested that the relationship between the individual and the organization may be better understood if analyses in terms of self-definition and self-categorization complemented the social exchange perspective (see also social exchange theory; P. M. Blau, 1964). However, as already noted, because the scale used to measure affective commitment includes identification items, and the two scales are highly correlated, this conclusion is premature.

Consistent with the present view, Sluss, Klimchak, and Holmes (2008) argued that perceived organizational support may increase not only felt obligation but also feelings of self-worth and esteem, leading to increased attractiveness of the organization and greater organizational identification. They found that perceived organizational support was positively related to employees' identification with the organization. Bell and Menguc (2002) similarly maintained that perceived organizational support would increase employees' identification with their organization. They found that perceived organizational support increased insurance sales agents' identification with their company, which in turn, increased the quality of service they rendered, as judged by customers.

Enhancement of self-esteem is one of the major principles of the social identity perspective (Dutton et al., 1994), just as reciprocity lies at the core of the social exchange perspective (van Knippenberg et al., 2007). If employees believe their organization is defined by qualities associated with competence, efficacy, virtue, or moral worth (Gecas, 1982), their identification with the organization becomes valued to the extent the organization conveys to employees they have such qualities. Accordingly, the organization's high regard for its employees, communicated through perceived organizational support, should increase self-enhancement through the employee's identification of valued organization characteristics as their own. Employees with high socioemotional needs would find their identification with the organization especially attractive. This helps explain the finding by Armeli et al. (1998) that the relationship between perceived organizational support and police issuance of driving-under-the-influence citations increased with the needs for esteem, approval, affiliation, and emotional support.

Wariness and Trust

Trust has been considered an important difference between short-term economic exchange and longer term social relationships. As discussed in Chapter 2, Shore et al. (2006) noted that employees' trust in the organization involves the expectation that their efforts will receive attention and reward. This allows employees to take a long-term view of their relationship with the organization and devote more energy on the organization's behalf without worrying that their efforts will be wasted. Trust also makes employees more willing to take on risky projects, if asked, with greater assurance that they will not have to bear unwarranted blame for failure.

Publicity given to reductions in workforce and employee benefits in recent decades has contributed to general mistrust of work organizations to treat employees equitably (Kanter & Mirvis, 1989; Mirvis & Kanter, 1992). Employees often have a reason to be mistrustful of organizations that look for ways to squeeze ever greater effort from employees without commensurate rewards. For example, employees who remain following an organizational downsizing typically do not receive new benefits appropriate with the resultant increased responsibilities. In such a situation, many employees believe that their organization holds them in low regard and ignores their interests (see also Andersson, 1996; McLean Parks & Kidder, 1994). The fraying of the employee–employer exchange relationship that has become widespread in the past several decades lessens employees' trust in their organization and their motivation to exceed minimal standards of performance or to help the organization in ways beyond the scope of specified job roles (Rousseau, 1995).

Considering the role of trust in social exchange relationships generally, let us start with interpersonal relationships and then apply the discussion to employee–organization relationships. In developing relationships, partners in interpersonal relationships evaluate benefits and costs at a conscious or nonconscious level to decide whether to increase or decrease their investment of resources (Drigotas & Rusbult, 1992; Rusbult & Farrell, 1983). In interpersonal relationships, the resources often exchanged involve investments of time and provision of socio-emotional rewards to a partner. Before partners become well acquainted, each has only tentative and incomplete information concerning (a) the resources possessed by the other, (b) one's own capacity to provide resources desired by the other, and (c) the other's reliability in reciprocating positive treatment. Relationships are enhanced to the extent that the evidence is good in all these regards. Thus, individuals expecting that their partners possessed or were likely to possess valued resources showed greater reciprocation of aid (Cotterell et al., 1992; Eisenberger et al., 1987; Pruitt, 1968).

However, such investments carry risk. Exchange relationships may be damaged when one individual repeatedly fails to receive the resources he or she feels is deserved. The undercompensated individual may question the other's willingness to live up to reciprocity obligations, lessening his or her investment in the relationship. Trust strengthens interpersonal relationships by increasing the willingness of partners to help meet the needs and interests one another with the expectation that they will be repaid in kind sometime in the future.

Suspicion about others' intentions to live up to their obligations may result not only from recent mistreatment but also from a generalized fear of mistreatment in social exchange (Cotterell et al., 1992; Eisenberger et al., 1987). Individual differences in generalized fear of exploitation have been found to influence the exchange of resources in interpersonal relationships (Cotterell et al., 1992; Eisenberger et al., 1987). Lynch et al. (1999) examined how a generalized fear of exploitation undermined employee work performance and how this poor performance was ameliorated by perceived organizational support.

Eisenberger et al. (1987) identified *reciprocation wariness* as a generalized cautiousness in reciprocating aid stemming from a fear of exploitation in interpersonal relationships. Some people focus more on the possible gains than the costs of investments in relationship development. Other people are concerned more with the dangers than benefits of reciprocation. Wary individuals believe the offer of aid or professions of friendship or romantic interest is often a mask used to take advantage of people (see also Rempel, Holmes, & Zanna, 1985). Persons receiving or extending aid may be mistreated by others who misuse the reciprocity norm. Because individuals giving aid often have the opportunity to select the time and type of repayment, they can place exorbitant demands on the recipient (Cialdini, 1993). Further, persons extending aid cannot be sure that the recipient will provide equitable compensation. Therefore, some degree of caution serves as a realistic protection against misuse of the reciprocity norm. Concern with misuse of the reciprocity norm produces a belief system or ideology of reciprocation wariness that favors caution when accepting or returning aid from others (Eisenberger et al., 1987; Cotterell et al., 1992).

Reciprocation-wary individuals express a general hesitance to accept help (Eisenberger et al., 1987). Being fearful that others will use the norm of reciprocity to exploit them if they respond generously to favorable treatment, wary individuals are hesitant to provide aid, return aid, or contribute a great deal to a social relationship until they are convinced that the other party can be counted on to act responsibly. As a personality variable, reciprocation wariness involves a general predisposition to fear and to attempt to avoid exploitation. This generalized cautiousness can be distinguished from situational influences on fear of exploitation, such as the identity of an exchange partner.

Eisenberger et al. (1987) studied the effects of wariness on reciprocation using a prisoner's dilemma bargaining task designed to mimic everyday situations in which cooperation by two participants would produce substantial gains but in which exploitation of one participant by the other could result in a short-term advantage. Students whose questionnaire responses indicated high reciprocation wariness returned less aid following beneficial treatment by their partner and viewed their benefactors less favorably than low-wary students (Eisenberger et al., 1987). High-wary individuals also showed less generosity in a bargaining task than low-wary individuals following receipt of a communication offering cooperation (Cotterell et al., 1992). Friends and roommates of high-wary persons viewed them as relatively selfish and uncaring (Cotterell et al., 1992). Students who were supervised by high-wary resident assistants evaluated those assistants as relatively unapproachable, hesitant to develop close relationships, and unresponsive to student needs (Cotterell et al., 1992).

High-wary persons show greater reciprocation of favorable treatment when they believe the exchange of resources is unlikely to result in their exploitation. When offered protection against mistreatment, wary individuals can behave generously. High-wary persons were more generous than low-wary individuals following the receipt of minimal aid; the return of this help allowed them to cautiously probe the intentions of others (Eisenberger et al., 1987). High-wary individuals were also more generous than low-wary individuals at the start of a bargaining task if assured of a large number of bargaining trials (Cotterell et al., 1992). High-wary individuals may have responded favorably to the expectation that the long-term interaction as provided opportunities to test the good faith of their partner. This evidence supports the interpretation that high-wary individuals are not indiscriminately selfish; they behave generously in situations that reduce the likelihood of exploitation.

As we discussed in Chapter 2, employees personify the organization, viewing it as having persisting motives and intentions. Reciprocation-wary individuals would doubt that efforts on behalf of the organization would be adequately repaid. They would likely be reluctant to invest their efforts beyond what their job explicitly required unless convinced the employer is committed to a strong exchange relationship. Obtaining the dedication and superior performance of reciprocation-wary employees may be especially difficult because of the widespread publicity concerning layoffs of long-term employees, increased workloads, and restrictions of employee benefits. Reciprocation-wary individuals may view such treatment of employees as confirmation of their suspicion that the organization cannot be counted on to satisfy its exchange obligations. On the basis of uncertainty concerning the organization's intent to reward high work effort, employees with strong reciprocation wariness may perform poorly.

Where perceived organizational support is an experience-based attribution concerning a particular organization's policies, norms, and procedures as they affect employees, reciprocation wariness is a persisting personality trait or disposition involving a fear of exploitation in social exchange relationships. The specificity of perceived organizational support to a particular exchange partner (one's organization) and its malleability due to experience differentiates perceived organizational support from the durable trait of reciprocation wariness. With retail employees in one study and employees from multiple organizations in a second study, My colleagues and I (Lynch et al., 1999) found that when perceived organizational support was low, employees with high reciprocation wariness performed more poorly than others low in reciprocation wariness. However, when perceived organizational support was high, employees with high reciprocation wariness performed as well or better than those low in reciprocation wariness.

We (Lynch et al., 1999) had anticipated that when perceived organization support was high, high-wary employees might show the same degree of performance as low-wary employees. We were surprised that under these circumstances, the performance of high-wary employees exceeded that of low-wary employees. Wary employees may be pleasantly surprised and relieved by indications that the organization values their contributions and cares about their well-being. According to Aronson and Lindner (1965), when aversive treatment is expected, favorable treatment reduces anxiety and thereby increases enjoyment of the treatment and liking for the benefactor. Thus, the expectation of aversive treatment has been found in experiments to lead college students to respond more positively to favorable treatment (e.g., Aronson & Lindner, 1965; Berscheid, Brothen, & Graziano, 1976; Burgoon & Lepoire, 1993; Burgoon, Lepoire, & Rosenthal, 1995; Mettee, Taylor, & Friedman, 1973). Reciprocation-wary employees may respond to perceived organizational support in a similar manner; unexpected favorable treatment may lessen anxiety, increase affective attachment to the organization, and motivate greater efforts on the organization's behalf. These findings suggest that although wary employees are hesitant to risk exploitation by performing beyond minimally required levels, perceived organizational support enhances confidence that the organization will fulfill its exchange obligations to them and thereby encourages greater effort.

Considering employees in general, those who trust their organization should be more willing to invest their resources of time and effort on its behalf, with the assurance that the organization can be relied on to reciprocate in the future. Perceived organizational support may enhance employees' investment in the organization by increasing trust. Several studies have reported a positive relationship between perceived organizational support and employees' trust in the organization, with consequences for affective organizational commitment (Albrecht & Travaglione, 2003; Z. X. Chen et al., 2005; Tan & Tan, 2000; Whitener, 2001).

Although trust seems to be important in interpersonal relationships and in the association of the employee with the organization, the study of interpersonal trust and, by extension, trust in the organization has been troubled by a myriad of conceptualizations, multiple measurement scales, and a general absence of correspondence between conceptualizations and their measurement. Two articles published in the 1990s attempted to clarify the concept of trust (Mayer, Davis, & Schoorman, 1995; Rousseau, Sitkin, Burt, & Camerer, 1998). Mayer et al.'s (1995) integrative model defined *trust* as

> the willingness of one party to be vulnerable to the actions of another party based on the expectation that the other party will perform a particular action important to the trustor, irrespective of the ability to monitor or control that other party. (p. 712)

In a similar vein, Rousseau et al.'s (1998) cross-discipline review defined *trust* as "a psychological state comprising the intention to accept vulnerability based upon positive expectations of the intentions or behavior of another" (p. 395). Both definitions include the intention to accept vulnerability as a primary component of the trust construct. Rousseau et al.'s definition contains perhaps the heart of what is meant by trust in employee–employer relationships. The employee accepts risk based on beliefs about the favorable intentions of the organization. Unfortunately, no scale seems to be available that adequately encompasses this insightful definition.

The part of the conception of trust concerning benevolent intentions of the organization is embedded in perceived organizational support. The employees' perception that the organization values one's contribution and cares about one's well-being implies favorable intentions toward the employee by the organization. In fact, some of the 36 items in the original full-length Survey of Perceived Organizational Support involve scenarios in which the perceived intentions of the organization are assessed, as for example, "The organization would take advantage of me if it had the opportunity," as well as more general items regarding a high regard for the employee. To such perceived intentions of the organization, Rousseau et al.'s (1998) definition of trust adds a behavioral component concerning a willingness to accept risk. Thus, part of the definition of trust is embedded in perceived organizational support, and we might expect to see a substantial relationship between employees' perceived organizational support and trust measures that include the organization's benevolence.

Considering the risk-taking component of trust, perceived organizational support should increase employees' willingness to take risk on behalf of the organization because the organization's favorable intent suggests that it will reward success generously and treat failure magnanimously. Such risk taking can include, for example, accepting assignments with a low probability of success or being willing to admit error. W. A. Kahn (1990) suggested that supportive managerial environments provide contexts in which employees feel safe taking the risks of showing vulnerability and acting without fear of negative consequences to self-image, status, or career. Such employee–employer relationships, characterized by "psychological safety," have a flexibility that allows employees to try and perhaps to fail without fearing the consequences.

In summary, trust associated with the benevolent intentions of the organization is a component of perceived organizational support. Contemporary views of trust add the dimension of a willingness of employees to place themselves at risk to aid the organization with the expectation that they will be protected in the case of failure. Perceived support has been found to be positively related to trust and helps overcome the trait of wariness that lessens performance.

Organizational Cynicism

Although researchers are divided on the definition of organizational cynicism, they generally agree that it involves a general disillusionment with, and distrust of, the organization (e.g., Treadway et al., 2004). For example, Bedeian (2007) defined *cynicism* as "an attitude resulting from a critical appraisal of the motives, actions, and values, of one's employing organization" (p. 11). Andersson (1996) referred to "an attitude characterized by frustration, hopelessness, and disillusionment, as well as contempt toward and distrust of business organizations" (p. 1395).

Recall that Rousseau et al.'s (1998) helpful definition of trust involves a willingness to place oneself at risk with the expectation the other individual or entity will look after one's best interests. Therefore, mistrust appears to be a key element in organizational cynicism. Cynics see a systemic source for their trust: They believe the organization's actions indicate a basic absence of such principles as integrity, honesty, and sincerity and that these principles are sacrificed to further the organization's narrow self-interest (J. Dean, Brandes, & Dharwadkar, 1998; Goldner, Ritti, & Ference, 1977; James, 2005). Actions of the organization are viewed as often inconsistent with stated policies based on a consistent motivation to further the interests of the power structure (J. Dean et al., 1998; Goldner et al., 1977).

In contrast, trust implies the assessment of the likelihood that the organization will take account of the employees' best interests and, at a more general level, will concern itself with the interests of all employees who contribute to its success. According to J. Dean et al. (1998), one major difference between cynicism and trust is that trust is conceptualized as a belief or expectancy and, as such, does not include affect. Cynicism is an attitude composed of an affective component, including hopelessness, disillusionment, and frustration, as well as a belief (Andersson, 1996). In other words, cynicism has a very distinctive negative affective component (James, 2005).

High executive compensation, poor managerial performance, and unjustified layoffs generate cynicism among employees (Andersson & Bateman, 1997). Naus, van Iterson, and Roe (2007) also found that high levels of role conflict and few opportunities for autonomous behavior contributed to organizational cynicism. Moreover, employees who felt that promises by the organization had been broken (i.e., psychological contract breach) held more cynical attitudes about their organization (Johnson & O'Leary-Kelly, 2003). Finally, Pugh, Skarlicki, and Passell (2003) demonstrated that the violation of the psychological contract by a former employer was positively related to employee cynicism toward a new employer.

Consequences of organizational cynicism include outcomes such as low job satisfaction and fewer self-reported organizational citizenship behaviors (Hochwarter, James, Johnson, & Ferris, 2004), and low organizational commitment (Abraham, 2000). Although most studies have focused primarily on negative outcomes related to cynicism, Andersson and Bateman (1997) showed that cynicism toward the organization reduced employee compliance with unethical requests made by managers.

Several studies have investigated the possible role of perceived organizational support in the development of organizational cynicism. Treadway et al. (2004) argued that low perceived organizational support leads employees to believe their organization ignores their efforts and contributions (Gouldner, 1960). As a result of this perceived failure to reciprocate, employees become frustrated and cynical with the organization. In agreement with this view, the authors found that leader political skill was positively related to perceived organizational support, leading to reduced cynicism. Part of the relationship between perceived organizational support and reduced cynicism was due to increased trust of the organization. James (2005), using a sample of employees from 17 schools, found that low perceived organizational support led to cynicism, which in turn was associated with burnout. Byrne and Hochwarter (2008) found negative relationships between perceived organizational support and cynicism among employees from a variety of organizations and in a second study with government employees. These findings suggest that perceived support leads to reduced organizational cynicism.

Job Involvement

Job involvement has been defined in diverse and often inconsistent ways. Kanungo (1979, 1982) helped focus the concept by restricting it to employees' identification with their job. Examples from the Kanungo's (1982) Job Involvement Questionnaire include "I live, eat and breathe my job" and "I consider my job to be very central to my existence" (p. 342). By engaging employees deeply in their work and making it a meaningful experience, employees' incorporation of jobs into their sense of self can have important positive effects on their productivity and morale.

Because of their conceptual similarities, organizational commitment and job involvement were described by Morrow and Goetz (1988) as two distinct aspects of work commitment. Research has confirmed that organizational commitment and job involvement are related but distinct (e.g., G. Blau, 1985; Hirschfeld & Feild, 2000). Both individual differences and situational factors have been emphasized as antecedents of job involvement. Thus, Rabinowitz and Hall's (1977) literature review included such factors as higher order need strength and values as individual determinants of job involvement, plus such factors as leader behavior, interpersonal relationships, and job characteristics as situational determinants of job involvement.

In our view, these individual differences and situational approaches are complementary. By fulfilling needs for esteem, approval, support, and affiliation (Armeli et al., 1998; Eisenberger et al., 1986), employees' perception of being valued and cared about by the organization should lead to the incorporation of job into self-image (Lawler & Hall, 1970) and, therefore, encourage a favorable motivational orientation toward the job. Effective leadership and positive discretionary acts by the organization and its representatives should also fulfill socio-emotional needs, leading employees to incorporate their jobs into their self-image.

The contribution of perceived organizational support to job involvement has been found to be less than its contribution to outcomes related to bonds to the organization, such as affective commitment and organizational identification. Rhoades and Eisenberger's (2002) meta-analytic review of the literature found that perceived organizational support accounted for about 10% of the variability in job involvement, much lower than for affective organizational commitment or organizational identification. The reason may be that employees' involvement in their job, as opposed to commitment to their organization, involves a number of aspects of the job that employees only moderately connect with voluntary actions by the organization, such as challenging aspects of the work and role clarity (Aryee, 1994). Still, given the diverse causes of job involvement, perceived support's contribution of approximately 10% is notable.

Work Engagement

Work engagement refers to a positive, fulfilling affective–motivational state characterized by *vigor*, involving high levels of energy and resilience while working; *dedication*, concerning a sense of significance, inspiration, and pride; and *absorption*, involving focus and concentration (Bakker, Schaufeli, Leiter, & Taris, 2008; Schaufeli, Salanova, González-Romá, & Bakker, 2002). Most researchers refer to employees' identification with their work as well (Bakker et al., 2008), raising some questions concerning the overlap between job involvement and work engagement. Researchers working on job involvement seem more interested in the relationship of work with self-image, whereas those concerned with work engagement seemed more concerned with the experiential and expressive aspects of work.

According to contemporary theories of work engagement and optimal experience, task concentration is a key element in developing intrinsic interest in one's work (Csikszentmihalyi & Lefevre, 1989; Eisenberger, Jones, Stinglhamber, Shanock, & Randall, 2005; González-Roma, Schaufeli, Bakker, & Lloret, 2006; Sonnentag, 2003). Perceived organizational support may increase work engagement in several ways. First, the expectation that the resources needed to carry out one's job well will be provided should increase intrinsic task interest. Second, the self-efficacy and expanded use of high-level skills, resulting from perceived organizational support, should make work more interesting. Third, perceived organizational support increases expected reward for high performance (Eisenberger et al., 1990), which has been found to enhance intrinsic task interest. Fourth, the positive valuation of one's current performance should meet needs for approval and esteem and therefore also increase intrinsic interest.

Kinnunen, Feldt, and Makikangas (2008) found that perceived organizational support was positively related to Finnish managers' vigor, dedication, and absorption or work, as well as being negatively related to turnover intentions. Work engagement is an exciting new area of study, and its relationship to perceived organizational support warrants much more attention.

Empowerment

Empowerment has become a buzzword in business culture, but it suffers from a lack of agreement concerning its meaning. Based on Thomas and Velthouse's (1990) view, Spreitzer (1995, 1996) defined empowerment as a positively valued experience that employees obtain directly from performing the task involving four contributing aspects that combine to form a gestalt: *impact* in terms of success, *meaningfulness* in the sense of goal or purpose, *competence,* and *self-determination* viewed a choice concerning whether and how to perform the task. However, it is unclear why these distinctive features should contribute to a single general mind state. Corsun and Enz (1999) found that perceived organizational support was positively related to perceived self-determination to only a small degree and not to self-efficacy or meaningfulness, when other supportive relationships were controlled for. However, their scale of organizational support had low internal reliability. Chow, Lo, Sha, and Hong (2006), also using their own measure of perceived organizational support with low internal reliability, found a positive relationship between perceived organizational support and an overall measure of empowerment. Using measures of low reliability lessens the ability to find relationship between variables. Moreover, using self-constructed measures of common constructs, without some justifiable reason, makes comparisons with other research findings difficult. More research needs to be done on this topic using the standard scale for assessing perceived organizational support.

Besides having a direct effect on empowerment, perceived organizational support might enhance the impact on management practices that contribute to empowerment. Butts et al. (2009) examined the effects of high-involvement work processes, involving a company's design of new practices for enhancing organizational productivity, management information sharing, performance-contingent reward, and career development on empowerment. Studying employees of a large national retailer, the researchers found that the high-involvement work practices led to empowerment, which increased affective organizational comment and reduced job stress. They argued that employees would view high work involvement practices either as manipulative or beneficial depending on the perceived intent of the organization. Thus, management's concern with employees' welfare, as reflected in perceived organizational support, should enhance the influence of high-involvement work practices on empowerment. As predicted, these relationships were stronger at high levels of perceived organizational support, and a positive relationship was found between empowerment and self-evaluated job performance when perceived organizational support was high. This study suggests that perceived organizational support can have a positive influence on employees' favorable reactions to high work involvement practices, viewing them more as a positive challenge than as a threat.

Summary and Implications

Perceived organizational support increases the favorableness of employees' attitudes and feelings toward their organization. Perceived organizational support is strongly related to employees' affective organizational commitment and their associated dedication to the organization's objectives and job retention. The conceptualization of affective organizational commitment remains contentious despite conceptual and empirical advances (Klein et al., 2009). Yet, the construct rightly continues to have great appeal because it relates to an important psychological phenomenon that needs explanation: the persisting emotional bond of the employee to the organization even when short-term incentives dictate otherwise.

Consistent with organizational support theory, perceived organizational support enhances affective commitment partly through the reciprocity norm, as indicated by findings that perceived support leads to felt obligation to the organization, which in turn leads to affective commitment (Eisenberger et al., 2001). Organizational support theory holds that perceived organizational support fulfills socioemotional needs (e.g., approval, esteem, affiliation) and by this means also contributes to affective commitment. Evidence is needed on this proposed role of need fulfillment in the relationship between perceived organizational support and affective organizational commitment.

Meyer and Allen's (1997) concept of normative commitment, originally thought to stem from socialization experiences that produce a sense of obligation to remain with one's employer, had little empirical success and evolved into the more general concept of a diverse set of obligations to the organization, including retention. The construct now is very similar to the felt obligation concept of organization support theory (Meyer & Herscovitch, 2001). Perceived support is closely tied to normative commitment. Because the relationship between perceived organizational support is stronger among employees who strongly endorse the reciprocity norm (see Chapter 2), the normative commitment resulting from perceived organizational support appears to reflect employees' conformity with this norm. At an experiential level, as Meyer and Allen (1997) put it, employees believe they ought to do the right thing by the organization for what the organization has done for them.

Continuance commitment, involving the costs of leaving the organization, such as implicit benefits, community ties, and lack of employment alternatives, shows little if any direct relationship with perceived organizational support. However, Gellatly et al. (2007) reported some tantalizing evidence concerning how continuance commitment combines with the other two forms of commitment. When affective commitment and normative commitment (felt obligation) were low, perceived organizational support was related to reduced continuance commitment. This suggests that in the absence of emotional ties to the organization, the necessity to remain with the organization is experienced as entrapment. According to self-determination theory (Deci & Ryan, 1985), the absence of choice in activities is inherently unpleasant. Favorable emotional ties to the organization appear to eliminate that unpleasant experience. Although individuals often experience their obligations as aversive, obligations within the context of perceived organizational support and affective commitment seem less burdensome to employees. Meeting obligations in these circumstances may the create satisfaction of aiding an organization that appreciates the aid and that responds in kind.

Perceived organizational support increases employees' incorporation of their organizational membership and social roles into their social identity. The fulfillment of socioemotional needs by perceived organizational support is one among several mechanisms that may contribute to employees' feeling at one with the organization. Thus, perceived organizational support increases employees' beliefs that they can further their self-interests as individuals (reward expectancies) and enhances their outlook that they have common interests with the organization.

Perceived organizational support has been found to increase trust in the organization, including reduced skepticism by employees with a permanent disposition to mistrust others (reciprocation wariness). Trust has been recognized as central to the development of strong social relationships. However, its study has been hampered by rich and varied meanings that have carried over to psychological research. Psychologists use diverse definitions of trust, often with scales that fail to accurately represent what is intended. Accepting Rousseau et al.'s (1998) invaluable definition of trust as employees' willingness to accept vulnerability on the basis of their expectation of the positive intentions of organization, it is clear that perceived organizational support incorporates the aspect of trust concerning the favorable orientation of the organization toward employees. That is, perceived organizational support inherently involves the employee's trust in the organization if, by *trust*, we mean employees' beliefs concerning the benevolent intentions of the organization directed toward the employee.

The added component of trust, involving employees' acceptance of risk on behalf of the organization, should be examined as a consequence of perceived organizational support. The dangers of ill founded and excessive risk taking in business are well illustrated by the recent global financial meltdown. Yet, without risk, there can be no creativity and innovation because any new activity involves uncertainty and the possibility that the resources devoted to the activity will not be fully recovered. For the individual employee, as for organizations as a whole, strict guidelines and oversight are necessary to prevent excessive risk. Now that we have a working definition of trust applicable to organizations, it is time that the risk taking component of trust be examined as an outcome of perceived organizational support.

Employees with high perceived organizational support are positively oriented toward their work as well as their organization. Perceived organizational support increases job involvement, which reflects employees' incorporation of their job into their social identity. For employees with high perceived organizational support, the job provides an important source of purpose and meaning. Perceived organizational support also increases work engagement, involving enhanced vigor, dedication, and absorption (Kinnunen et al., 2008). Perceived organizational support encourages employees to become more excited and engrossed in their work by indicating the organization's appreciation of employees' accomplishments and by signaling a readiness to provide aid when needed. The number of studies examining the influence of perceived organizational support on job involvement and work engagement is currently very small. But the initial positive findings are exciting.

Behavioral Outcomes of Perceived Organizational Support

7

My colleagues and I (Eisenberger et al., 1990) investigated how perceived organizational support influenced the creative performance of hourly and managerial employees of a large steel plant that was threatened with closure because of foreign competition. The plant needed new technology to compete effectively, and opinions were divided concerning whether the company to which the plant belonged could be convinced to keep it open. Some managers and employees believed that central headquarters had decided to close the plant and were keeping the decision a secret to prevent a backlash until operations could be closed down. Others believed that central headquarters identified the plant strongly with the company and valued the contributions and welfare of the employees of the plant, who for generations had done the hard and dangerous work associated with steel production. The more optimistic employees felt that if they could obtain sufficient productivity gains with their current equipment through cooperation between labor and management, central headquarters would reciprocate by introducing the new technology needed to compete with foreign producers, allowing the plant to remain open. According to organizational support theory, employees with high perceived organizational support are more likely to believe that the company would be responsive to their efforts on behalf of the organization, and behave accordingly.

We (Eisenberger et al., 1990) asked everyone in the plant for "any suggestion you have for ways management can be kept better informed of your ideas for small or large changes that will improve productivity." We evaluated the creativity of the suggestions on the basis of the combination of their originality and practical utility. For hourly employees and managers alike, the creativity of their responses was strongly associated with perceived organizational support. One interesting aspect of the findings is that the respondents had been told that they would not be identified individually. Thus, employees were not responding out of an expectation for personal short-term gain but based on a longer term orientation toward aiding the company.

The positive influences of perceived organizational support on various behaviors beneficial to the organization, together with explanations that have been offered for these effects, are presented in Figure 7.1. The explanations listed for each outcome in the figure, and discussed in detail in the chapter, are those proposed by researchers to explain their findings for the positive relationships between perceived organizational support and seven kinds of employee behaviors favorable to the organization. From one to four of the same explanations have been proposed to explain each outcome: felt obligation, fulfillment of socioemotional needs, increased reward expectancy, and anticipation of help when needed to carry out one's job better. We believe it likely that future research will implicate all four mechanisms in every one of the outcomes. The greater the felt obligation resulting from perceived organizational support should result in a generalized desire to be helpful to the organization in all the behaviors. Fulfillment of socioemotional needs should increase the employees' identification with, and affective commitment to, the organization, increasing their desire for positive outcomes for the organization. An increased reward expectancy for high performance should raise the instrumental value of all these types of cooperative actions. And anticipated help when needed should decrease the expected costs in time and effort of all the activities and therefore make them more palatable. Now, we turn to the evidence concerning behaviors beneficial to the organization that arise from perceived organizational support.

Job Performance

Inrole performance refers to the activities that employees are expected to carry out as a regular part of their job. In contrast, organizational *extra-role performance* involves job activities that go above and beyond those dictated by formal role requirements and organizational policies.

FIGURE 7.1

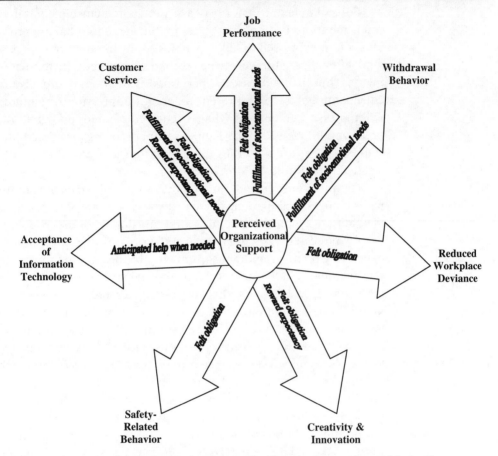

Behavioral outcomes of perceived organizational support favorable to the organization and proposed underlying mechanisms.

Extrarole behaviors can be directed primarily toward aiding the organization or individuals linked to it, such as fellow employees and customers. George and Brief (1992) included in their concept of *organizational spontaneity* aiding fellow employees, taking actions to protect the organization from risk, offering constructive suggestions, and gaining knowledge and skills beneficial to the organization. Dennis Organ's (1988; Konovsky & Organ, 1996) classification of *organizational citizenship* behaviors has been widely embraced in research studies. However, these kinds of extrarole behavior are difficult to differentiate empirically (LePine, Erez, & Johnson, 2002). This problem may arise in part because supervisors who often assess employee performance give positive evaluations across the various dimensions (a halo effect), especially when rushed, when asked to evaluate many employees, or when they do not have good firsthand knowledge of employees' behavior in the category being judged.

For example, the majority of assessed sportsmanship items involve resentments and complaints about the organization that are probably most often expressed to fellow employees rather than to supervisors, who, after all, are unlikely to be respond sympathetically to such comments. Thus, in many cases, supervisors' evaluations of organizational citizenship behaviors represent a general impression of employees' willingness to go beyond what is required of them on behalf of the organization. Viewed in this light, assessments of organizational citizenship behaviors are a useful general measure that can often be distinguished from inrole performance.

Organizations depend on employees not only to engage in inrole performance but also to help out in many ways that are not formally specified but are essential to the successful functioning of the organization. Employees can greatly help or harm the organization on a daily basis depending on their favorable or unfavorable orientation toward it. As one example, members of the psychology department at the University of Delaware, where we worked, were being temporarily housed on the first floor of an administration building while our home building was being renovated. Above us, on the second floor, were administrative employees who were permanently housed there. It seemed very important to these employees to leave by 5:00 p.m. Seldom was one of them seen after that. The building had only one bathroom, which was located on the second floor. One day at 5:05 p.m., I went up to the second floor to use the bathroom and found great amounts of water pouring rapidly out of one of the toilets and into the hallway; there was a danger of substantial flood damage to both floors. One employee happened to be left on the second floor, and he was quickly gathering his materials together. I said to him, "We've got a real flood coming out of one of the toilets in the bathroom. Can you help me get the phone number to call maintenance?" He instantly replied, "It's not my problem," and went home.

Such a refusal to engage in extrarole behavior to aid the organization is influenced by perceived organizational support. Another interesting example involves employees' willingness to participate in organizational surveys. Spitzmüller, Glenn, Barr, Rogelberg, and Daniel (2006) found that college students who consciously decided not to take part in a survey conducted by their school had lower perceived organizational support and greater concern about being taken advantage of in social exchange relationships than students who passively failed to participate or those who did participate. Students with low perceived organizational support evidently felt little inclination to aid their school by taking part in the survey.

Results of numerous studies suggest that, overall, employees who feel supported by their organization work harder at their jobs and perform better than do those with low perceived organizational support. Perceived organizational support was found to be positively related to evaluative and objective measures of standard job activities (e.g., Armeli et al., 1998) and extrarole behaviors (e.g., Shore & Wayne, 1993; Wayne et al., 1997; Witt, 1991). The meta-analytic literature review by Rhoades and Eisenberger (2002) showed a small relationship between perceived organizational support and both inrole performance and extrarole performance directed toward individuals. Perceived support also showed a moderate relationship of perceived organizational support with extrarole performance directed toward the organization.

Perceived organizational support may be more weakly related to inrole than extrarole performance because inrole performance is constrained by supervision, producing a relatively high baseline for all employees. Further, in some cases the job itself may allow limited opportunities for variation in work quality or speed of inrole performance. Thus, extrarole performance may be a more effective way than inrole performance for most employees to reciprocate perceived organizational support and thereby receive the benefits of being considered an excellent employee (Rhoades & Eisenberger, 2002).

Measures of performance associated with perceived organizational support beyond assessments by supervisors have been obtained. For example, my colleagues and I (Armeli et al., 1998) found that perceived organizational support was positively related to speeding tickets issued and drunk driving arrests made by state police. It is notable that the extent of both activities had little influence on the officers' formal evaluations. The informal quota for speeding tickets was easily met by officers at the end of each month because the required number was not excessive and because most motorists drove faster than the speed limit. Arrests for drunk driving were even more divorced from evaluations because, although figures were kept for each officer, it was recognized that catching drunk drivers was a low probability occurrence. Drunken driving arrests were not formally used to determine pay increases.

At the police academy, the cadets were told that the one activity they could do most to prevent deaths was to make drunk driving arrests, and such arrests were viewed as an important part of the state police organization's mission. Yet, because observing erratic drivers was difficult and related to chance, the department did not evaluate patrol officers on the number of drunken driving arrests they made. From the officers' viewpoint, making many such arrests would aid one's reputation and might informally affect one's evaluations, but there was no guarantee. Balanced against these possible gains were the costs of searching for and processing drunk drivers. Being successful at finding drunk drivers required considerable diligence. And in finding such drivers, officers would subject themselves to considerable unpleasantness. Such drivers often do not follow directions clearly. Some become aggressive and even violent. If the drivers did prove to be drunk, considerable time and effort was often involved in transportation of the arrestee's vehicle, filling out the arrest report, and perhaps appearing in court to testify. So, all in all, being vigilant for drunk drivers was a very difficult task. Many patrol officers instead took the easy alternative of spending much of their time parked in their cars, parked out of view, paying little attention to traffic and responding primarily to emergency calls.

Yet perceived organizational support was positively related to traffic ticket citations and drunken driving arrests, more so for patrol officers with strong socioemotional needs. The drunken driving arrests especially were an activity that allowed patrol officers to pay back the organization in an important way for high perceived organizational support. Moreover, as discussed in the preceding chapter, because perceived organization support contributes to employees' identification with, and involvement in, their work, here was an activity that helped give the officers more purpose and meaning to their lives and that, although often tedious, could engender greater interest because of its importance. Finally, with high perceived organizational support came the expectation that this activity, kept at diligently, would in the long run be noticed and appreciated.

Several previously discussed studies detailed how basic organizational support mechanisms influence the perceived organizational support–performance relationship. These findings suggest that employees who feel supported by their organization are more likely to feel obligated to care about the organization's welfare and help it reach its objectives, and this felt obligation, in turn, increases their inrole and extrarole performance (e.g., Eisenberger et al., 2001). It should be noted that the widespread use of cross-sectional procedures to gather evidence on the relationship of perceived organizational support with job performance leaves uncertain the causal order of the observed associations. Although organizational support theory suggests that perceived organizational support leads to higher employee performance (see also Rhoades & Eisenberger, 2002), the effect might occur in the opposite direction, or both directions. For example, high-performing employees feel more supported and valued by the organization. Although obtaining repeated measures of perceived organizational support, performance, and other variables of interest requires added time and effort and convincing organizations to cooperate is often difficult, the obtained gain in knowledge is substantial.

We obtained preliminary evidence on the issue of the direction of causality between perceived organizational support and performance (Z. Chen, Eisenberger, Johnson, Sucharski, & Aselage, 2009). Perceived organizational support and extrarole performance were examined twice, the occasions separated by a 3-year interval, among employees of an electronic and appliance sales organization. We found that perceived organizational support was positively associated with a temporal change in extrarole performance. In contrast, the relationship between extrarole performance and temporal change in perceived organizational support was not statistically significant. These findings provide evidence that perceived organizational support leads to extrarole performance. As previously noted (see Chapter 4), in these cross-lagged panel designs, in which the variables are measured two or more times, significant findings are more indicative of relationships than are nonsignificant findings. So the evidence indicates that perceived organizational support leads to performance and is inconclusive concerning the possibility that high performance leads to perceived organizational support.

A promising area for future research concerns how the relationship between perceived organizational support and performance is influenced by employees' dispositions. As discussed in Chapter 2, consistent with the view that the relationship between perceived organizational support and performance is partly due to the norm of reciprocity, the relationship between perceived organizational support and extrarole performance was greater among employees who strongly endorsed the norm of reciprocity as applied to work (Ladd & Henry, 2000; Witt, 1991). As described in Chapter 2, the importance of socioemotional need fulfillment in outcomes of perceived organizational support is indicated by the finding that the relationship between perceived organizational support and police patrol officers' performance was greater among officers with high needs for esteem, affiliation, emotional support, and social approval (Armeli et al., 1998).

As discussed in Chapter 6, employees with a strong disposition to mistrust others (*reciprocation wariness*) were poorer performers than others low in reciprocation wariness. However, when perceived organizational support was high, such high-wary employees performed as well or better than those low in reciprocation wariness (Lynch et al, 1999).

Byrne and Hochwarter (2008) found in a study with state employees that perceived organizational support was negatively related to organizational cynicism, a general mistrust and disillusionment with their work organization. They then examined the relationship between perceived organizational support and job performance and how employees' cynicism intervenes in this link. The authors found that highly cynical employees construe levels of support negatively. Specifically, both inrole and extrarole performance for cynics were highest when perceived organizational support was at a moderate level only. Conversely, inrole and extrarole performance for cynics were lowest when perceived organizational support was either high or low. They explained the result indicating that performance is low under conditions of high perceived organizational support for cynical employees by suggesting that those employees perceive organizational support as manipulation rather than behavior undertaken to cultivate an acceptable social exchange relationship. Evidently, knowing that one is cared about and valued by an organization whose values and actions one finds corrupt and upsetting fails to have much a positive effect. Inspection of the figures presented by these investigators suggests it is possible that high-cynicism employees with high perceived organizational support might still have been outperforming high-cynicism employees with low perceived organizational support. This interesting effect reported by Byrne and Hochwarter (2008) warrants replication and extension.

Withdrawal Behavior

Withdrawal behavior refers to employees' voluntary lessening of active participation in the organization. High levels of employee turnover reduce the profitability for firms that use skilled employees because of the expense of recruiting and replacing them (Reichfield, 1996). Inadequate staffing, resulting from high turnover, also lessens the ability of remaining employees to carry out their jobs satisfactorily. For example, a study with frontline staff at Burger King restaurants found that turnover was related to food waste and increased customer waiting time, with a loss of sales and profits (Kacmar, Andrews, Van Rooy, Steilberg, & Cerrone, 2006).

Retention of organizational membership, high attendance, and punctuality provide publicly identifiable ways for employees to reciprocate perceived organizational support. The relationship of perceived organizational support to behavioral intention to leave (i.e., turnover intention) have been assessed, as has been such actual withdrawal behaviors as voluntary turnover, absenteeism, and tardiness. The latest meta-analytic review of the literature (Kurtessis et al., 2009) shows a substantial negative relationship between perceived organizational support and turnover intention, and a modest but reliable relationship between perceived organizational support and actual turnover.

The far greater relationship between perceived organizational support with turnover intention than with actual turnover suggests that low perceived organizational support increases employees' inclination to leave the organization, but actual leaving is also influenced by continuance commitment, including such factors as accumulated resources at work that may be lost, one's romantic partner's job needs and preferences, and the extent of available job opportunities. T. R. Mitchell and Lee (2001) noted the importance of strong attachments to people and groups at work and in the community as strong influences that may also prevent individuals from leaving their jobs. As discussed in Chapter 1, age is a major factor that reduces mobility in the United States. Employers have a strong bias toward hiring younger workers both because they can be paid less than older workers and they are believed to be more set in their ways and more likely be unhealthy.

Perceived organizational support has also been found to reduce other withdrawal behaviors, such as absenteeism and tardiness (e.g., Eder & Eisenberger, 2008; Shore et al., 2006). As with job performance, the association between perceived organizational support and absenteeism appears to be based on employees' endorsement of the norm of reciprocity as applied to work. Eisenberger et al. (1986) found that the relationship between perceived organizational support and absenteeism was greater among those employees who were more accepting of the reciprocity norm.

Withdrawal behavior that violates company norms and harms the organization blends into the category of workplace deviance, which we discuss next. Withdrawal behavior is influenced by norms established by coworkers. Coworkers have long been considered an important normative influence on the prosocial and antisocial behavior of employees (Ehrhart & Naumann, 2004; J. Greenberg, 1997; Homans, 1950). For example, the frequency of absenteeism among individual workgroup members has been found to be related to the absenteeism of the workgroup (Mathieu & Kohler, 1990), and this relationship is associated with perceived workgroup norms encouraging such withdrawal behavior (Gellatly, 1995). Also, G. Blau (1995) found that the tardiness of individual employees was related to the tardiness of others in their workgroup.

When the workgroup engages in a high level of withdrawal behavior without punishment by the organization, individual employees may reap the personal benefits of high withdrawal behavior by simply conforming to the group's norms. If the group has a high level of absenteeism or tardiness, then the individual employee should feel safer to engage in similar actions than in a group in which such withdrawal behavior occurs at a low rate. In addition, when workgroup withdrawal behavior is high, employees may believe that they will face the group's criticism for violating the group's standard (see also Bandura, 1986; Bandura, Adams, & Beyer, 1977; Mars, 1974).

Despite the potentially strong influence of the workgroup on the individual employee's behavior and the potential rewards associated with withdrawal behaviors, some employees manage to resist the temptation to arrive late frequently or to neglect job tasks. Paul Eder and I suggested that this resistance may also be influenced by employees' reciprocal exchange relationship with their organization (Eder & Eisenberger, 2008). In deciding whether to conform to high workgroup withdrawal behavior, individuals may pay attention to their obligation to return favorable treatment received from the organization.

We (Eder & Eisenberger, 2008) argued that withdrawal behavior, even in the presence of coworkers who also engage in it, may be a negative experience for employees high in perceived organizational support. We reasoned that the reciprocity norm obliges employees to reciprocate perceived organizational support by acting in ways that benefit the organization. In addition, perceived organizational support should lead employees to incorporate their roles as effective employees into their self-image, increasing their desire to refrain from harming the organization. Accordingly, we found that high perceived organizational support completely eliminated the positive relationship between tardiness of individual members of workgroups and that of the rest of the members of their workgroup. A second study, using a more general measure of withdrawal behavior involving taking undeserved work breaks, spending time in idle conversation, and neglecting aspects of the job one is obligated to perform, reported similar, although not as strong, effects.

These results suggest that perceived organizational support deters conforming to coworker norms, which benefit the individual employee at a cost to the organization. Employees would view such behaviors as violation of their positive exchange relationship with the organization. Therefore, employees with high perceived organizational support would be motivated to meet their exchange obligations by remaining fully engaged in their work activities. Further, by fulfilling socioemotional needs and increasing the incorporation of employees' organizational membership and roles into their self-identity, perceived organizational support would increase resistance to harmful coworker norms by identifying harm to the organization with harm to oneself.

Workplace Deviance

One of the my students at my previous university, whom we will call Emily, took a temporary summer job working at an office of the Delaware Department of Revenue, where she and her coworkers were responsible for answering questions phoned in about taxes. Emily soon observed that her coworkers found these calls quite annoying. The inquiries interfered with conversations among the employees about their lives, movies, sports, and so on. So during these long interludes from work, the employees simply kept a button pushed down on their phones that created a busy signal for callers. The supervisor came to check on the employees' performance once a week and went away happy each time, having been shown falsified figures indicating that large numbers of phone calls had been answered and taxpayers' questions addressed. Emily, however, took her job seriously and never pressed the phone button, creating the busy signal, to engage in personal pursuits. Further, when Emily could not answer a taxpayer's question, she took the unusual step of researching the answer, violating the norm of her coworkers that complex questions should receive either a response involving a guess or the taxpayer's need to consult an accountant or tax attorney.

Early in Emily's employment, the coworkers tried to reason with her in a friendly way. "Take a break from work" or "Never mind the calls. Come chat," they said. Or, "Don't bother looking up difficult questions. That's for the accountants." Because friendly persuasion did not work, they began to isolate her socially. They were further angered when she refused to inflate her numbers of phone calls answered to jibe with their own exaggerated records. Her truthful log of fewer phone calls answered might raise uncomfortable questions about the possible reasons for the disparity. So they complained to the supervisor. Emily was not a team player. She was unfriendly and arrogant. She was unhelpful to callers. The supervisor, who was more interested in the smooth operation than the effectiveness of the tax office, fired Emily.

Workgroup counterproductive or deviant behavior involves a violation of organizational norms that may be directed toward the organization or other employees (Bennett & Robinson, 2000). Some workplace deviance involves acts of aggression against coworkers or the organization in which there are active attempts to do harm, such as spreading negative rumors about the organization or a disliked colleague. Other forms of workplace deviance are more passive and often reflect placing one's own needs and interests ahead of organizational norms. Surveying a random selection of employees, Bennett and Robinson (2000) found that a third of the individuals reported they had intentionally worked slowly during the preceding 6 months, a third had come late to work without permission, and half had taken longer work breaks than allowed (Bennett & Robinson, 2000). The costs of such counterproductive behaviors have been estimated to run as high as $200 billion per year (K. R. Murphy, 1993).

As discussed in Chapter 2, one way in which employees reciprocate unfavorable treatment by the organization and its agents (supervisors and managers) is by trying to harm the instigator in ways that violate organizational norms. Employees' beliefs that they have been strongly mistreated, especially when their dignity has been violated, would be more likely to strongly elicit the negative norm of reciprocity (see Chapter 2) and result in active attempts to do harm. In contrast, minor mistreatment received from the organization would be more likely to elicit passive types of workplace deviance.

As indicated by the preceding examples, some kinds of employee withdrawal behavior and passivity have been treated as forms of workplace deviance when they violate workplace norms. Thus, a high level of absenteeism or a reduced pace of work involve workplace deviance when they violate organizational norms. Perceived organizational support may increase the resistance to the allure of deviant behaviors that involve inattention to work, excessive socializing, and aggression.

Colbert, Mount, Harter, Witt, and Barrick (2004) suggested that perceived organizational support would reduce such workplace deviance by increasing employees' felt obligation to care about the organization's welfare, thus making it more likely that employees would follow organizational norms. Conversely, employees with low perceived organizational support were argued to feel more frustrated because of a lack of support toward achieving their goals and so be more likely to engage in hostile workplace behavior. Colbert et al. (2004) found that perceived organizational support was related to reduced interpersonal deviance involving such behaviors as making fun of others at work and acting rudely toward them. These investigators also considered how personality might interact with perceived organizational support to influence interpersonal deviance. Because individuals high in agreeableness tend to be compliant, considerate, and tolerant, they should be less likely to engage in interpersonal deviance even when they are frustrated in their goals by a lack of organizational support.

Accordingly, Colbert et al. (2004) found that the relationship between low perceived organizational support and deviance was greatly reduced among highly agreeable employees. Thus, employees, who by their personality, tend to comply with organizational norms are not much further influenced by low perceived organizational support. It is those who tend toward deviance that are primarily influenced. This finding is interesting in view of results that personality variables show only small relationships with perceived organizational support. The ways in which personality variables interact with perceived organizational support to influence behavioral outcomes is an important topic for future research.

C. L. Pearce and Giacalone (2003) reported that the perceived support of the workgroup by the organization decreased a variety of deviant behaviors by group members that interfere with group performance such as trying to look busy while doing nothing, coming in late, and leaving early. As we discussed in Chapter 4, employees form perceptions of support from organizational units, such as the workgroup, department, and division, and local facility, as well as from the entire organization. Thus, perceived workgroup support should create an obligation to help the workgroup enhance its effectiveness and not engage in deviant activities that harm its functioning.

Creativity and Innovation

Creative performance refers to behavior that is novel and has high quality or utility (Mumford & Gustafson, 1988). Innovation usually carries the additional implication that the creative idea has been transformed into a useful product (Scott & Bruce, 1994). Creative contributions are important for employees such as research scientists and product designers whose jobs primarily concern innovation. Creativity by employees performing jobs that do not directly require innovation also has value for organizations. For example, manufacturing employees have been found to provide effective suggestions to increase productivity and reduce production costs (Carrier, 1998). Employees' enjoyment of their work for its own sake (intrinsic job interest) appears to make a significant contribution to their creativity (Shalley, Zhou, & Oldham, 2004).

Employees who have high perceived organizational support and therefore feel their work contributions are strongly valued by the organization may take a greater intrinsic interest in their jobs, resulting in more thoughtful ways to improve performance. In addition, the increased obligation felt by employees with high perceived organizational support to repay the organization and increased expectancy of reward should be channeled into creative performance when the organization indicates that creativity and innovation are priorities. As discussed in the introduction to this chapter, My colleagues and I (Eisenberger et al., 1990) found that hourly and managerial employees of a steel plant with high perceived organizational support made more creative anonymous suggestions for enhancing the plant's productivity. Thus, these employees acted in the best long-term interest of the company in the absence of any possibility of immediate personal gain.

Some evidence has been reported that organizational climate, involving the organization's encouragement and assistance in enhancing creativity, has the intended effect of fostering creativity and innovation (e.g., Scott & Bruce, 1994; Zhou & George, 2001). By encouraging one important aspect of employee performance, such a climate can serve as a precursor to perceived organizational support. We noted in Chapter 3 that organizational support for specific organizational objectives, such as creativity, differs from perceived organizational support in important ways. Perceived support for creativity should increase perceived organizational support primarily for those employees who value creativity. For other employees who feel threatened by the necessity to be more creative, an organizational climate fostering creativity might reduce perceived organizational support.

Safety-Related Behavior

Worker safety depends on a responsible attitude by management, involving the expenditure of time and resources, and the cooperation of employees who, human nature being what it is, may be attentive to only the most salient safety hazards. I viewed the interplay of motivational and engineering issues in employee safety while carrying out research in chicken processing plants. The temperatures are kept very low so that bacteria do not grow in the chicken. Thus, workers coming from 90-degree Fahrenheit summer temperatures wear warm clothes. Chicken catchers obtain the live chickens from pens. After electrocution, the chickens are stripped of feathers and placed on hooks which move rapidly down the disassembly line. Here, the so-called *leg men, wing men, leg women, wing women,* and so on slice off edible chick parts with sharp knives many times a minute. Some of the chickens are stripped of bone and sent to the artists of the factory, the *fat tuckers,* whose job it is to package the fillets in an appealing manner by tucking the fat under the meat so that it cannot be see under the clear wrapping by potential supermarket customers.

The processing plant is a dangerous place. The floors are hosed with water periodically to remove oil but remain wet and slippery at all times. Employees wear Kevlar gloves that cover part of their hands, but with quick slashing motions and close quarters, it is easy to cut one's own or a coworker's face or arm, particularly because employees must reach up high to slice the chickens and thus have reduced muscular control. Repetitive injuries are frequent because the same basic motions are repeated numerous times a day with little letup. Rush orders sometimes come in, increasing the number of hours worked and tiring the employees. With low wages and uncomfortable working conditions, turnover is often great.

In these conditions, the employer plays a key role in maintaining or neglecting safety. Many such plants are not union organized, so there may be little pressure for safety. So long as the employer follows the letter of the law regarding safety, if not the spirit, there will be limited negative consequences for a high rate of accidents. Employees lack the middle-class ethic of seeking redress for injuries in court, and government agencies punish repeated safety violations, if at all, with small fines. Thus, all but an egregious series of accidents usually go ignored.

In more enlightened chicken processing plants, the picture is brighter. Managers recognize that uncomfortable and unsafe working conditions and poor pay result in high turnover, making it difficult to maintain enough trained workers to deal effectively with variable production demands. They use human engineering information and employee suggestions to cut down on injuries by such means as lowering the height of the disassembly line, giving short workers a base to stand on so that they do not have to reach up, and placing stations farther apart to prevent injuries from coworkers. More frequent breaks and job rotation may be used to reduce repetitive stress syndrome. Safety is continually stressed to employees, and the credibility of management is enhanced by its active steps. Concern with safety goes beyond having a safer workforce, with its positive effects on perceived organizational support and its outcomes.

Hofmann and Morgeson (1999) noted that the traditional emphasis on workplace safety as an engineering problem has been supplemented recently with the recognition that organizational factors also play a major role. These researchers suggested that social exchange influences employees' willingness to communicate safety concerns to management. Such reports are important because even well-meaning managers may overlook important safety problems that can be observed by line workers. Hoffman and Morgeson viewed such safety communication as a form of extrarole behavior in which such communication constitutes helpful actions for the organization in return for the organization's favorable treatment of the employee. They found that perceived organizational support was positively related to employees' self-reports of safety problems to the organization. Haines, Merrheim, and Roy (2001) reported that perceived organizational support was positively related to employees' attitudes toward a safety incentive program in which employees shared monetary rewards based on how well their plant met its safety objectives. Mearns and Reader (2008) reported that perceived organizational support among employees working on British offshore oil and gas installations was positively related to self-evaluated safety behaviors.

Tucker, Chmiel, Turner, Hershcovis, and Stride (2008) found that perceived organizational support specifically for safety was positively related to a belief that coworkers supported safety behavior, which in turn, led to self-reports of voicing of increased safety concerns to coworkers, management, and the union. These authors argued that perceived organizational support for safety would act in much the same way as more general perceived organizational support, indicating the organization's favorable positive valuation of employees. Tucker et al. suggested that employees would reciprocate, in part, by convincing fellow employees to express their safety concerns, and the findings supported their suggestion. From the viewpoint of organizational support theory, management's support for greater safety, if viewed as a voluntary attempt made to increase employees' welfare, would enhance perceived organizational support and indicate to employees that the way to repay such support would entail greater safety-related behavior. Some evidence that management's commitment specifically to safety has broader implications for how employees view the organization is suggested by findings that management's safety commitment was positively associated with affective organizational commitment, job satisfaction, and performance (Michael, Evans, Jansen, & Haight, 2005).

In sum, perceived organizational support appears to increase favorable employee attitudes toward safety behavior. Employees with high perceived organizational support are more willing to engage in safety behaviors. Of course, the relationship between perceived organizational support and safety is probably bidirectional: The promotion of safety is one indication that the organization is concerned with employees' welfare. We noted in Chapter 3 the distinction between perceived organizational support and perceived support for specific organizational objectives, the latter not necessarily indicating positive valuation of employees. However, to the extent that safety programs on the part of the organization are viewed as voluntary, as opposed to meeting government regulations, they may contribute greatly to perceived organizational support, and cooperation with them may be enhanced by perceived organizational support. Such cooperation may be strongly influenced by the way safety programs are presented. If couched in terms of employees' health and welfare in a very concrete way, safety programs should be much more effective and contribute more to perceived organizational support than if presented as lifeless set of rules that must be followed because, well, they are rules.

Acceptance of Information Technology

Over the past 3 decades, the availability of information technology (IT) within organizations has increased tremendously. IT, with its capacity to process, store, and transmit information, has replaced what used to be done by many individuals, often with greater efficiency. For example, FedEx's tracking of packages promotes efficiency and consumer confidence. Electronic recording of medical records eliminates wasted time and mistakes when patients continually try to recreate their medical histories on new visits to physicians. On the other hand, many employees use computers haphazardly and ineffectually because the systems they are provided do not work well, they have received inadequate training and support, or their own fear of advanced technology prevents them from taking full advantage of the technology. Supplying customer service representatives with IT has not prevented a general decline in customer service in recent years as experienced by anyone who spends much time phoning most large providers of computers, phone service, and insurance, to name a few.

On the other hand, when IT is done right, information can be retrieved quickly and efficiently, providing excellent customer service (Sergeant & Frenkel, 2000; Stone & Good, 2002). More generally, IT has considerable potential for aiding organizational effectiveness and productivity (see also Curley, 1984). Somewhat circularly, the level of IT usage has been widely used as a measure of its success (DeLone & McLean, 1992). Current evidence suggests that a favorable attitude toward the use of IT, termed *acceptance*, contributes to its use. Many managers and subordinates are unwilling to accept the systems supplied them, often limiting their use (Swanson, 1988; Young, 1984).

Understanding why people accept or reject IT has proven to be one of the most challenging issues in information systems research (Davis, Bagozzi, & Warshaw, 1989). In part, this may be due to the wide array of different measures of beliefs, attitudes, and satisfaction that have been used, frequently without adequate theoretical or psychometric development. One promising approach to IT acceptance and use involves a behavioral intention approach based on the theory of reasoned action (Fishbein & Ajzen, 1975). This technology acceptance model (Davis, 1989, 1993) is one of the most influential accounts of IT user behavior (Chau, 1996; Igbaria, Guimaraes, & Davis, 1995).

The technology acceptance model holds that external variables (e.g., training, intrinsic motivation) influence the individual's perception of the ease of use and usefulness of a particular technology, which in turn, produces a favorable or unfavorable attitude toward the technology. This attitude results in a behavioral intention regarding the use of the technology that affects actual system use. Davis (1989) found that perceived usefulness of IT is a stronger predictor of employees' usage intention than is perceived ease of use.

Several studies have examined how the so-called external variables affect perceived ease of use and usefulness of IT. Magni and Pennarola (2008) attempted to integrate social exchange theory into the technology acceptance model. These investigators argued that users' adoption of a newly introduced technology is related to their beliefs about their exchange relationships with the team members, the supervisor, and the organization as a whole. Without the perceived support of others, employees may be hesitant to adopt new technology. Their ideas are represented in Figure 7.2.

Among the results of greatest interest, they found that perceived usefulness and ease of use of technology were influenced by perceived organizational support and team-member exchange (i.e., the individuals' belief that they had high-quality relationships with other workgroup members), as well as by the typically studied external variables. In turn, both perceived usefulness and ease of use were related to the employees' intention to use the new system for data and information retrieval.

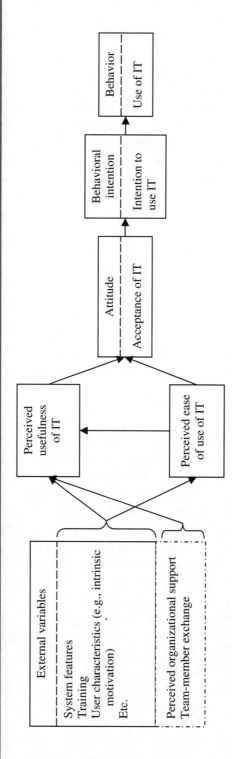

FIGURE 7.2

Representation of Magni and Pennarola's (2008) integration of the technology acceptance model with social exchange theory. IT = information technology.

Future research should examine how exchange relationships with the team members, the supervisor, and the organization affect actual user behavior. As Magni and Pennarola (2008) suggested, the findings indicate that when users perceive a good relationship with teammates (i.e., a high level of team-member exchange), they may be more likely to refer to their team to get information concerning the new technology. They thus activate informational channels within the group, increasing knowledge sharing among team members concerning how to manage the new technology and about the way in which the new technology may support their task accomplishment (see also S. M. Murphy, Wayne, Liden, & Erdogan, 2003). Additionally, when perceived organizational support is high, they may turn more to institutional support to help them learn and manage the new system.

Customer Service

I am a very picky shopper. On my weekly trip to the supermarket, I want my Asian Spicy frozen veggie burgers and Lucerne low-fat ice cream. No substitutes will do. When these products are on sale, I want a full shelf of them so I can stock up. The slim, raven-haired beauty who stocks the freezer chest (my perceptions perhaps exaggerated by my love for her frozen products) generally approaches me to tell me that both are in stock or, if not, to explain why they are temporarily unavailable and to let me know she has ordered more. On sale days, she excuses herself to bring out cartons of veggie burgers and ice cream so I can load up. Because she has been so good to me, I feel I am letting her down when I do not buy veggie burgers or ice cream. On occasion, when she has approached me to tell me that she had made sure the shelves were well-stocked, I have bought the items even though my own freezer was well-stocked. I cannot let the freezer lady down.

High service quality has received considerable attention as a way for organizations to maintain a loyal customer base in the face of competition (C. H. Hui, Chiu, Yu, Cheng, & Tse, 2007; Schneider, Holcombe, & White, 1997). Parasuraman, Zeithaml, and Berry (1988) described *service quality* as a customer's global judgment of superior treatment during encounters with service personnel, involving such categories as *responsiveness* (e.g., perceived willingness and promptness of aid), *assurance* (e.g., capacity of service personnel to inspire trust and confidence) and *empathy* (e.g., caring, individualized attention to customers' needs; Roberts, Varki, & Brodie, 2003). C. H. Hui, Chiu, et al. (2007) argued that high service quality is promoted by allowing service employees considerable discretion to improve on standard practice. For example, service personnel may be given the discretion to offer an upgraded product or service or respond rapidly to urgent customer requests. High service quality has been found to be related to customer satisfaction and loyalty (e.g., Han, Kwortnik, & Wang, 2008; Rogelberg, Barnes-Farrell, & Creamer, 1999; Schneider, Ehrhart, Mayer, Saltz, & Niles-Jolly, 2005). However, there is little theory or research examining the processes by which service quality contributes to satisfaction and loyalty.

Because high service quality is discretionary and tailored to customers' individual needs, customers are likely to view such treatment as an indication that the provider feels the customer is valued and important. Customers receiving high service quality thus feel more assured that the provider can be counted on in the future to fashion products and services to meet their wants and needs. Accordingly, Han et al. (2008) found that service quality was positively related to trust that the provider will reliably fulfill its service promises. Such trust should help build long-term exchange relationships conducive to customer loyalty.

Consistent with organizational support theory, Masterson's (2001) analysis of social exchange in organizations emphasizes the obligation of employees to repay favorable treatment received from the organization. Masterson suggested that service employees' receipt of favorable treatment would have a trickle-down effect on their treatment of customers. Masterson found that service employees who perceived they were treated fairly responded by treating customers well.

When organizations emphasize favorable treatment of customers as an objective, one way of reciprocating perceived organizational support is through higher quality customer service. Employees of various service-based organizations who had high perceived organizational support stated a desire to provide good customer service (Susskind et al., 2003), and service employees with high perceived organizational support were rated by their customers as more attentive, courteous, and concerned about customers' best interest than employees with low perceived organizational support (Bell & Menguc, 2002). Vandenberghe et al. (2007) suggested that perceived organizational support would increase service quality of fast food workers owing both to reciprocity and its role as a socioemotional resource in reducing the emotional labor associated with the necessity to display the pleasant emotions and act in a prescribed, repetitive manner. Thus, a server in a fast food restaurant may be required to smile and converse pleasantly with customers for extended periods of time. To make the job of restaurant workers yet more difficult, they are generally required to be pleasant even when the rudeness of customers evokes anger and desire to respond in kind based on the negative norm of reciprocity (Eisenberger et al., 2004). Vandenberghe et al. found that perceived organizational support was positively related to customer ratings of the helpfulness of the fast food workers.

Duke, Goodman, Treadway, and Breland (2009) provided direct evidence on the role of perceived organizational support in influencing emotional labor. Perceived organizational support was negatively related to self-reports of emotional labor among service employees. Perceived organizational support also reduced the negative relationship between emotional labor and job satisfaction, and made a nonsignificant relationship between emotional labor and performance into a positive one.

Liao, Toya, Lepak, and Hong (2009) examined how a high-performance work system for bank employees would influence perceived organizational support and, in turn, customer service. Bank employees evaluated the extent to which their work system incorporated facets that would promote their human capital, including extensive service training, information sharing, incorporation of self-management service teams and receptivity to suggestions, compensation contingent on service quality, interdepartmental support, and discretion in resolving customer complaints and customizing service. Employees' favorable assessment of the work system was positively related to perceived organizational support, which was related to increased service performance as rated by supervisors.

These studies indicate that employees take the opportunity to provide high customer service when they perceive that it provides a way to reciprocate for perceived organizational support. Thus, part of the effect may be due to the obligation to repay the organization for perceived support and the expectation, based on such support, that treating customers well, an important part of their jobs, will be noticed and rewarded. In addition, perceived support's influence on job involvement and work engagement may play a role. Taking one's job more seriously and becoming more engrossed in the work may cause employees to be more careful and thoughtful in dealing with customers.

Negative Consequences of Perceived Organizational Support

We have discussed evidence that perceived organizational support results in attitudinal and affective outcomes that are usually considered favorable for employees. Employees with high perceived organizational support trust the organization, are more satisfied with their jobs and experience less stress, feel a greater emotional commitment to the organizational, and so on. Employees with high perceived organizational support also show behavioral outcomes that are favorable to the organization, including increased inrole performance, greater organizational citizenship behavior, increased creativity and innovation, reduced withdrawal behavior and lessened workplace deviance, among others. This constellation of outcomes is normally beneficial for employees and the organization.

Yet, perceived organizational support does not always have positive consequences. Based on the norm of reciprocity, perceived organizational support produces a felt obligation to help the organization reach its objectives. Perceived organizational support also increases employees' incorporation of their organizational membership and role status into their self-identity, increasing the extent to which they view the organization's outcomes as their own and the desire to aid the organization. These processes can be used by organizations and their representatives to demand unreasonable amounts of work from employees. Employees can be asked to be on call nights, weekends, and vacations, and even made to feel guilty when they take the full vacation time. This is particularly true in the United States. American workers employed a year or more received an average of 9 days of paid vacation, whereas almost every country in Europe has a statutory minimum number of at least 20 paid vacation days (Allegretto, 2005).

The employee's organizational identification and affective organizational commitment, resulting from perceived organizational support, can also cause employees to become complicit with poorly planned, risky, or unethical activities. Employees with high perceived organizational support may feel a conflict between supporting current management in behavior that harms the organization or the general public versus following their own ethical principles. Employees with high perceived organizational support may initially point out what they consider incompetence or malfeasance with the expectation that the organization will be thankful that they are protecting it and will be grateful for their dedication. However, sometimes top management is more concerned with protecting the power structure than the company. Further, unethical behavior may be part of a management strategy that loyal employees are expected to support.

Whistle-blower is a term for an individual who risks his or her career to reveal waste or fraud by an employer. The term is a bit misleading. Most whistle-blowers do not realize they are starting trouble but are simply trying to do a good job. Myron and Penina Glazer (1986) studied 55 whistle-blowers and found that most did not understand that their actions might involve strong retribution, including intimidation, demotion, and firing. One whistle-blower, Demetrios Basdekas, an engineer who worked for the U.S. agency that regulates nuclear power plants, refused to license a plant that he believed was unsafe. His punishment began with isolation:

> I was put in an office with no windows and no heat controls, a building that used to be the FBI storage building. That would be OK if there was no other space available. But right across the hall from me there was a nice office with windows, heat controls, desk, chars, table, the whole works, and it was empty. (Glazer & Glazer, 1986, p. 39)

Basdekas was refused a promotion for 11 years. His fate was actually mild compared with that of most other whistle-blowers, because he was not fired. The attitudinal and affective consequences of perceived organizational support, involving identification and affective commitment, increase the difficulty of continuing to follow one's conscience and fight objective organizational practices once management makes clear to the employee that such actions constitute disloyalty.

Perceived organizational support, without effective ethical guidelines and constraints, can also lead to risky or illegal behaviors by employees motivated to benefit the organization or protect the organization from harm by hiding the organization's poor performance or misdeeds.

Summary and Implications

Perceived organizational support has a variety of positive behavioral outcomes, including inrole and extrarole job performance, reduced withdrawal behavior and workplace deviance, increased creativity, greater safety-related activities, more acceptance of IT, and enhanced customer service. According to organizational support theory, perceived organizational support creates a felt obligation to help the organization achieve its objectives. Perceived organizational support also meets socio-emotional needs, increasing employees' identification with the organization and affective emotional commitment. As a result, employees have an increased tendency to view the organization's outcomes as their own and care more about the organization, both of which should increase organizational involvement. Perceived organizational support also increases the expectations of future aid when it is needed to do one's job more effectively and of reward for greater efforts on the organization's behalf, both of which should increase activities helpful to the organization. Additionally, perceived support may increase performance by enhancing the favorableness of employees' orientation toward their work, including self-efficacy and excitement about the work itself (work engagement). Employees with high perceived organizational support may also wish to aid the organization because of an increased centrality of their organizational role in their self-image and a greater engagement in the work itself.

Evidence linking perceived organizational support to various kinds of employees' positive orientation toward the organization and work was described in Chapter 6, and we previously discussed research relating perceived organizational support to employees' acceptance of the norm of reciprocity. However, additional research is needed showing how these factors affect the relationship between perceived organizational support and various behavioral outcomes. There is evidence, for example, that the reciprocity norm and fulfillment of socioemotional needs play an important role in the relationship of perceived organizational support with inrole and extrarole performance (see Chapter 2), but there is less evidence on the other proposed mechanisms involving performance as an outcome.

One important area for future research concerns the determinants of how employees with high perceived organizational support channel their increased efforts on behalf of the organization. Employees have limited time and energy. Those with high perceived organizational support may increase their organizational involvement in a variety of ways. What determines the direction of their efforts? The organization's culture, goals, and objectives and the employee's work roles may influence specific ways that an employee with high perceived organizational support chooses to make a greater contribution to the organization. For example, for a secretary whose presence or absence contributes greatly to the workflow of others, increased work attendance may be the behavioral change that best aids the organization. For a salesperson working for the same company, the organization's emphasis on expanding the customer base might cause him or her to increase customer contacts in order to be helpful.

Managing for Perceived Organizational Support

8

Perceived organizational support is generally beneficial for organizations, managers, and employees. Employees who feel supported experience greater well-being, are more positively oriented to the organization, and behave in various ways to foster the interests of managers and the organization. The present chapter considers three approaches to enhancing perceived organizational support: (a) managers can engage in supportive behaviors and promote human resources policies that foster perceived organizational support; (b) organizations can train managers to be more supportive; and (c) organization leaders can help create a more supportive organizational culture.

Supportive Managerial Behaviors and Human Resources Policies

Figure 8.1 provides a list of supportive behaviors and human resources policies that managers can use to increase the perceived organizational support of their subordinates. We begin by examining two key overriding principles, described in

FIGURE 8.1

Overarching Principles	• Communicate the voluntary nature of the favorable actions and the involuntary nature of the unfavorable actions. • Display sincerity through consistent speech and actions.
Supportive Treatments	• Treat applicants fairly, respectfully, and courteously. • Maintain open channels of communication. • Communicate the discretionary nature of favorable actions and the involuntary nature of unfavorable actions. • Provide employees with the needed resources to perform their jobs effectively. • Reward achievable high performance generously. • Provide meaningful training and developmental programs that promote personal growth and knowledge, and further career goals. • Provide employees with autonomy in fulfilling their job responsibilities. • Obtain information on and quickly resolve conflicting job responsibilities. • Eliminate continual work overload. • Provide assurance during times of stress. • Provide job security through a stated goal of avoiding layoffs whenever possible. • Promote fairness in the way policies and rewards are administered.

List of supportive managerial behaviors and human resources practices.

Chapter 2, that apply to the various kinds of supportive behaviors to be considered.

OVERARCHING PRINCIPLE: ENGAGE IN DISCRETIONARY HELPFUL BEHAVIOR

When managers provide subordinates with training, coaching, and equipment, and when they design and implement human resources policies, they should do more to be helpful than what is simply required. Treating employees favorably adds little to perceived organizational support when employees believe that the organization is forced to because of such factors as governmental regulations, contractual obligations, or a competitive labor market (Eisenberger et al., 1997). To enhance perceived organizational support, managers should communicate the voluntary nature of their favorable actions and involuntary nature of unfavorable actions and, therefore, the organization's benevolent intent.

For example, both the content of training provided employees and the reasons given for training help determine the extent to which training contributes to perceived organizational support. Employees often view training programs as based on management's self-interest and without benefits for employees. However, when training is framed as a way to increase the capability of employees to make important contributions, and elements are included that contribute to personal development, such training contributes to perceived organizational support. Thus, it is important that employees and managers evaluate training programs to be sure they are worthwhile and include opportunities for personal growth in work-related skills rather than being restricted entirely to narrow work functions.

As Sisodia et al. (2007) noted, many organizations rated by employees as excellent places to work, such as The Container Store, UPS, Caterpillar, and Southwest Airlines, have extensive educational training and mentoring programs that are used to motivate employees and enhance their skills throughout their careers. Increasingly, organizations are introducing corporate "universities" staffed by their own experienced trainers. Such training increases perceived organizational support when it is conducive to personal growth in work related skills.

OVERARCHING PRINCIPLE: DEMONSTRATE SINCERITY THROUGH CONSISTENT SPEECH AND ACTION

When managers give praise, awards, bonuses, and other indications that they find employees' contributions noteworthy, they should follow through with consistent actions. Compliments, awards, and other forms of favorable treatment, when based on the superior performance of employees, are important sources of perceived organizational support. Because such favorable treatment is discretionary, it indicates the organization's high regard for employees. However, the value of such stated positive valuations depends on their perceived sincerity. Telling an employee he or she has a terrific idea raises the expectation that the manager will act on it. Giving repeated high performance evaluations to an employee raises the expectation that there will be favorable consequences for the employee.

Stated positive valuations that are presented to everyone or to a single person regardless of performance degrade their value because employees believe the organization does not care about the employees' performance. Compliments delivered to employees independent of performance come to be ignored. They become meaningless—employees simply stop paying attention to them. Repeated compliments, if not followed by help on the job or substantive rewards, are eventually taken by employees as social conventions rather than meaningful communications. Further, compliments and other rewards, when presented independently of performance, have been found to reduce interest and performance in activities that people find enjoyable (Deci & Ryan, 1985; Eisenberger, Pierce, et al., 1999). For compliments, awards, and other kinds of favorable treatment to increase perceived organizational support, they must be presented in a discriminating manner and followed by meaningful favorable consequences.

Another undesirable outcome of the receipt of stated positive valuations and other rewards, when they are presented independently of performance or for minimal performance, is a sense of entitlement. Employees come to attribute their easy work requirements and the rewards they receive for it as their right, and they become angry when the organization interferes with this right. Consider American postal workers. Their political clout produces a salary high enough that the waiting list of well-qualified applicants is invariably much greater than the number of positions available. As a consultant to a postal facility, I talked with a union official who struggled to retain his composure as he angrily described a supervisor's new practice of periodically observing mail carriers to determine whether individual routes could be enlarged. The union official had justified concerns about an unreasonable speedup. But several mail carriers in the same office said their current routes were short enough to be completed at a leisurely pace. One carrier expressed surprise on the first day of his route when he finished in time to return to the post office before noon rather than at 2:30 in the afternoon as the job "required." His fellow workers were enraged. "Never, never act that way again," they told him. These employees had become accustomed to a low level of performance, for which they continually received pay raises that they considered themselves entitled to. Sincerity means giving reward where reward is due, not independently of performance. Praise and rewards should be based on achievements.

Many savvy companies, such as Southwest Airlines and W. L. Gore and Associates, communicate to employees that they value them and care about their well-being because of their actual contributions to the organization's success. These two companies assign considerable autonomy in decision making to employees, allowing employees to use their skills and ingenuity to solve problems and plan ahead. Employees at Southwest and Gore understand that they are valued conditionally based on their contributions. Honest mistakes are acceptable. However, praise is never indiscriminate. Both companies are careful to compliment and reward performance when deserved, resulting in very high levels of perceived organizational support.

Treat Job Applicants Fairly and Give Them Emotional Support

For most job applicants, the selection process produces considerable anxiety. We found that employees who felt that their job interviewer had treated them fairly and provided emotional support developed an anticipation of future perceived organizational support in the organization (Stinglhamber, Eisenberger, Stewart, et al., 2010). If hired, this perceived support would carry over into organizational life. Although job interviews need to deal realistically with unpleasant as well as favorable aspects of the job, interviewers should promote anticipated perceived organizational support, by setting the applicant at ease by acting in a courteous and friendly manner and directing full attention to what he or she has to say. To display fairness, the applicant should have a full opportunity to discuss his or her strengths and have his or her questions answered.

Maintain Open Channels of Communication

Management's downward communication of useful information that helps employees do their job better contributes to perceived organizational support (M. W. Allen, 1992). Opportunities for upward communication are also important, ranging from individual contacts via e-mail to responses on surveys. Top managers often live in a bubble, cut off from all but a small coterie of advisers who tell them what they want to hear. Obtaining information and opinions from employees can help break through the groupthink engendered in such situations and enhance employees' view that management values their input.

Explain Motivation for Well-Meaning Actions

The motives that employees attribute to management for favorable or unfavorable treatment have a considerable influence on perceived organizational support. Favorable treatment that appears discretionary greatly increases perceived organizational support, and unfavorable treatment that appears discretionary greatly reduces perceived organizational support. When presenting favorable changes in job conditions or human resources benefits, communication of the discretionary nature of the actions and their benefits for employees will enhance perceived organizational support.

Managers often simply assume that employees will understand there is a benevolent intent behind favorable treatment. Not so. For example, for 30 years, I taught at a university where each year I received a letter enumerating the extra money beyond salary the university contributed on my behalf through taxes and various human resources programs, such as health, retirement, and educational plans. Yet, the yearly letters failed to carry the intended punch because there was little in them to indicate what had changed for the better over 30 years or what the university was doing beyond what was required by government regulations or the union contract. After several years, I stopped reading the letters.

The importance for perceived organizational support of explaining well-meaning actions also applies to unfavorable treatment of employees, such as denial of customary pay increases or rejection of a proposed new project. Social accounts involving apologies and explanations for poor treatment have been found quite effective in reducing the blame employees place on the organization (e.g., Bies, 1987; J. Greenberg, 1990). Managers are not always able to fulfill explicit promises or reasonable expectations of subordinates. Left without explanation, such unexpected poor treatment often produces a substantial decrease in perceived organizational support.

Because of findings that social accounts help mitigate blame, they hold great promise for lessening the consequences negative treatment of employees on perceived organizational support. Mitigating accounts should be particularly effective in lessening the drop in perceived organizational support because they assert that the organization was forced to act by sources outside its control. Just as the effects of favorable treatment on perceived organizational support are enhanced by the appearance of the organization's discretion, the loss of perceived organizational support following unfavorable treatment should be lessened by the appearance of a lack of organizational discretion (Eisenberger et al., 1997). For example, managers might accurately identify unusually small pay raises as resulting from the organization's financial difficulties caused by a slowing in sales of a major product line. Employees' perception that the organization was forced by external circumstances to engage in unfavorable treatment should lessen the decrement in perceived organizational support.

In the short run, social accounts can often be effective even when they are untrue and disguise willful mistreatment. Clever managers can construct plausible social accounts that distort reality because employees often have limited access to relevant information concerning management's prerogatives. Moreover, most employees want to believe that they are valued and cared for by the organization. This belief fulfills socioemotional needs and suggests the possibility of better future treatment. Therefore, they would like to accept social accounts as true and reflecting management's positive regard.

However, repeated excuses for unfavorable treatment begin not to be believed, and employees come to feel patronized. In this case, social accounts not only lose their effectiveness but are likely to boomerang as employees come to view managers as thinking so little of them that they believe they can be fooled with repeated lies. If the organization is generally truthful with employees, social accounts will tend to be believed and will cushion perceived organizational support against unfavorable treatment on occasions when it is necessary.

Provide Needed Job-Related Resources

Managers should provide employees with the resources they need to perform their jobs effectively, including information, supplies, and equipment. As we have stressed, discretionary actions count far more than nondiscretionary actions in influencing perceived organizational support. Repeated attention to helping employees do their jobs better, with effective resources, contributes more to perceived organizational support than waiting to supply resources as a matter of necessity after a long period of neglect.

In one research organization with which I am familiar, the employee in charge of fixing broken equipment always responded to requests (except those from department heads) with the words "no way." When employees told him of the urgency of their requests, he showed them a large stack of papers that he told them were requests more urgent than theirs. He bragged to intimates that the stack was filled mostly not with work orders but random papers to make it appear he was busy. He was thus able to spend most of his time lounging in his office, listening to his radio. Employees whose work was hampered by malfunctioning equipment and who complained to management got nowhere because managers got their own requests filled promptly and did not care about their subordinates' problems.

Complaints by employees to the department heads were ignored. After all, the department heads were getting the service they needed. These top managers knew that raising the issue with the errant equipment fixer might result in his firing, which would cause a temporary inconvenience to themselves. Yet, their subordinates took the message to be that the department heads cared nothing about their welfare. This lack of support frustrated and lowered the perceived organizational support of employees who were denied the resources needed to do their jobs effectively.

Reward Achievable High Performance

Rewards in the form of awards and pay increases should be provided for high performance. Expected rewards for high performance have been found to increase employees' interest in their job (Eisenberger, Rhoades, & Cameron, 1999) and perceived organizational support (Eisenberger et al., 1990). Rewards should be based on realistic expectations and provided on a sliding scale to prevent a winner-take-all atmosphere in which only the highest performers are satisfied. Group rewards can be combined with individual rewards to promote cooperation.

Many employees are put off by their own lack of available rewards for high performance and the organization's tolerance for others who fail to do a good job. High pay for poor performers violates many employees' sense of fairness. This lack of differentiation among employees also questions the sincerity of organizations' claims to reward superior performers.

When I began research with organizations, I was surprised by the large number of employees who complained about other employees not pulling their weight. Lazy or incompetent employees often obtain more resources and rewards than they deserve at the expense of effective employees. Equally important, these poor performers increase the workload of the other employees who must pick up the slack. Perceived organizational support does not rest on unconditional favorable treatment of all employees. Employees want coworkers to shoulder their fair share of job responsibilities.

I was once sent a new supervisor for counseling who had been promoted to the position because he was very amiable and a hard worker. He wanted more than anything else to maintain his old friendly relationships with all his subordinates and was unwilling to provide negative feedback to poor performers. Hard-working employees complained to him that they had to take up the responsibilities of lazy employees. The hard workers blamed the company for providing a supervisor who was unable to establish performance standards. The supervisor insisted that everything would work out if everyone "just got along." Rather than change his ways, he chose to go back to his old job. He was replaced by another individual as supervisor who was careful to insist on, and reward, equitable efforts by all employees.

Generous rewards for achievable high performance increase perceived organizational support. On the other hand, some organizations place unrealistic demands for reward on employees, leading to increased stress and lower perceived organizational support. Telesales employees often are expected to make a handful of sales a day because it is difficult to convince prospective customers on first contact to purchase a new product. At many companies, the incentives are sufficient for only a minority of these salespeople to earn enough to afford to remain at their jobs. Here, the necessity of unrealistically high performance leads to low self-efficacy and low perceived organizational support.

Rewards should be based on reasonable expectations concerning what employees can achieve with their present skills or with additional training that the organization provides. Opportunities for reward need to be sufficiently broad to prevent a winner-take-all atmosphere in which only a limited number of highly qualified employees believe they have a chance to succeed and continue to try, with the remainder giving up. This can be achieved by scaling rewards to the degree of achievement and providing a combination of individual and group awards. For example, in the credit card division of Bank of America in Wilmington, Delaware, employees may be rewarded for exceeding their personal sales records during bonus periods while their workgroup is entered in a competition with other workgroups for group awards.

Provide Developmental Opportunities

Meaningful training and educational programs that promote personal growth and knowledge should be provided. Veteran workers in most organizations are offered fewer developmental training courses than newer workers, despite the veterans' appreciation of such opportunities and consequent strengthening of perceived organizational support (Armstrong-Stassen & Ursel, 2009). Also, programs of mentoring and career guidance help establish that the organization cares enough about employees to be concerned with their future. However, such programs will be effective only to the extent that mentors are competent and show genuine interest in the welfare of their advisees. This suggests that mentoring should be established as a prestigious activity and assigned only to individuals who are both knowledgeable in their fields and possess good interpersonal skills.

As previously discussed, training programs that communicate the organization's belief in the employees' important contributions to its welfare should be distinguished from narrowly based training that simply instructs employees on routine aspects of their job or involves bureaucratic requirements having little value. Too often, corporate training involves poorly designed attempts to ward off legal liabilities or reduce the workload of administrators. For example, I and other researchers at my former university were required to take a federally mandated course on ethics in human research. The uninformed instructors went through the motions, indicating they cared neither for the issues nor us. To consume the scheduled course time, the instructors even went into detail on the definition of a human being. Another required training course involved how to keep credit card records, forcing researchers to sit through information that only administrators needed to know. The university communicated the message through its training it thought so little of its researchers that it was willing to waste their time with meaningless course materials. Here was the perfect opportunity taken by management to use discretionary action to lower perceived organizational support.

Deciding what developmental training opportunities will be good for participants should take into account the career goals of individual employees. Some excellent employees are perfectly satisfied with their current job responsibilities and resent patronizing attempts to help them "improve themselves." I had a secretary who begged me to leave her alone after I tried to enrich her job by taking her to various meetings to understand the functioning of the department. Rather than have a conversation with her about what she wanted out of her job, I had incorrectly and arrogantly assumed she would welcome this additional education to more fully understand the role of her job and as a possible step to advancement. The key is to offer, rather than require, optional training and developmental experiences that move employees to greater skills.

Employees with a high need for achievement or desire for career advancement will be more likely to take advantage of such opportunities. Developmental training, especially if linked to opportunities for greater job responsibilities, will be understood as an indication that employees are important to the organization, leading to greater perceived organizational support.

Provide Autonomy for Individuals and Workgroups

Giving employees leeway in how to carry out their jobs, including scheduling, work procedures, and task variety, conveys the organization's trust in the employees' judgment and abilities, and allows employees to explore new ways to carry out their jobs more effectively. Autonomy may also allow a reduction in the layers of bureaucratic oversight produced when employees' activities are micromanaged. Autonomy conveys confidence in employees' abilities and judgment and thereby increases perceived organizational support.

Large bureaucratic structures often inhibit employee autonomy and the flexibility to get work done in the most effective manner. Moreover, individualized attention may suffer in large organizations, reducing attention to individual needs and talents. Therefore, it might be supposed that organizational size is negatively related to perceived organizational support. However, as described in Chapter 3, a quantitative review of research studies (Kurtessis et al., 2009) revealed only a small negative relationship between organizational size and perceived organizational support. Informal employee reports suggest that organizational inflexibility and an entrenched, uncooperative bureaucracy do detract from perceived organizational support but that these factors are little related to organizational size.

Supportive organizations, even large organizations, find ways to deal effectively with these potential problems. As explained in Chapter 4, Gore, the manufacturer of breathable clothing fibers, keeps its individual facilities small to prevent overbearing and unnecessary layers of bureaucracy. With the goals of flexibility and innovation, Gore also engages in careful planning to provide streamlined management, a high level of autonomy for workgroups, and good lines of communication and cooperation across factories. We previously noted the high level of perceived organizational support at Gore. As shown by Gore, reducing bureaucracy and increasing autonomy can play important roles in increasing perceived organizational support.

Reduce Role Conflict and Work Overload

As discussed in Chapter 3, role conflict and work overload lead to stress and show moderate negative relationships with perceived organizational support. Role conflict has a stronger negative association than work overload with perceived organizational support, perhaps because many employees believe the nature of their work, rather than decisions of the organization, are primarily responsible for high workloads. Some employees may also suspect that economic constraints or competitive pressures prevent the organization from hiring the additional personnel that would allow lower workloads. In contrast, conflicting work responsibilities are viewed as more voluntary and remediable than work overload and, therefore, as an indication of organizational support.

To foster perceived organizational support, employees need to be able to let managers know about conflicts in job responsibilities and to have the conflicts quickly resolved. Instead, managers often ignore the job conflict because the solution often involves the trouble of careful planning or splitting the job in two and assigning a second employee to take the second job. My wife, Joanne, taught schoolchildren who had learning disabilities for 40 years in various settings and loved helping them develop their academic skills and become more self-confident. Recognized for her careful preparation and streetwise ability to implement education theory in a practical way, Joanne wrote two well-received books for educators on teaching children with learning disabilities and served as a peer coach for other teachers. Yet, she finally met a situation she could not handle. To save money, the school district assigned Joanne a class of children with learning disabilities and, at the same time, an administrative job involving management of the individualized learning plans for all children in the district with emotional problems. Each job was to be done half-time, but the administrative job actually required her full attention if she was to carry it out properly. Focusing on teaching was incompatible with doing a good job as an administrator. When Joanne pointed out these difficulties, higher level administrators dithered, continuing to respond with small measures designed to try to placate her without addressing the major role conflict.

Joanne could have simply reduced her efforts and done a lackadaisical work, but this would have violated her strong sense of professionalism and love of teaching. This was one of the richest school districts in the state, yet the administrators complained that the school district was too financially strapped to work out a solution that might involve hiring additional personnel. Joanne's perceived organizational support dropped precipitously. She walked into the administrative office one day and said she was going to quit at the end of the academic term. "You mean retire?" they asked. "No, quit," she responded. A picture of a smoothly functioning school district was important to the administrators, and they paid Joanne a substantial bonus to "retire" rather than "quit." The school had lost a good administrator and teacher because of the inflexibility of its administrators and was forced to deal with the new problem of hiring additional qualified personnel. The managers' insensitivity to role conflict cost them more trouble than if they had dealt with it in a timely way.

Role conflict is often a sign of disorganization in which an employee has multiple supervisors who assign tasks that are incompatible or a single supervisor who assigns tasks without thinking through their implications. In Joanne's case, administrators failed to consider the fact that they were really dealing with two distinct jobs that could not be simultaneously handled well. Then, when the facts were laid out before them, it seemed easier to let Joanne suffer than to try to find a solution to the problem. Perceived organizational support is enhanced when managers take the time to go over work tasks with employees before making important changes in assigned responsibilities to make sure no role conflict is involved.

We have discussed the use of work overload by companies like Wal-Mart that count on low-skilled, low-wage employment and tolerate high turnover by disgruntled employees. This approach has limited applicability. Wal-Mart is remarkably effective in procuring goods at low prices, especially from China, and tracking its goods from supplier to customer. It became successful as the prime mover of this well-executed strategy. However, work overload is not a cost-effective strategy in organizations that rely on employee loyalty and creativity or high service quality. Upscale competitor Costco, which provides much better customer service and treatment of employees, has higher sales and profits per square foot of store space than Wal-Mart.

Excess work is sometimes required to get projects done, and employees with high perceived organizational support see the need for the extra effort and frequently take on the extra load without being asked. However, repeated overload often represents poor planning and a lack of concern for employees' welfare. When surges in work reoccur, managers would do well to ask themselves how careful planning would reduce their occurrence. By reducing role conflict and overload, employers signal their positive valuation of employees, increase perceived organizational support, and enhance employees' satisfaction and motivation.

Provide Assurance During Times of Stress

Managers can help employees faced with stressful work situations by providing assurance in such forms as empathy for the employee's difficulties, confidence in the employee's abilities, and offers of aid as needed. The sincerity principle is important here. Employees will soon learn that concern for the employees' welfare is meaningless if not followed by action or that statements about the employees' abilities are obvious exaggerations. By keeping perceived organizational support high, employees will respond more effectively to stressors. Thus, Wallace et al. (2009) found that employees with high perceived organizational support worked harder than those with low perceived organizational support when faced with such work hindrance stressors as politics, role ambiguity, red tape, job security, and a stalled career. And they worked especially hard at high levels of stressors that could be construed as positive challenges, such as the number of projects, time at work, volume of work, time pressures, and amount and scope of responsibility.

Provide Job Security

Organizations can increase perceived organizational support by establishing a stated goal in their mission statements of avoiding layoffs and making this known to employees. Employees can be told that there are no guarantees but because the organization values its employees highly, it will try to avoid layoffs based on economic reasons whenever possible.

Feelings of job insecurity are widespread among employees. Fear of losing one's job seems to have greater detrimental effects on employees' psychological well-being than in the past because of the increased risks now associated with unemployment. With a loss of one's job may come medical costs that have ballooned in recent years and are a leading cause of bankruptcy. Defined retirement benefit plans have been largely eliminated, and many more employees now need to remain employed until an older age than before. Personal debt has ballooned and individuals have fewer resources to fall back on. Downsizings, mergers, and bankruptcies, resulting in layoffs, receive more attention than ever before by business-oriented news media thereby increasing employees' apprehension about being laid off.

Not only are employees more concerned than in the past over job security, but they also believe the organization has substantial control over offering job security to its workforce. Four fifths of a diverse sample of employees that I and colleagues studied (Eisenberger et al., 1997) believed that their organization had high or medium control over retaining or laying off employees. Therefore, perceived organizational support is substantially related to job security (Rhoades & Eisenberger, 2002). It is true that the implicit guarantees of lifetime job security in most large U.S. organizations have disappeared and are beginning to fray in Western Europe and Japan. But it is also the case that employees have a strong belief in implicit job security at most employee-supportive organizations. At companies such as Southwest Airlines or Google, employees know that because their contributions are valued and the organization cares about their welfare, top management will not institute a downsizing unless required by dire economic difficulties. Such employee-supportive organizations generally manage their growth wisely and attempt to retain employees in times of economic distress by finding ways to cut costs without eliminating employees.

Promote Fairness in Evaluation, Compensation, and Promotion

Fairness in the way policies are followed and fairness in the outcomes of those policies are strongly related to perceived organizational support. Fair procedures are more strongly associated with perceived organizational support in mechanistic organizations that emphasize formal procedures and rules, as opposed to more fluid, organic organizations (Ambrose & Schminke, 2003). This makes sense because procedures and rules are more salient and important for employees' work experiences in mechanistic organizations.

As previously noted, a quantitative review of the research findings indicates that perceived fairness of pay of employees at various levels in the organizational hierarchy is highly related to perceived organizational support, whereas the absolute level of pay shows little relationship to perceived organizational support (Kurtessis et al., 2009). Thus, what counts for perceived organizational support is not how much pay a person receives per se but the amount of pay relative to the person's inputs (qualifications, efforts, and accomplishments) and the pay received by others within and outside the organization.

Managers should reward achievement rather than simply loyalty. This is sometimes more easily said than done, especially in those organizations in which organizational politics is prevalent. Perceived organizational politics, involving the pursuit of personal gain at the expense of the organization's welfare and the fair treatment of others, is a strong enemy of perceived organizational support. Perceived organizational politics is particularly strong when employees view high-level managers, who should serve as exemplars, as the ones getting ahead and rewarding subordinates for loyalty at the expense of others who have done a good job (Byrne et al., 2005; Hochwarter et al., 2003). Top managers need to set a standard of good conduct in this regard by creating the reality and appearance of fairness in their treatment of subordinates. Outstanding employees should be rewarded regardless of whose protégés they may be. Managers should avoid surrounding themselves with individuals who hesitate to give them a realistic picture of the organization. Creative input for organizational change should be encouraged and rewarded from all sources. Admittedly, this is a difficult ideal to achieve. But many successful companies that value human capital, such as the ones discussed in this book, have gone a long way in rewarding achievement rather than loyalty.

Train Leaders to Promote Perceived Organizational Support

Studies are needed to establish procedures for training managers to promote perceived organizational support. A substantial research literature, discussed in Chapter 4, indicates that perceived organizational support is increased when employees believe they are supported by their supervisors and have positive relationships with the supervisors. Because employees view supervisors as representatives of the organization, favorable treatment received from them promotes perceived organizational support. Therefore, training supervisors to be more supportive in their roles of directing, evaluating, and coaching employees will contribute to perceived organizational support.

A step in this direction is suggested by research on training that fosters organizational justice, a major antecedent of perceived organizational support. Because organizational justice leads to perceived organizational support, procedures effective in enhancing perceived fairness of organizations should also contribute to perceived organizational support. The following discussion draws heavily from a valuable book chapter by Daniel Skarlicki and Gary Latham (2005), who described lessons they learned from a small number of studies, most of them unpublished, on training leaders to treat subordinates more fairly. Skarlicki and Latham were the researchers in most of the studies and had firsthand knowledge about opportunities and perils in training managers to behave in ways that promote subordinates' beliefs that they are being treated fairly by the organization. The positive relationship between perceived fairness, involving the application of procedures and rules and their outcomes, and perceived organizational support was discussed in Chapter 3. We now describe and adapt the principles presented by Skarlicki and Latham for training leaders to foster perceived organizational support.

CARRY OUT A NEEDS ANALYSIS

A needs analysis should establish the kinds of support that managers should be providing. Strategies for implementing such support should also be considered. An *organizational analysis* offers input concerning how perceived organizational support fits in with the goals of the organization. How will the organizational culture and power centers adapt to the training? If enhancing perceived organizational support is solely a goal of the human resources department or group of midlevel managers who lack substantial support of upper management in the project, substantial spade work will have to be done to bring others on board in order to give the project a chance of success. A *person analysis* identifies the kinds of organizational representatives who will be trained. Should the training, for example, be confined to first-line supervisors or should higher level managers be included?

If first-line supervisors themselves are not feeling supported, this raises the issue of whether they will be enthusiastic about providing increased support to their subordinates. Supervisors' perceived organizational support has been found to influence the extent to which their subordinates feel supported by them, leading to an increase in perceived organizational support (Shanock & Eisenberger, 2006). In the case of low perceived support on the part of supervisors, higher level managers may need to be included in the training to enhance the perceived organizational support of the first-line supervisors.

A *task analysis* identifies the behaviors essential for the leader to meet the goals for training. Structured interviews and surveys, including data previously gathered by the organization, should be used to establish the kinds of support that are most important for managers to provide. A funnel technique might be used, starting with general questions so that important areas will not be omitted from consideration. Then specifics can be addressed. One might find, for example, that nurses in a hospital indicate that job stress and burnout are highly important issues for them and that perceived organizational support is being hindered by a lack of respect from doctors and administrators, lack of communication by supervisors and upper managers concerning upcoming changes in procedures and policies, and failure to obtain needed supplies in a timely manner. An understanding of factors influencing perceived organizational support will allow the identification of behaviors that managers can be taught to reduce these problems and lessen the likelihood of similar problems in the future.

The task analysis should also examine the kinds of outcomes that should be considered to evaluate the training program's success. In the example of the nurses, perceived organizational support might be assessed through questionnaires before and after training. Patient satisfaction scores, medical outcomes, and voluntary employee turnover might also be obtained.

USE OPTIMAL TRAINING PRINCIPLES

Skarlicki and Latham (2005) recommended that training programs incorporate active participation, distributed practice, presentation of materials in a meaningful way, and knowledge of results. Trainees need to be able to practice behaviors leading to perceived organizational support in a risk-free environment. Participants can be provided with basic principles of organizational support theory, embodied in specific steps relevant to the current job setting, and can carry out role-playing exercises. In the hospital example, supervisor trainees would be armed with lessons in the etiology of perceived organizational support, methods of active listening, and techniques for displaying socioemotional support to subordinates. Then they might take part in role-playing exercises in which they enact management situations described by nurses as problematic.

Skarlicki and Latham (2005) noted considerable data from experimental psychology that distributed practice of lessons usually produces greater learning than continuous practice. These authors recommended that in addition to providing trainees feedback from trainers and other trainees during training sessions, trainees be given homework assignments to try out on the job so that they can receive naturalistic feedback. The authors recommended that the training be made meaningful by introductory statements framing the training as an opportunity. We suggest that trainers provide examples from other highly successful organizations, as well as the present organization, concerning outcomes of enhancing the organizational support of subordinates. Managers should be shown how it is in their personal best interest as well as the organization's to enhance perceived organizational support by the recommended procedures.

PROMOTE TRANSFER OF TRAINING

For training in perceived organizational support to be effective, trainees need to apply what they have learned in training to their regular job settings. Skarlicki and Latham (2005) suggested that five training principles make important contributions to transfer of training: expectancies of desirable outcomes, self-efficacy, similarity between training and the job situation, realistic examples, and relapse preventions.

Skarlicki and Latham (2005) argued that trainees need to understand the relationship between their actions and desirable outcomes (*expectancies of desirable outcomes*). As previously noted, success stories from within and outside the organization can help illustrate the effectiveness of variables important for enhancing perceived organizational support. Stress should also be placed on the value of perceived organizational support for outcomes important for attendees and favored by the larger organization. For example, the supervisor's annual evaluation might be changed to incorporate support for subordinates as assessed by their own managers and subordinates.

Confidence in one's ability to successfully employ the skills taught in training (*self-efficacy*) will contribute to transfer. The most effective method of increasing self-efficacy is *enactive mastery* (Bandura, 1986), involving a series of small steps in which employees see themselves getting progressively better. Enactive mastery can be accomplished in role-playing and homework assignments. *Vicarious experience*, in which trainees model important skills, is also useful.

Similarity between training and the job should be enhanced to promote transfer. Information obtained from the needs analysis can be used to make issues examined in the training situation as relevant as possible to the job context. Issues that have the greatest potential for increasing perceived organizational support in the organization being studied are prime candidates for use. But training should go beyond rote learning to the teaching of general principles. Trainees should be taught enough concerning organizational support theory (e.g., organizational discretion and sincerity) to be able to promote perceived organizational support as new issues arise.

Transfer can also be promoted by the using varied and realistic examples. Varied examples gleaned through the needs analysis can strengthen learning.

WORK TO PREVENT RELAPSE

A major problem with newly learned behaviors that depend on motivation is their maintenance following the end of training. This difficulty is exacerbated when the new behavior requires considerable effort and attention and the payoff is long-term. In their own research, Skarlicki and Latham (2005) used the establishment of a support group and a refresher session after the training program was completed to maintain trained behaviors. To be still more effective, we recommend, as described earlier, that performance of the new skills be incorporated into attendees' evaluations.

CARRY OUT A TRAINING EVALUATION

Using training at a single facility, with before-and-after measures, creates the classic problem that many variables besides training may be responsible for a change in subordinates' perceived organizational support. Because random assignment of participants to the training group and control group is often impractical or has deleterious side effects, a quasi-experimental design can be used in which half the facilities or units within a facility receive training. The remaining facilities or units, matched with the experimental facilities on relevant variables, serve as the control group. Ideally, there would be a control group that receives a diluted form of the training that lacks the specialized elements thought to enhance perceived organizational support and a second control group that receives no training at all but is simply assessed on the same key measures as the other groups. Because a controlled demonstration of perceived organizational support training would be a new and important advance in the research literature, a single-control group of either type would be very welcome.

Skarlicki and Latham (2005) suggested evaluating the effectiveness of the training with three types of measures. *Reaction* measures are especially useful for determining the need for midcourse corrections in training. *Learning* measures assess participants' knowledge of the principles and information conveyed in training. *Behavioral* measures assess changes in the behavior of the trainees. For example, the trained group and a control condition that receives minimal or no training could be compared before and after the training program, inrole and extrarole performance, absenteeism, and objective measures of organizational success.

Cultural Organizational Support

SAS is the largest privately held developer of statistical software, with annual revenues of $800 million and 5,000 employees. In a typical year, some 25,000 people apply for less than 200 jobs. Voluntary turnover is a miniscule 2% annually. The North Carolina company's culture strongly promotes the valuation of contributions and concern for the welfare of all employees. According to the cofounder and CEO Jim Goodnight, "My chief assets drive out the gate each day. My job is to make sure they come back" ("SAS ranks No. 1," 2010; D. A. Kaplan, 2010; Stellard, 2010). Employees find it easy to identify with CEO Jim Goodnight, who spends some of his time writing code like many of his employees. Employees who in most companies would be paid on the basis of the number of hours worked are salaried, which lessens uncertainties of income. Benefits are generous, equivalent to about 40% of employees' pay. Work schedules are flexible, and there are no limitations on annual sick leave. The company avoided layoffs during the recent financial meltdown both to demonstrate loyalty to employees and maintain a pool of talented employees. Direct communication with management is facilitated through one-on-one conversations and small group meetings. Ninety-eight percent of employees responded favorably to a combined index of the organization's credibility, respect for employees, fairness, pride in employees' accomplishments and the organization's products, and camaraderie.

We refer to organizationwide positive valuation of employees' contributions and concern for their welfare as *cultural organizational support*. We have discussed supportive treatment by workgroups, departments, organizational hierarchies, and social networks. Still more widespread strengthening of perceived organizational support occurs when the underlying values of the organization promote a favorable valuation of employees' contributions and regard for their well-being. Often spurred by founders' intuitive understanding of the importance of nurturing human capital, cultural organizational support can markedly increase the breadth of perceived organizational support in the organization.

Organizational culture refers to shared values and ideologies and resulting norms concerning appropriate behavior as held by employees at all levels in the organizational hierarchy. Schein (1990, as cited by Casper, Weltman, & Kwesiga, 2007, p. 480) characterized organizational culture as

> a pattern of basic assumptions, invented, discovered, or developed by a given group, as it learns to cope with its problems of external adaptation and internal integration, that has worked well enough to be perceived as valid and, therefore, is taught to new members as the correct way to perceive, think, and feel in relation to those problems. (p. 111)

Many organizations we have discussed, such as SAS, Southwest Airlines, Costco, Google, Smucker's, and Gore, have cultures that view employees as constituting important human capital, and this positive valuation promotes perceived organizational support. For example, Southwest Airlines views the effective performance of its workforce as essential to its success and recognizes and encourages both skill development and dedication through such policies as developmental training experiences, job autonomy, and implicit guarantees against arbitrary layoffs.

Wegmans markets provides another example of cultural organizational support, as Sisodia, Wolfe, and Sheth (2007) discussed in their book *Firms of Endearment.* Wegmans sees its workforce as a strong asset and hence provides extensive training. Department managers are sent on trips to learn firsthand about products. The company promotes primarily from among current employees. As at Southwest Airlines, workers are given considerable latitude to work out problems with customers without consulting managers.

Wegmans' recognition that employees make an important contribution is combined with an interest in employees' welfare. Wegmans provides above-average wages, affordable health insurance, and a generous retirement plan. These benefits have resulted in higher than average labor costs of 15% to 17% of sales. But this supportive culture has strongly benefited Wegmans. Employees rate Wegmans highly in surveys of the best place to work, and they show it in their loyalty and enthusiasm. The turnover rate for full-time employees is 6% in an industry with an average turnover rate that exceeds 100%. Well-trained, knowledgeable, satisfied, and motivated employees treat customers well, thereby increasing customer satisfaction. This dedicated workforce contributes to sales per square foot that are 50% higher than the average for the industry.

To take one more example, consider Gore, the manufacturer of synthetic waterproof fibers. After a probationary period, employees are viewed as making a primary contribution to the organization's success. Formal job titles and rank mean little—useful contributions by all employees are held in the highest regard. When I asked to survey a sample of Gore employees concerning perceived organizational support, I was told by a manager, "Okay, but I know that our employees will score extremely high. It's a pointless exercise."

I initially thought this answer smug. In the first place, although Gore has an excellent reputation for supportive treatment of employees, the individual talking to me might have been one of those managers who simply lacks empathy and therefore fails to understand the true beliefs of his employees. Second, I knew that Gore's unusual practice of telling new employees to find a way to fit in their workgroups, giving them little direction, followed later by stringent evaluation by coworkers, created initial distress among many new employees. Did the survivors of this stringent screening process really feel so highly supported by the company?

Yet, the manager was correct. Gore's positive treatment of employees following probation, including training to increase personal strengths and opportunities for creative contributions, resulted in higher scores on perceived organizational support than any of the dozens of organizations I had examined at that time. The culture of positive valuation of employees and a concern with their welfare had strongly enhanced the employees' perceived organizational support.

Organizations differ in the value of the resources they are willing to invest in their employees (Tsui et al., 1997). To the extent that employees are viewed as human capital, making important contributions to the organization's success, top managers will be more likely to provide developmental training opportunities and other resources that develop the potential of employees. In a study of 10 companies, Tsui et al. (1997) found that employees performed better on central tasks, showed higher citizenship behavior, and expressed greater affective organizational commitment in firms that promoted heavy investment of resources in employees. Results were similar for extrarole behavior, whether the companies encouraged strong involvement by employees or not; however, supervisors reported they perceived employees were less likely to quit when employee involvement was encouraged. Supportive culture should enhance the kinds of investment strategies reported by Tsui et al., with widespread effects on employees' perceived organizational support.

Supportive culture is especially effective in transmitting perceived organizational support to employees because it reinforces the message of positive valuation through a variety of policies and procedures and individual actions carried out by many organizational members. When organizational actions are guided by a positive valuation of employees, the cumulative effect is substantial and noticeable to the great majority of employees. We have discussed how employees personify the organization to meet socioemotional needs and to assess the value of increased efforts on the organization's behalf. In supportive organizational cultures, most employees' personification of the organization involves the attribution of benevolence toward employees and appreciation of their contributions.

Supportive organizational cultures contribute to perceived organizational support partly through objectives that make use of employee skills and through human resource practices that amply reward employee contributions and enhance employee welfare. Interpersonal contact plays an important role in conveying support. Employees are encouraged to provide each other with socioemotional support and resources that aid others. We previously described such support as *multiplier effects* (see Chapter 4) because when one employee supports another, the recipient is likely to help several others. Thus, supervisors' perceived organizational support increased perceived supervisor support and performance among subordinates (Shanock & Eisenberger, 2006). Favorable treatment received from coworkers with whom employees had socioemotional and instrumental ties increased perceived organizational support (Hayton et al., 2009), probably because coworkers are identified with the organization to some degree. Therefore, favorable treatment from coworkers was interpreted as favorable treatment received from the organization. These effects suggest how interpersonal contact spreads perceived organizational support widely in supportive organizational cultures.

Perceived organizational support is spread both by favorable treatment received from others and by the sharing of opinions by employees who believe the culture is supportive. Employees who exchange advice in the organization's social networks convince others of the organization's support and thereby spread perceived organizational support. This is indicated by similar levels of perceived organizational support among employees who regularly share advice with each other (Zagenczyk, Scott, Gibney, Murrell, & Thatcher, 2010). Because of favorable organizational procedures and policies, supportive interactions with a variety of organization members and the favorable opinions of others concerning organizational support, supportive organizational culture promotes perceived organizational support throughout the organization.

Supportive organizational cultures often provide pleasant working conditions and generous fringe benefits. Many organizations that evaluate and reward employees on the basis of their accomplishments also offer a baseline of favorable treatment for all. As at Google, these benefits may include subsidized child care, meals, exercise rooms, transportation, and generous retirement plans. At first glance, such across-the-board generous treatment seems to contradict our argument that rewards presented independently of performance, such as pay or praise, lessen employees' view that the organization is sincere about its interest in high performance.

However, although some resources are best linked to individual and group performance, others like the ones we mentioned above are best provided freely because they contribute to the entire group's cohesion and sense of identification with the organization. A supportive organizational culture in which employees are treated benevolently as a group and are also held accountable and rewarded for good performance fosters perceived organizational support. Within Google's overall group identity by employees, differentiation based on quality of performance provides the recognition needed to motivate employees.

One drawback of generous, noncontingent benefit packages is that employees may begin to take them for granted and as a matter of entitlement rather than seeing them as the result of the organization's part of its exchange relationship with employees. To the extent that employees take benefits for granted, the benefits no longer lead to felt obligation and affective commitment to the organization. This entitlement reaction becomes somewhat muted when employees are reminded in literature and talks that they are treated in a special way because the organization respects them and expects much of them.

Distinction Between Cultural Organizational Support and Perceived Organizational Support

Cultural organizational support should be distinguished from perceived organizational support. Perceived organizational support concerns perceptions of one's own support by the organization. It is a belief of the individual employee. Cultural organizational support refers to the organization's valuation of employees' welfare and well-being generally. Cultural organizational support differs from perceived organizational support in several major ways:

- Cultural organizational support refers to a general positive valuation of employees whereas perceived organizational support refers to the inference by a single employee concerning his or her own support.
- As an aspect of organizational culture, cultural organizational support is durable. In companies with established high cultural organizational support, founders who strongly valued organizational support have propagated it with like-minded top managers, management practices, and organizational structures that are consistent with their vision. In contrast, perceived organizational support is an individualized belief that is no longer present when the individual leaves the organization.
- Cultural organizational support involves a widespread emphasis on how employees should be valued as opposed to perceived organizational support, which involves a belief concerning one's current valuation.
- Perceived organizational support involves the employee's global belief concerning the extent to which the organization values his or her contributions and cares about his or her well-being. Cultural organizational support typically involves positive valuation of employees' contributions and their welfare; however, one of these elements is sometimes present without the other.

The human capital view of employees (see Chapter 1) generally involves an appreciation of employees' contributions and an understanding that promoting employees' welfare is in the company's best interest. The marginal capital view generally promotes the disparagement of employees' contributions and lessens concern for their welfare. However, contrary to this typical dichotomy, some organizations value employees' contributions but care little about their well-being. For example, many high-prestige organizations are able to hire talented graduating students from exclusive universities and give them important work while demanding exorbitant work hours or offering little pay. Well-known teaching hospitals often obtain freshly minted physicians for internships but, owing to the medical profession's hierarchical culture and tradition of mistreating newcomers, give them excessive work hours and case loads, resulting in great stress and inadequate treatment for patients. Other organizations care about employees' well-being but place little value on their contributions. This latter situation involves the patronizing view by some firms that although employees may not have much contribution to make, the organizations are morally or legally required to take good care of them. This outlook is common in nations of the European Union, where laws dictate longer vacations than in the U.S. and make firing employees more difficult, and where labor-management cooperation remains a more sustained tradition than in the United States.

In employees' eyes, a positive valuation of one's contributions is inseparable from how much the organization cares about one's well-being. An instance of treatment indicating either high caring or high appreciation of the employee's contributions will increase perceived organizational support. An instance of treatment indicating either low caring or low appreciation of the employee's contributions will reduce perceived organizational support. Organizations are not so uniformly consistent in combining valuations of contributions with caring about welfare. An example of an organization that values employees' contributions but not their welfare is the U.S. Federal Aviation Administration's orientation toward air traffic controllers. The importance of the job for preventing plane crashes is recognized by the agency, and the controllers are well trained. However, the controllers are given antiquated computer systems to keep track of flights in an overburdened transportation system. The constant vigilance necessary to prevent collisions results in burnout among most controllers. The controllers typically quit to take less well paying jobs after less than 10 years on the job because of the high stress.

Some supportive organizational cultures value employees' contributions and care about employees' welfare but take a restrictive ingroup–outgroup view of human capital, viewing a limited set of employees as possessing the talents and skills that will move the organization forward, while relegating the remaining employees to temporary or part-time relationships (Shore, Porter, & Zahra, 2004) or simply providing them with fewer opportunities than the ingroup. Differential treatment of employees, depending on their contributions, is reasonable to a degree. And organizations may wish to outsource functions that they are not particularly good at. Yet, treating some employees as though they are incapable of making useful contributions is a self-fulfilling prophesy that damages an organization's prospects. All employees can contribute to the organization's success through diligent and thoughtful performance; all can harm the organization's prospects through lazy and thoughtless actions.

Part-time and temporary employees respond positively to discretionary favorable treatment with perceived organizational support, just as full-time, long-term employees do (Gakovic & Tetrick, 2003; see Chapter 3). Temporary employees who want to find a full-time job with the organization may be more likely to be motivated than those just there for seasonal employment. However, they also have socioemotional needs that they wish to have fulfilled, and they respond positively to favorable discretionary treatment and negatively to unfavorable treatment.

Organizations that take a negative view of groups of employees do themselves a disservice. Some lower level employees will rise through the ranks if given the opportunity. Others will make notable contributions at their own level. An annual increase in the profitability of several percent a year due to providing widespread support is a nice counterweight against the colossal errors sometimes made by superstars.

Positive valuation of employee contributions and concern for welfare at all levels of the organizational hierarchy produces a dedicated, high-morale workplace, as has been shown in such companies as Gore, Google, and Wegmans. Systematic research has only just begun to examine organizational support of employees as a cultural value. Mauseth (2008) reported a positive relationship between the strength of clan culture and perceived organizational support. On the basis of Cameron and Freeman's (1991) typology, *clan culture* is characterized by the dominant attributes of cohesiveness, participation, teamwork, and sense of family; by a leadership style involving mentoring, facilitation, and a parent figure; by bonding involving loyalty, tradition, and interpersonal cohesion; and by strategic direction involving development of human resources, commitment, and morale. Although we define *supportive organizational culture* more narrowly as involving a positive valuation of employees' contributions and well-being, Mauseth's results suggest that supportive organizational culture enhances perceived organizational support.

As previously noted in Chapter 4, founders of a number of highly successful companies we have discussed, such as Costco, Southwest Airlines, Google, and Gore, demonstrated an intuitive understanding of the importance of supportive organizational culture. They selected top executives who favored supportive values and who helped spread them through policies and objectives. In contrast, many organizations see less value in recognizing and developing human capital because they are dominated by a short-term profit mentality or put their faith predominantly in a specialized strategy (e.g., developing technology, promoting low cost) without recognizing the important contribution that rank-and-file employees can make to the organization's success. Changing from a culture that values employees only marginally to an employee-supportive culture is likely to be sparked only by an organizational crisis or a change in top management.

Perceived Organizational Support—Today and in the Future

9

The extensive research we have reviewed suggests the value of considering employees' relationship with their work organization from the employees' viewpoint. Employees' general perception concerning their valuation and caring by the organization is important to them. Perceived organizational support affects employees' well-being, the positivity of their orientation toward the organization, and behavioral outcomes favorable toward the organization. Organizational support theory organizes and explains the major findings concerning perceived organizational support and spurs new areas of research. We begin this final chapter by summarizing organizational support theory and what has been learned concerning perceived support from the accumulated large number of research studies. Then we consider some useful new directions for research and conclude by examining the choice that organizations must make between treating employees supportively and treating them as if they have little value.

What Is Known About Perceived Organizational Support

Organizational support theory holds that employees personify the organization, thinking of it as a powerful individual with a benevolent or malevolent orientation toward them. To meet socioemotional needs (e.g., approval, esteem, affiliation, emotional support) and assess the value of greater efforts on the organization's behalf, employees form a general perception concerning the degree to which the organization values their contributions and cares about their well-being. Because most employees accept the norm of reciprocity as applied to work, perceived support increases their felt obligation to help the organization achieve its objectives. Additionally, by meeting socioemotional needs, perceived organizational support contributes to employees' incorporation of their membership status and work roles into their social identity.

Favorable discretionary acts by the organization, that is, actions that appear voluntary as opposed to being forced by external circumstances (e.g., governmental regulations, contractual obligations, competitive job market), are taken by employees as strong indicators of perceived organizational support. Highly discretionary actions by the organization were found to have a 6 times greater influence on perceived organizational support than actions over which the organization was perceived to have little choice (Eisenberger et al., 1997). Thus, communicating the voluntary nature of favorable discretionary acts and the involuntary nature of unfavorable actions should contribute considerably to perceived organizational support. Sincerity of positive valuations also has an important influence on perceived organizational support: Compliments and positive evaluations must be discriminating and followed up by supplying implied resources so employees will believe they are appriciated.

We discussed the diverse positive consequences of perceived organizational support for employees' subjective well-being (see Chapter 5): Employees who feel supported are happier at work, more satisfied with their jobs, believe they make more important contributions to the organization's success, feel less stressed, and find that their work interferes less with their home life. Perceived organizational support leads to a positive orientation toward the organization (see Chapter 6): Employees who feel supported are more emotionally committed, more trusting, and less cynical. They identify more with their organization. They find their jobs more central to their identity and are more engaged and intrinsically interested in the work itself. Employees who feel supported by their organization are more helpful to the organization (see Chapter 7): They perform better in standard job responsibilities and engage more in other job activities that aid the organization reach its objectives. Supported employees take part in fewer withdrawal behaviors such as tardiness, absenteeism, or turnover. They carry out fewer violations of organizational norms, ranging from the discourtesy in treating others to work slowdowns. They are more creative and respond more favorably to organizational initiatives such as safety programs and new technology, and they treat customers with more consideration.

As discussed in Chapter 3, work experiences have considerable influence on perceived organizational support. Prior to the beginning of employment, future employees begin to anticipate low or high support from information received from such sources as organizational representatives, media, and friends. After employment begins, the fairness of procedures and outcomes provided to employees has a strong relationship with perceived organizational support. In contrast, employees' observation of self-centered political behavior by managers that is harmful to the organization and others' careers has a devastating effect on perceived organizational support. Perceived organizational support is also positively related to such antecedents as rewards and favorable job conditions, effective communication channels from and to managers, organizational support for values held by employees, and support for specific objectives favored by employees.

Employees form general perceptions concerning their valuation from such deliverers of support as supervisors, workgroups, local facilities, departments, and divisions (see Chapter 4). Perceived support has been found to generalize from organizational representatives to the organization as a whole. One important influence on such generalization is *organizational embodiment*, the extent to which employees identify the supervisor with the organization. In some cases, as in loose conglomerates, an embedded unit in the organization may be more meaningful to employees than the more encompassing nominal organizational entity. The researcher's decision to focus on a particular organizational unit in terms of perceived support depends on what is meaningful for employees and the purposes of the analysis. Organizational support is contagious: Supervisors who experience perceived organizational support treat their subordinates more favorably (Hayton et al., 2009; Shanock & Eisenberger, 2006). Also, support spreads across social networks within the organization. Favorable treatment has been found effective in increasing perceived organizational support for employees both in traditional work roles and in nonstandard roles, including part-timers, contracted employees, and those on overseas assignments.

Organizational support theory has recently been extended to consider its relationship with psychological contract theory (Chapter 3), to individuals other than employees, and to organizations with unique characteristics (Chapter 4). First, Coyle-Shapiro and Conway (2005) found that current incentives rather than fulfillment of past promises were responsible for the relationship between the psychological contract and perceived organizational support. The possible limits of this important finding warrant investigation. Second, perceived organizational support provided to military personnel was found to operate similarly in many respects to civilian organizations. Military recruitment, performance, and retention are difficult practical issues for voluntary armed forces when civilian jobs are plentiful. The militaries of many nations have strong cultures. The extent to which perceived organizational support is part of those cultures and contributes to their acceptance may vary trans-nationally is an important topic for future research. Third, a well-developed research area extends organizational support theory to employees' affective commitment to their employee union (Shore et al., 1994; Tetrick et al., 2007). Yet to be investigated is the nature of what activities union members believe are discretionary and should therefore strongly influence perceived union support. Fourth, customers were found to form general perceptions concerning the extent to which a given organization that provided services or products cared about their satisfaction and valued them as customers (Shanock & Eisenberger, 2009). Such perceived provider support operated in much the same way as perceived organizational support, being dependent on the perceived favorableness of discretionary treatment and working through felt obligation and affective commitment to enhance loyalty behavior. Fifth, volunteer members of an organization with high perceived organizational support were found to take greater pride in their membership, leading to greater affective organizational commitment (Boezeman & Ellemers, 2007, 2008).

Cultures of organizational support (Chapter 8), such as those found at Southwest Airlines, Costco, Google, W. L. Gore and Associates and Wegmans, consider most employees to be valued human capital who provide important contributions to the organization's success. In such cultures, the positive valuation of employees becomes incorporated into policies and procedures and helps guide the actions of organizational agents at all levels of the organizational hierarchy. As a result, employees develop a high level of perceived organizational support. The most common source of cultures of organizational support is the vision, power, and organizing ability of successful founders who put in place successors and managers who share their vision. Changes to such a supportive culture from one that places modest value on employees' contributions are typical of conditions promoting major cultural shift, usually occurring only when the organization experiences a shock that initiates a new top management team with a mandate for change.

Managers who work within a supportive culture are provided generous resources to cultivate the human capital of subordinates, such as developmental training opportunities and technical support. But all managers, regardless of the culture in which they work, can enhance the perceived support of subordinates by providing more favorable work experiences (see Stinglhamber & Vandenberghe, 2004). Employees place great emphasis on whether favorable treatment is discretionary and whether positive valuations are sincere (see Chapter 2). The supervisor's provision of favorable discretionary treatment and sincere positive valuation goes a long way to increase perceived organizational support. With these principles in mind, a variety of favorable work experiences, discussed in Chapter 3, can be used to cultivate perceived organizational support and thereby increase employees' productivity. Training techniques to provide managers with the encouragement and skills to enhance subordinates' perceived organizational support were presented in Chapter 8.

New Research Directions

Throughout this book we have discussed new research directions to extend knowledge of perceived organizational support. We highlight some of these areas plus additional ones we think are particularly likely to advance the understanding of the influence of perceived organizational support in organizations.

CAUSAL RELATIONSHIPS

More studies are needed to assess the direction of perceived organizational support's relationship with other variables of interest. For example, we have good evidence that perceived organizational support leads to affective organizational commitment because when employees were assessed on both measures at two points in time, perceived organizational support was found to be associated with a change in affective organizational commitment (Rhoades et al., 2001). By contrast, in most studies the relationship between perceived organizational support and other variables has been established on the basis of a single simultaneous measurement. Thus, the direction of the relationship between perceived organizational support and the second variable is assigned solely on the basis of theory.

This paucity of research using repeated measures is a general problem in the study of employee behavior. It is time consuming and difficult to get organizations to agree to survey their employees on multiple occasions, and often scientific journals do not see the value of giving page space to studies whose main focus involves providing evidence concerning causality. Yet, such studies are exactly what are needed to build a solid foundation of knowledge.

ORGANIZATIONAL SINCERITY

We have suggested how employees view the expression of positive valuation by an organizational representative depends partly on perceived sincerity. Indiscriminate praise given to most employees, regardless of performance, and encouragement for a particular undertaking without subsequent provision of implied tangible support, are examples of insincerity that should lessen perceived organizational support. This principle makes sense on the basis of organizational support theory and what is known about the decremental effects of noncontingent approval on attention (Eisenberger et al., 1974). More empirical evidence is needed on the effects of employee perceptions of sincerity on perceived organizational support.

MATERIAL EXPECTATIONS

Perceived organizational support provides for the immediate fulfillment of socioemotional needs. Believing that the organization values one's contribution and cares about one's well-being makes one feel esteemed, accepted, integrated into a significant social structure, and in the case of stressful situations, provides empathy and consolation. Perceived support is also valued as an indication of reward for high effort and the availability of needed resources for carrying out one's job well. Only a small amount of research has been carried out relating perceived support to reward expectancies (Eisenberger et al., 1990). Beyond a single item on the Survey of Perceived Organizational Support ("The organization is willing to extend itself in order to help me perform my job to the best of my ability"), the responses to which correlated highly with other items, we are aware of no research concerning the basic assumption of organizational support theory that perceived organizational support increases employees' expectation of future aid. Such expectations concerning aid deserve more research attention.

ANTICIPATED PERCEIVED ORGANIZATIONAL SUPPORT

We discussed evidence that information about employment benefits influenced prospective employees' anticipation of perceived organizational support (Casper & Buffardi, 2004). Further, fairness of treatment and supportive treatment during the job selection process were also positively related to prospective employees' anticipated perceived organizational support (Stinglhamber, Eisenberger, Stewart, et al., 2010). These initial findings raise the issue of how perceived organizational support anticipated prior to employment influences employees' successful adjustment to the organization. For example, encouraged by the promise of supportive treatment, do employees with high anticipated perceived organizational support work harder in the belief that their efforts will be attended to and rewarded? With the anticipation of support, do they engage in more active information seeking concerning their organizational roles?

COMMUNICATIONS

We have noted evidence that management's communication of high-quality job information and comments reflecting various kinds of organizational support contribute to perceived organizational support (M. W. Allen, 1992, 1995). A related untapped area of communications research concerns social accounts, which deal with apologies and explanations for unfavorable treatment in interpersonal relationships (Bies, 1987; Sitkin & Bies, 1993). In Chapter 3, we reviewed evidence that social accounts have been found to lessen aversive reactions by employees to managers whom they believe have mistreated them. Social accounts may mitigate the impact of instances of aversive treatment of employees by placing the mistreatment in a larger context of caring and concern for the employees. Thus, one would expect that social accounts would lessen the loss of perceived organizational support when organizations find it necessary to treat employees unfavorably on occasion. Although social accounts apply to aversive treatment, employees' interpretation of favorable treatment should also be influenced by accounts that managers may provide for them. When favorable treatment is left unexplained, employees in some cases may attribute it to a by-product of a policy that was not intended to help them (e.g., the provision of new information technology, which may be seen as based on a desire by management to help itself) or as an action forced on the organization (e.g., an enhancement of medical insurance benefits, which may be seen as complying with new government regulations). When the context of favorable treatment does not make the organization's discretion clear, added explanation should be especially effective. Research on how explanations for both unfavorable and favorable treatment provided by the organization affect perceived organizational would be valuable.

SELF-EFFICACY

Bandura's (1986) concept of *self-efficacy* refers to confidence in being able to carry out an activity using current skills. Self-efficacy theory strongly emphases a belief in one's own capabilities as a prerequisite for behavioral change. Bandura (1986) and Gist and Mitchell (1992) maintained that the nature of the task and external feedback influence self-efficacy. How much effort the individual has to expend, the task's difficulty, and the amount of help required are examples of the information individuals use to determine self-efficacy (Bandura, 1986, pp. 401–402). Self-efficacy theory has had remarkable success in suggesting ways to overcome behavioral deficiencies involving various activities, including phobias, academic achievement, and sports performance. Bandura argued that self-efficacy has a number of positive influences on subjective well-being owing to such factors as increased intrinsic interest in a previously failed activity and lessened stress and despondency. The theory's application to understanding employee well-being has considerable potential.

Bandura (1986) argued that self-efficacy is most predictive of specific domains of activities rather than broad aspects of behavior. However, researchers have found it useful to assess employees' self-efficacy with respect to their broad aspects of job performance. As previously noted, Erdwins, Buffardi, Casper, and O'Brien (2001) found that perceived organizational support was positively related to self-efficacy, which in turn was negatively related to reduced interference of work with home life.

One omission in self-efficacy theory concerns how individuals decide on their competence when criteria for competence are vague. In many jobs, employees are heavily dependent on the social determination of success for defining competence. Consider the car salesperson's task of selling a car. The salesperson's success involving a particular transaction involving the sale of a new car consists of a complex function involving the selling price of the car, the price paid for any trade-in, the cost to the dealer of the car, the declining value of the car with age, the size of unsold inventory of similar models on the lot, any service contract that the customer is induced to buy, and so on. Self-efficacy is influenced by the relative weights the sales manager places on these different factors. To the extent that these differential values are not carefully communicated to the car salesperson, perceived organizational support fills the gap by indicating positive valuation of his or her performance over a sustained period of time. The greater the ambiguity concerning what constitutes competent performance, the more we would expect perceived organizational support to contribute to self-efficacy by conveying that the organization views the employee's contribution as valuable.

GOAL SETTING

Goal setting theory (Locke & Latham, 2002) emphasizes the importance of clear, established goals for motivating and sustaining performance. Hutchison and Garstka (1996) reported that the opportunity to participate in the formulation of work objectives during performance appraisals was positively related to employees' perceived organizational support. From the viewpoint of goal setting theory, of even greater interest is the possible contribution of perceived organizational support to employees' commitment to assigned organizational goals and employees' self-selection of difficult goals. These effects would be expected for several reasons. First, perceived organizational support leads to a felt obligation to help the organization reach its objectives and an affective commitment to the organization, both of which should enhance employees' desire to accomplish more for the organization. Second, perceived organizational support communicates that greater resources are available when needed from the organization to help the employee to reach a goal, increasing its ease of attainment. Third, by conveying the organization's positive valuation of the employee's contributions, perceived organizational support may increase self-efficacy, which goal setting theory assumes is an antecedent of the selection of high personal goals.

MULTIPLIER EFFECTS

Recent findings suggest that recipients of organizational support treat others more supportively. Supervisors who feel highly supported by the organization have subordinates who report that those supervisors treat them supportively. The subordinates, in turn, show increased perceived organizational support and performance (Erdogan & Enders, 2007; Shanock & Eisenberger, 2006). Thus, support provided to managers trickles down the organizational hierarchy (see also Masterson, 2001); in effect, the organization's favorable treatment of managers is multiplied through the managers' favorable treatment of subordinates.

Another transmission of organizational support occurs in the organization's social networks. Perceived organizational support increases with the number of relationships the employee has in the network that are useful or provide friendship and emotional support (Hayton et al., 2009; Zagenczyk, Scott, Gibney, Murrell, & Thatcher, 2010). The mechanisms underlying such contagion of support should be investigated because the findings are of substantial theoretical and practical significance. Supervisors and, more generally, members of organizations' social networks who receive support may treat others more supportively because (a) they observe others modeling support as an appropriate behavior and (b) treating others supportively may be a way to reciprocate one's own supportive treatment.

RISK TAKING

As discussed in Chapter 6, Rousseau et al. (1998, p. 395) defined *trust* as a psychological state involving a willingness to accept vulnerability on the basis of the expectation of the benevolent intentions of the other individual. Perceived organizational support incorporates employees' beliefs about the organization's benevolent intentions but only implies the second half of this definition of trust, which involves a willingness to put oneself at risk. Risk taking concerns actions that may yield high returns but whose outcomes are uncertain (Chiles & McMackin, 1996; Wiseman & Gomez-Mejia, 1998). Employee risk taking may include accepting tasks that pose difficult problems or involve taking unconventional public positions. The excessive risk taking that contributed to the recent worldwide economic crisis notwithstanding, informed risk taking is an essential element in business innovation. When asked by managers to help the organization by accepting a task with a limited likelihood of success or when expressing an unpopular view may help the organization, employees with high perceived organizational support may be more likely to engage in high-risk behaviors for the benefit of the organization with the expectation that the organization will appreciate and reward such dedication.

ORGANIZATION-LEVEL DIFFERENCES IN SUPPORT

Most studies of perceived organizational support consider the employee as an individual. However, variations in supportiveness occur from one workgroup to another, in part because some supervisors are more supportive than others (Erdogan & Enders, 2007; Shanock & Eisenberger, 2006), and from one organization to another. We have discussed how the supportive cultures of such organizations as Google, Costco, Southwest Airlines, Wegmans, Smucker's, and Gore enhance perceived organizational support while the devaluing cultures of such companies as Wal-Mart and U.S. Airways lessen perceived organizational support. In a study of 10 organizations, Tsui et al. (1997; see Chapter 8) found that those companies emphasizing human capital had employees who performed better on central tasks, showed higher citizenship behavior, and expressed greater affective organizational commitment. Further, Mauseth (2008) found that clan culture was positively related to perceived organizational support. These promising findings call for more systematic study of the relationships of supportive culture, strategies, and objectives of entire organizations with perceived organizational support.

ORGANIZATIONAL INTERVENTIONS

Founders of organizations have an excellent opportunity to build management teams and establish policies that promote supportive cultures. High-level managers can influence the perceived support of many employees through supportive policies and objectives that emphasize human capital. Supervisors can enhance the support of subordinates in the course of fulfilling their responsibilities to evaluate, direct, train, and coach subordinates. Research is needed on practical ways to implement supportive treatments. The processes described by organizational support theory that influence the strength of the relationship between favorable work experiences and perceived organizational support (e.g., organizational discretion, sincerity, organizational embodiment) can be taught to supervisors to increase their skills in promoting perceived organizational support.

The Choice for Organizations

Organizations and individual managers face a choice between treating employees as human capital or marginal capital. Favorable discretionary treatment may be used to increase perceived organizational support, with positive outcomes for employees' subjective well-being, positive orientation toward the organization, and behavioral outcomes that benefit the organization. Alternatively, organizations and managers may view the majority of employees as marginal capital, capable of making a minimal contribution to the organization's success. These alternative approaches have a major impact on employees' lives. Employees with high perceived organizational support are happier than those at other companies. They work harder and smarter, and they provide better service to customers. In contrast, employees who work at organizations that view them as marginal capital are less happy, more stressed, and more likely to leave for other jobs.

As we previously noted, the companies included in *FORTUNE*'s list of the 100 best U.S. companies for which to work, reflecting supportive treatment of employees, produced much greater long-term returns to shareholders than the average returns of the broad stock indexes ("Great workplaces," 2010). Why then do only a minority of organizations pursue human capital policies that result in high perceived organizational support? Part of the reason is the reward structure for CEOs and managers. In the United States, top managers are generally rewarded with stock options and bonuses for short-term gains, which are often produced at a cost to the long-term health of the company. Career-oriented managers in many organizations understand that the path to promotion or upward moves to other organizations depends on short-term success, defined in terms of cash flow and profit. These goals, in turn, stem from top management's desire to raise stock prices as quickly as possible. When managers are rewarded only for meeting short-term goals, they often find it beneficial for their careers and financial status to cut back on the resources necessary for promoting human capital, including support of subordinates. This tyranny of the stock market has been resisted by organization founders, investors, and managers who have a long-term view of success.

So this really is the choice: Do what looks best for the next quarterly report or act to promote the long-term well-being of employees and the organization. It will be interesting to see which organizations and their managers have the foresight and courage to look to the future and treat their employees supportively.

References

Abraham, R. (2000). Organizational cynicism: Bases and consequences. *Genetic, Social, and General Psychology Monographs, 126,* 269–292.

Albrecht, S., & Travaglione, A. (2003). Trust in public-sector senior management. *International Journal of Human Resource Management, 14,* 76–92. doi:10.1080/09585190210158529

Allegretto, S. A. (2005, August 24). *U.S. workers enjoy far fewer vacation days than Europeans.* Economic Policy Institute. Retrieved from http://www.epi.org/economic_snapshots/entry/webfeatures_snapshots_20050824

Allen, D. G., Shore, L. M., & Griffeth, R. W. (1999). *A model of perceived organizational support.* Unpublished manuscript, University of Memphis, Memphis, TN, and Georgia State University, Atlanta.

Allen, D. G., Shore, L. M., & Griffeth, R. W. (2003). The role of perceived organizational support and supportive human resource practices in the turnover process. *Journal of Management, 29,* 99–118. doi:10.1177/014920630302900107

Allen, M. W. (1992). Communication and organizational commitment: Perceived organizational support as a mediating factor. *Communication Quarterly, 40,* 357–367.

Allen, M. W. (1995). Communication concepts related to perceived organizational support. *Western Journal of Communication, 59,* 326–346.

Allen, T. D. (2001). Family-supportive work environments: The role of organizational perceptions. *Journal of Vocational Behavior, 58,* 414–435. doi:10.1006/jvbe.2000.1774

Allen, T. D., Herst, D. E. L., Bruck, C. S., & Sutton, M. (2000). Consequences associated with work-to-family conflict: A review and agenda for future research. *Journal of Occupational Health Psychology, 5,* 278–308. doi:10.1037/1076-8998.5.2.278

Amabile, T. M. (1983). Brilliant but cruel: Perceptions of negative evaluators. *Journal of Experimental Social Psychology, 19,* 146–156. doi:10.1016/0022-1031(83)90034-3

Ambrose, M. L., & Schminke, M. (2003). Organization structure as a moderator of the relationship between procedural justice, interactional justice, perceived organizational support, and supervisory trust. *Journal of Applied Psychology, 88,* 295–305. doi:10.1037/0021-9010.88.2.295

Anderson, E. W., Fornell, C., & Lehmann, D. R. (1994). Customer satisfaction, market share, and profitability: Findings from Sweden. *Journal of Marketing, 58,* 53–66. doi:10.2307/1252310

Andersson, L. (1996). Employee cynicism: An examination using a contract violation framework. *Human Relations, 49,* 1395–1418. doi:10.1177/001872679604901102

Andersson, L., & Bateman, T. (1997). Cynicism in the workplace: Some causes and effects. *Journal of Organizational Behavior, 18,* 449–469. doi:10.1002/(SICI)1099-1379(199709)18:5<449::AID-JOB808>3.0.CO;2-O

Aquino, K., & Griffeth, R. W. (1999). *An exploration of the antecedents and consequences of perceived organizational support: A longitudinal study.* Unpublished manuscript, University of Delaware, Newark, and Georgia State University, Atlanta.

Aristotle. (1941). *The basic works of Aristotle* (R. McKeon, Trans.). New York, NY: Random House.

Armeli, S., Eisenberger, R., Fasolo, P., & Lynch, P. (1998). Perceived organizational support and police performance: The moderating influence of socioemotional needs. *Journal of Applied Psychology, 83,* 288–297. doi:10.1037/0021-9010.83.2.288

Armstrong-Stassen, M. (1997). The effect of repeated management downsizing and surplus designation on remaining managers: An exploratory study. *Anxiety, Stress, and Coping, 10,* 377–384. doi:10.1080/10615809708249310

Armstrong-Stassen, M., Cameron, S. J., Mantler, J., & Horsburgh, M. E. (2001). The impact of hospital amalgamation on the job attitudes of nurses. *Canadian Journal of Administrative Sciences–Revue Canadienne Des Sciences De L'Administration, 18,* 149–162.

Armstrong-Stassen, M., & Ursel, N. D. (2009). Perceived organizational support, career satisfaction, and the retention of older workers. *Journal of Occupational and Organizational Psychology, 82,* 201–220. doi:10.1348/096317908X288838

Arnett, D. B., German, S. D., & Hunt, S. D. (2003). The identity salience model of relationship marketing success: The case of nonprofit marketing. *Journal of Marketing, 67,* 89–105. doi:10.1509/jmkg.67.2.89.18614

Aronson, E., & Lindner, D. (1965). Gain and loss of esteem as determinants of interpersonal attractiveness. *Journal of Experimental Social Psychology, 1,* 156–171. doi:10.1016/0022-1031(65)90043-0

Aryee, S. (1994). Job involvement: An analysis of its determinants among male and female teachers. *Canadian Journal of Administrative Sciences-Revue Canadienne Des Sciences De L'Administration, 11,* 320–330.

Aselage, J., & Eisenberger, R. (2003). Perceived organizational support and psychological contracts: A theoretical integration. *Journal of Organizational Behavior, 24,* 491–509. doi:10.1002/job.211

Ashforth, B. E., & Mael, F. A. (1989). Social identity theory and the organization. *Academy of Management Review, 14,* 20–39. doi:10.2307/258189

Auletta, K. (2009). *Googled: The end of the world as we know it.* New York, NY: Penguin Press.

Avolio, B. J., Bass, B. M., & Jung, D. (1999). Reexamining the components of transformational and transactional leadership using the Multifactor Leadership Questionnaire. *Journal of Occupational and Organizational Psychology, 7,* 441–462.

Aycan, Z. (1997). Acculturation of expatriate managers: A process model of adjustment and performance. In Z. Aycan (Ed.), *Expatriate management: Theory and research* (pp. 1–40). Greenwich, CT: JAI Press.

Bakker, A. B., Schaufeli, W. B., Leiter, M. P., & Taris, T. W. (2008). Work engagement: An emerging concept in occupational health psychology. *Work and Stress, 22,* 187–200. doi:10.1080/02678370802393649

Bandura, A. (1986). *Social foundations of thought and action: A social cognitive theory.* Englewood Cliffs, NJ: Prentice Hall.

Bandura, A., Adams, N., & Beyer, J. (1977). Cognitive processes mediating behavioral change. *Journal of Personality and Social Psychology, 35,* 125–139. doi:10.1037/0022-3514.35.3.125

Bass, B. M. (1985). Leadership: Good, better, best. *Organizational Dynamics, 13,* 26–40. doi:10.1016/0090-2616(85)90028-2

Becker, H. S. (1960). Notes on the concept of commitment. *The American Journal of Psychology, 66,* 32–40.

Becker, T. E. (1992). Foci and bases of commitment: Are they distinctions worth making? *Academy of Management Journal, 35,* 232–244. doi:10.2307/256481

Becker, T. E. (2009). Interpersonal commitments. In H. J. Klein, T. E. Becker, & J. P. Meyer (Eds.), *Commitment in organizations: Accumulated wisdom and new directions* (pp. 137–178). New York, NY: Routledge/Taylor & Francis.

Becker, T. E., & Kernan, M. C. (2003). Matching commitment to supervisors and organizations to in-role and extra-role performance. *Human Performance, 16,* 327–348. doi:10.1207/S15327043HUP1604_1

Bedeian, A. (2007). Even if the tower is "ivory," it isn't white: Understanding the consequences of faculty cynicism. *Academy of Management Learning & Education, 6,* 9–32.

Behson, S. J. (2002). Which dominates? The relative importance of work–family organizational support and general organizational context on employee outcomes. *Journal of Vocational Behavior, 61,* 53–72.

Bell, S. J., & Menguc, B. (2002). The employee–organization relationship, organizational citizenship behaviors, and superior service quality. *Journal of Retailing, 78,* 131–146. doi:10.1016/S0022-4359(02)00069-6

Bennett, R. J., & Robinson, S. L. (2000). Development of a measure of workplace deviance. *Journal of Applied Psychology, 85,* 349–360. doi:10.1037/0021-9010.85.3.349

Bennett, R. J., & Robinson, S. L. (2003). The past, present, and future of workplace deviance research. In J. Greenberg (Ed.), *Organizational behavior: The state of the science* (2nd ed., pp. 247–281). Mahwah, NJ: Erlbaum.

Berkowitz, L., & Friedman, P. (1967). Some social class differences in helping behavior. *Journal of Personality and Social Psychology, 5,* 217–225. doi:10.1037/h0024198

Berscheid, E., Brothen, T., & Graziano, W. (1976). Gain–loss theory and the "law of infidelity": Mr. Doting versus the admiring stranger. *Journal of Personality and Social Psychology, 33,* 709–718. doi:10.1037/0022-3514.33.6.709

Bhanthumnavin, D. (2003). Perceived social support from supervisor and group members' psychological and situational characteristics as predictors of subordinate performance in Thai work units. *Human Resource Development Quarterly, 14,* 79–97. doi:10.1002/hrdq.1051

Bies, R. J. (1987). The predicament of injustice: The management of moral outrage. *Research in Organizational Behavior, 9,* 289–319.

Bies, R. J., & Moag, J. S. (1986). Interactional justice: Communication criteria of fairness. In R. J. Lewicki, B. H. Sheppard, & M. H. Bazerman (Eds.), *Research on negotiation in organizations* (pp. 43–55). Greenwich, CT: JAI Press.

Bies, R. J., & Shapiro, D. L. (1987). Interactional fairness judgments: The influence of causal accounts. *Social Justice Research, 1,* 199–218. doi:10.1007/BF01048016

Bies, R. J., Shapiro, D. L., & Cummings, L. L. (1988). Causal accounts and managing organizational conflict: Is it enough to say it's not my fault? *Communication Research, 15,* 381–399. doi:10.1177/0093650 88015004003

Black, J. S., & Stephens, G. K. (1989). The influence of the spouse on American expatriate adjustment and intent to stay in Pacific Rim overseas assignments. *Journal of Management, 15,* 529–544. doi:10.1177/014920638901500403

Blau, G. (1985). The measurement and prediction of career commitment. *Journal of Occupational Psychology, 58,* 277–288.

Blau, G. (1995). Influence of group lateness on individual lateness: A cross-level examination. *Academy of Management Journal, 38,* 1483–1496. doi:10.2307/256867

Blau, P. M. (1964). *Exchange and power in social life.* New York, NY: Wiley.

Boezeman, E. J., & Ellemers, N. (2007). Volunteering for charity: Pride, respect, and the commitment of volunteers. *Journal of Applied Psychology, 92,* 771–785. doi:10.1037/0021-9010.92.3.771

Boezeman, E. J., & Ellemers, N. (2008). Pride and respect in volunteers' organizational commitment. *European Journal of Social Psychology, 38,* 159–172. doi:10.1002/ejsp.415

Bok, D. (2004). *Universities in the marketplace: The commercialization of higher education.* Princeton, NJ: Princeton University Press.

Boorstin, J. (2004). 1 J. M. Smucker. *Fortune, 149,* 58–59.

Bradley, B. L. (1997). *The relationships between perceived organizational support, institutional orientation and affective, continuance, and normative commitment in the Canadian military* (Unpublished doctoral dissertation). University of Calgary, Alberta, Canada.

Brinberg, D., & Castell, P. (1982). A resource exchange approach to interpersonal attractions: A test of Foa's theory. *Journal of Personality and Social Psychology, 43,* 260–269. doi:10.1037/0022-3514.43.2.260

Brockner, J., Dewitt, R. L., Grover, S., & Reed, T. (1990). When it is especially important to explain why: Factors affecting the relationship between managers explanations of a layoff and survivors' reactions to the layoff. *Journal of Experimental Social Psychology, 26,* 389–407. doi:10.1016/0022-1031(90)90065-T

Brough, P., O'Driscoll, M. P., & Kalliath, T. J. (2005). The ability of "family-friendly" organizational resources to predict work–family conflict and job and family satisfaction. *Stress and Health, 21,* 223–234. doi:10.1002/smi.1059

Buchanan, B. (1974). Building organizational commitment: The socialization of managers in work organizations. *Administrative Science Quarterly, 19,* 533–546. doi:10.2307/2391809

Buchanan, B. (1975). To walk an extra mile. *Organizational Dynamics, 3,* 67–80. doi:10.1016/0090-2616(75)90041-8

Buffardi, L. C. (2007). Perceived organizational support and work family issues. In R. Eisenberger (Chair), *Perceived organizational support: Future directions.* Panel discussion conducted at the Annual Meeting of the Society of Industrial and Organizational Psychology, New York, NY.

Buffardi, L. C., Ford, M. T., Kurtessis, J. N., & Stewart, K. A. (2009). New perspectives on perceived organizational support: Meta-analytic update of antecedents. In Z. Byrne & R. Eisenberger (Co-chairs), *Perceived organizational support: New directions.* Symposium conducted at the meeting of the Society of Industrial and Organizational Psychology, New Orleans, LA.

Buffardi, L. C., Smith, J. L., O'Brien, A. S., & Erdwins, C. J. (1999). The impact of dependent-care responsibility and gender on work attitudes. *Journal of Occupational Health Psychology, 4,* 356–367. doi:10.1037/1076-8998.4.4.356

Burgoon, J. K., & Lepoire, B. A. (1993). Effects of communication expectancies, actual communication, and expectancy disconfirmation on evaluations of communicators and their communication behavior. *Human Communication Research, 20,* 67–96. doi:10.1111/j.1468-2958.1993.tb00316.x

Burgoon, J. K., Lepoire, B. A., & Rosenthal, R. (1995). Effects of preinteraction expectancies and target communication on perceiver reciprocity and compensation in dyadic interaction. *Journal of Experimental Social Psychology, 31,* 287–321. doi:10.1006/jesp.1995.1014

Buss, A. H. (1983). Social rewards and personality. *Journal of Personality and Social Psychology, 44,* 553–563. doi:10.1037/0022-3514.44.3.553

Buttle, F., & Burton, J. (2002). Does service failure influence customer loyalty? *Journal of Consumer Behaviour, 1,* 217–227. doi:10.1002/cb.67

Butts, M. M., Vandenberg, R. J., DeJoy, D. A., Schaffer, B. S., & Wilson, M. G. (2009). Individual reactions to high-involvement work processes: Investigating the role of empowerment and perceived organizational support. *Journal of Occupational Health Psychology, 14,* 122–136. doi:10.1037/a0014114

Byrne, Z. S., & Cropanzano, R. (2001). History of organizational justice: The founders speak. In R. Cropanzano (Ed.), *Justice in the workplace: From theory to practice* (Vol. 2, pp. 3–26). Mahwah, NJ: Erlbaum.

Byrne, Z. S., & Hochwarter, W. A. (2008). Perceived organizational support and performance: Relationships across levels of organizational cynicism. *Journal of Managerial Psychology, 23,* 54–72. doi:10.1108/02683940810849666

Byrne, Z. S., Kacmar, C., Stoner, J., & Hochwarter, W. A. (2005). The relationship between perceptions of politics and depressed mood at work: Unique moderators across three levels. *Journal of Occupational Health Psychology, 10,* 330–343. doi:10.1037/1076-8998.10.4.330

Byron, K. (2005). A meta-analytic review of work–family conflict and its antecedents. *Journal of Vocational Behavior, 67,* 169–198. doi:10.1016/j.jvb.2004.08.009

Caceres, R. C., & Paparoidamis, N. G. (2007). Service quality, relationship satisfaction, trust, commitment, and business-to-business loyalty. *European Journal of Marketing, 41,* 836–867. doi:10.1108/03090560710752429

Caligiuri, P. M., & Lazarova, M. (2001). Strategic repatriation policies to enhance global leadership development. In M. E. Mendenhall, T. M. Kèuhlmann, & G. K. Stahl (Eds.), *Developing global business leaders: Poli-*

cies, processes, and innovations (pp. 243–256). Westport, CT: Quorum Books.

Cairns, R. B. (1970). Meaning and attention as determinants of social reinforcer effectiveness. *Child Development, 41,* 1067–1082.

Camerman, J., Cropanzano, R., & Vandenberghe, C. (2007). The benefits of justice for temporary workers. *Group & Organization Management, 32,* 176–207. doi:10.1177/1059601102287112

Cameron, K., & Freeman, S. (1991). Culture, congruence, strength, and type: Relationship to effectiveness. *Research in Organizational Change and Development, 5,* 23–58.

Capon, J., Chernyshenko, O. S., & Stark, S. (2007). Applicability of civilian retention theory in the New Zealand military. *New Zealand Journal of Psychology, 36,* 50–56.

Carrier, C. (1998). Employee creativity and suggestion programs: An empirical study. *Creativity and Innovation Management, 7,* 62–72. doi: 10.1111/1467-8691.00090

Cascio, W. F. (1993). Downsizing: What do we know? What have we learned? *Academy of Management Executive, 7,* 95–104.

Casper, W. J., & Buffardi, L. C. (2004). Work–life benefits and job pursuit intentions: The role of anticipated organizational support. *Journal of Vocational Behavior, 65,* 391–410. doi:10.1016/j.jvb.2003.09.003

Casper, W. J., Weltman, D., & Kwesiga, E. (2007). Beyond family-friendly: The construct and measurement of singles-friendly work culture. *Journal of Vocational Behavior, 70,* 478–501. doi:10.1016/j.jvb.2007.01.001

Cavanaugh, M. A., Boswell, W. R., Roehling, M. V., & Boudreau, J. W. (2000). An empirical examination of self-reported work stress among US managers. *Journal of Applied Psychology, 85,* 65–74. doi:10.1037/0021-9010.85.1.65

Chau, P. Y. K. (1996). An empirical assessment of a modified technology acceptance model. *Journal of Management Information Systems, 13,* 185–204.

Chen, Z., Eisenberger, R., Johnson, K. M., Sucharski, I. L., & Aselage, J. (2009). Perceived organizational support and extra-role performance: Which leads to which? *The Journal of Social Psychology, 149,* 119–124. doi:10.3200/SOCP.149.1.119-124

Chen, Z. X., Aryee, S., & Lee, C. (2005). Test of a mediation model of perceived organizational support. *Journal of Vocational Behavior, 66,* 457–470. doi:10.1016/j.jvb.2004.01.001

Chiles, T. H., & McMackin, J. F. (1996). Integrating variable risk preferences, trust, and transaction cost economics. *Academy of Management Review, 21,* 73–99. doi:10.2307/258630

Chow, H. S., Lo, W. C., Sha, Z., & Hong, J. (2006). The impact of developmental experience, empowerment, and organizational support on catering service staff performance. *International Journal of Hospitality Management, 25,* 478–495. doi:10.1016/j.ijhm.2005.03.002

Christmas Nightmare For US Airways And Its Passengers. (2004, December 26). *ConsumerAffairs.com.* Retrieved from http://www.consumer affairs.com/

Cialdini, R. B. (1993). *Influence: Science and practice* (3rd ed.). New York, NY: HarperCollins.

Cialdini, R. B., Green, B. L., & Rusch, A. J. (1992). When tactical pronouncements of change become real change: The case of reciprocal persuasion. *Journal of Personality and Social Psychology, 63,* 30–40. doi:10.1037/0022-3514.63.1.30

Clark, M., & Mills, J. (1979). Interpersonal attraction in exchange and communal relationships. *Journal of Personality and Social Psychology, 37,* 12–24. doi:10.1037/0022-3514.37.1.12

Clay, R. (2008). The corporatization of higher education. *Monitor on Psychology, 39,* 50.

Cobb, A., & Wooten, K. (1998). The role social accounts can play in a justice intervention. In R. Woodman & W. Pasmore (Eds.), *Research in organizational change and development* (Vol. 11, pp. 73–115). Greenwich, CT: JAI Press.

Cobb, S. (1976). Social support as a moderator of life stress. *Psychosomatic Medicine, 38,* 300–314.

Cohen, S., & Wills, T. A. (1985). Stress, social support, and the buffering hypothesis. *Psychological Bulletin, 98,* 310–357. doi:10.1037/0033-2909.98.2.310

Colbert, A. E., Mount, M. K., Harter, J. K., Witt, L. A., & Barrick, M. R. (2004). Interactive effects of personality and perceptions of the work situation on workplace deviance. *Journal of Applied Psychology, 89,* 599–609. doi:10.1037/0021-9010.89.4.599

Colquitt, J. A. (2001). On the dimensionality of organizational justice: A construct validation of a measure. *Journal of Applied Psychology, 86,* 386–400. doi:10.1037/0021-9010.86.3.386

Colvin, G., & Huey, J. (January 11, 1999). The Jack and Herb show. *Fortune, 139,* 163.

Connelly, C. E., Gallagher, D. G., & Gilley, K. M. (2007). Organizational and client commitment among contracted employees: A replication and extension with temporary workers. *Journal of Vocational Behavior, 70,* 326–335. doi:10.1016/j.jvb.2006.10.003

Conway, N., & Briner, R. B. (2002). A daily diary study of affective responses to psychological contract breach and exceeded promises. *Journal of Organizational Behavior, 23,* 287–302. doi:10.1002/job.139

Cook, J., & Wall, T. (1980). New work attitude measures of trust, organizational commitment and personal need nonfulfillment. *Journal of Occupational Psychology, 53,* 39–52.

Corsun, D. L., & Enz, C. A. (1999). Predicting psychological empower-ment among service workers: The effect of support-based relationships. *Human Relations, 52,* 205–224. doi:10.1177/001872679905200202

Costa, P. T., & McCrae, R. R. (1985). *The NEO Personality Inventory Man-ual.* Odessa, FL: Psychological Assessment Resources.

Cotterell, N., Eisenberger, R., & Speicher, H. (1992). Inhibiting effects of reciprocation wariness on interpersonal relationships. *Journal of Person-ality and Social Psychology, 62,* 658–668. doi:10.1037/0022-3514.62.4.658

Cotton, C. A. (1982). A Canadian military ethos. *Canadian Defence Quar-terly, 12,* 10–17.

Coyle-Shapiro, J. A. M., & Conway, N. (2005). Exchange relationships: Examining psychological contracts and perceived organizational sup-port. *Journal of Applied Psychology, 90,* 774–781. doi:10.1037/0021-9010.90.4.774

Coyle-Shapiro, J. A. M., & Kessler, I. (2000). Consequences of the psy-chological contract for the employment relationship: A large scale survey. *Journal of Management Studies, 37,* 903–930. doi:10.1111/1467-6486.00210

Coyle-Shapiro, J. A. M., Morrow, P. C., & Kessler, I. (2006). Serving two organizations: Exploring the employment relationship of contracted employees. *Human Resource Management, 45,* 561–583. doi:10.1002/hrm.20132

Coyle-Shapiro, J. A. M., & Shore, L. M. (2007). The employee-organization relationship: Where do we go from here? *Human Resource Management Review, 17,* 166–179. doi:10.1016/j.hrmr.2007.03.008

Cropanzano, R., & Byrne, Z. S. (2001). When it's time to stop writing pro-cedures: An inquiry into procedural injustice. *Human Resource Manage-ment Review, 11,* 31-54.

Cropanzano, R., & Greenberg, J. (1997). Progress in organizational justice: Tunneling through the maze. In C. L. Cooper & I. T. Robertson (Eds.), *International review of industrial and organizational psychology* (pp. 317–372). New York, NY: Wiley.

Cropanzano, R., Howes, J. C., Grandey, A. A., & Toth, P. (1997). The relationship of organizational politics and support to work behaviors, attitudes, and stress. *Journal of Organizational Behavior, 18,* 159–180. doi:10.1002/(SICI)1099-1379(199703)18:2<159::AID-JOB795>3.0.CO;2-D

Crowne, D. P., & Marlowe, D. (1964). *The approval motive.* New York, NY: Wiley.

Csikszentmihalyi, M. (1990). *Flow: The psychology of optimal experience.* New York, NY: Harper & Row.

Csikszentmihalyi, M., & Lefevre, J. (1989). Optimal experience in work and leisure. *Journal of Personality and Social Psychology, 56,* 815–822. doi:10.1037/0022-3514.56.5.815

Curley, K. F. (1984). Are there any real benefits from office automation. *Business Horizons, 27,* 37–42. doi:10.1016/0007-6813(84)90055-7

Dando-Collins, S. (2002). *Caesar's legion.* Hoboken, NJ: Wiley.

Danheiser, P. R., & Graziano, W. G. (1982). Self-monitoring and cooperation as a self-presentational strategy. *Journal of Personality and Social Psychology, 42,* 497–505. doi:10.1037/0022-3514.42.3.497

Davis, F. D. (1989). Perceived usefulness, perceived ease of use, and user acceptance of information technology. *Management Information Systems Quarterly, 13,* 319–340. doi:10.2307/249008

Davis, F. D. (1993). User acceptance of information technology: System characteristics, user perceptions and behavioral impacts. *International Journal of Man-Machine Studies, 38,* 475–487. doi:10.1006/imms.1993.1022

Davis, F. D., Bagozzi, R. P., & Warshaw, P. R. (1989). User acceptance of computer technology: A comparison of two theoretical models. *Management Science, 35,* 982–1003. doi:10.1287/mnsc.35.8.982

Dean, A. (2007). The impact of the customer orientation of call center employees on customers' affective commitment and loyalty. *Journal of Service Research, 10,* 161–173. doi:10.1177/1094670507309650

Dean, J., Brandes, P., & Dharwadkar, R. (1998). Organizational cynicism. *Academy of Management Review, 23,* 341–352. doi:10.2307/259378

Deci, E. L., Koestner, R., & Ryan, R. M. (1999). A meta-analytic review of experiments examining the effects of extrinsic rewards on intrinsic motivation. *Psychological Bulletin, 125,* 627–668. doi:10.1037/0033-2909.125.6.627

Deci, E. L., & Ryan, R. M. (1985). *Intrinsic motivation and self-determination in human behavior.* New York, NY: Plenum.

De Cremer, D., Stinglhamber, F., & Eisenberger, R. (2005). Effects of own versus other's fair treatment on positive emotions: A field study. *The Journal of Social Psychology, 145,* 741–744. doi:10.3200/SOCP.145.6.741-744

Dekker, I., & Barling, J. (1995). Workforce size and work-related role stress. *Work and Stress, 9,* 45–54. doi:10.1080/02678379508251584

DeLone, W. D., & McLean, E. R. (1992). Information systems success: The quest for the dependent variable. *Information Systems Research, 3,* 60–95. doi:10.1287/isre.3.1.60

DePaulo, B. M., Brittingham, G. L., & Kaiser, M. K. (1983). Receiving competence-relevant help: Effects on reciprocity, affect, and sensitivity to the helper's nonverbally expressed needs. *Journal of Personality and Social Psychology, 45,* 1045–1060. doi:10.1037/0022-3514.45.5.1045

Diener, E., Scollon, C. N., & Lucas, R. E. (2004). The evolving concept of subjective well-being: The multifaceted nature of happiness. In P. T. Costa & I. C. Siegler (Eds.), *Advances in cell aging and gerontology* (Vol. 15, pp. 187–220). Amsterdam, The Netherlands: Elsevier.

Diener, E., Suh, E. M., Lucas, R. E., & Smith, H. L. (1999). Subjective well-being: Three decades of progress, *Psychological Bulletin, 125,* 276–302.

Dobreva-Martinova, T., Villeneuve, M., Strickland, L., & Matheson, K. (2002). Occupational role stress in the Canadian forces: Its association with individual and organizational well-being. *Canadian Journal of Behavioural Science-Revue Canadienne Des Sciences Du Comportement, 34,* 111–121. doi:10.1037/h0087161

Downes, M., & Thomas, A. S. (1999). Managing overseas assignments to build organizational knowledge. *Human Resource Planning, 22,* 33–48.

Drigotas, S. M., & Rusbult, C. E. (1992). Should I stay or should I go: A dependence model of breakups. *Journal of Personality and Social Psychology, 62,* 62–87. doi:10.1037/0022-3514.62.1.62

Duke, A. B., Goodman, J. M., Treadway, D. C., & Breland, J. W. (2009). Perceived organizational support as a moderator of emotional labor/outcomes relationships. *Journal of Applied Social Psychology, 39,* 1013–1034. doi:10.1111/j.1559-1816.2009.00470.x

Dupré, K. E., & Day, A. L. (2007). The effects of supportive management and job quality on the turnover intentions and health of military personnel. *Human Resource Management, 46,* 185–201. doi:10.1002/hrm.20156

Dutton, J. E., Dukerich, J. M., & Harquail, C. V. (1994). Organizational images and member identification. *Administrative Science Quarterly, 39,* 239–263. doi:10.2307/2393235

Eder, P., & Eisenberger, R. (2008). Perceived organizational support: Reducing the negative influence of coworker withdrawal behavior. *Journal of Management, 34,* 55–68. doi:10.1177/0149206307309259

Edwards, J. (2002, June). Timeline of Personhood Rights and Powers. *ReclaimDemocracy.org.* Retrieved from http://www.reclaimdemocracy.org/personhood/personhood_timeline.pdf

Edwards, M. R. (2005). Organizational identification: A conceptual and operational review. *International Journal of Management Reviews, 7,* 207–230. doi:10.1111/j.1468-2370.2005.00114.x

Ehrhart, M. G., & Naumann, S. E. (2004). Organizational citizenship behavior in work groups: A group norms approach. *Journal of Applied Psychology, 89,* 960–974. doi:10.1037/0021-9010.89.6.960

Eiriz, V., & Wilson, D. (2006). Research in relationship marketing: Antecedents, traditions, and integration. *European Journal of Marketing, 40,* 275–291. doi:10.1108/03090560610648057

Eisenberger, R. (1989). *Blue Monday: The loss of the work ethic in America.* New York, NY: Paragon House.

Eisenberger, R., Armeli, S., Rexwinkel, B., Lynch, P. D., & Rhoades, L. (2001). Reciprocation of perceived organizational support. *Journal of Applied Psychology, 86,* 42–51. doi:10.1037/0021-9010.86.1.42

Eisenberger, R., Cotterell, N., & Marvel, J. (1987). Reciprocation ideology. *Journal of Personality and Social Psychology, 53,* 743–750. doi:10.1037/0022-3514.53.4.743

Eisenberger, R., Cummings, J., Armeli, S., & Lynch, P. (1997). Perceived organizational support, discretionary treatment, and job satisfaction. *Journal of Applied Psychology, 82,* 812–820. doi:10.1037/0021-9010.82.5.812

Eisenberger, R., Fasolo, P., & Davis-LaMastro, V. (1990). Perceived organizational support and employee diligence, commitment, and innovation. *Journal of Applied Psychology, 75,* 51–59. doi:10.1037/0021-9010.75.1.51

Eisenberger, R., Huntington, R., Hutchison, S., & Sowa, D. (1986). Perceived organizational support. *Journal of Applied Psychology, 71,* 500–507. doi:10.1037/0021-9010.71.3.500

Eisenberger, R., Jones, J. R., Stinglhamber, F., Shanock, L., & Randall, A. T. (2005). Flow experiences at work: For high need achievers alone? *Journal of Organizational Behavior, 26,* 755–775. doi:10.1002/job.337

Eisenberger, R., Kaplan, R. M., & Singer, R. D. (1974). Decremental and nondecremental effects of noncontingent social approval. *Journal of Personality and Social Psychology, 30,* 716–722. doi:10.1037/h0037449

Eisenberger, R., Karagonlar, G., Stinglhamber, F., Neves, P., Becker, T. E., González-Morales, M. G., & Steiger-Mueller, M. (2010). Leader–member exchange and affective organizational commitment: The contribution of supervisor's organizational embodiment. *Journal of Applied Psychology, 95,* 1085–1103. doi: 10.1037/a0020858

Eisenberger, R., Lynch, P., Aselage, J., & Rohdieck, S. (2004). Who takes the most revenge? Individual differences in negative reciprocity norm endorsement. *Personality and Social Psychology Bulletin, 30,* 787–799. doi:10.1177/0146167204264047

Eisenberger, R., Pierce, W. D., & Cameron, J. (1999). Effects of reward on intrinsic motivation –Negative, neutral, and positive: Comment on Deci, Koestner, and Ryan (1999). *Psychological Bulletin, 125,* 677–691. doi:10.1037/0033-2909.125.6.677

Eisenberger, R., Rhoades, L., & Cameron, J. (1999). Does pay for performance increase or decrease perceived self-determination and intrinsic motivation? *Journal of Personality and Social Psychology, 77,* 1026–1040. doi:10.1037/0022-3514.77.5.1026

Eisenberger, R., Stinglhamber, F., Shanock, L. R., Jones, J. R., & Aselage, J. (2009). *Extending the social exchange perspective of perceived organizational support: Influences of collectivism and competitiveness* (Unpublished manuscript). University of Delaware, Newark.

Eisenberger, R., Stinglhamber, F., Vandenberghe, C., Sucharski, I. L., & Rhoades, L. (2002). Perceived supervisor support: Contributions to perceived organizational support and employee retention. *Journal of Applied Psychology, 87,* 565–573. doi:10.1037/0021-9010.87.3.565

Eisenberger, R., Sucharski, I. L., Yalowitz, S., Kent, R. J., Loomis, R. J., Jones, J. R., . . . McLaughlin, J. P. (2010). The motive for sensory pleasure: Enjoyment of nature and its representation in painting,

music, and literature. *Journal of Personality, 78,* 599–638. doi:10.1111/
j.1467-6494.2010.00628.x

Ellis, A. D. (2008). *The impact of corporate social responsibility on employee attitudes and behaviors* (Unpublished doctoral dissertation). Arizona State University, Tempe.

Erdogan, B., & Enders, J. (2007). Support from the top: Supervisors' perceived organizational support as a moderator of leader–member exchange to satisfaction and performance relationships. *Journal of Applied Psychology, 92,* 321–330. doi:10.1037/0021-9010.92.2.321

Erdogan, B., Kraimer, M. L., & Liden, R. C. (2004). Work value congruence and intrinsic career success: The compensatory roles of leader–member exchange and perceived organizational support. *Personnel Psychology, 57,* 305–332. doi:10.1111/j.1744-6570.2004.tb02493.x

Erdwins, C. J., Buffardi, L. C., Casper, W. J., & O'Brien, A. S. (2001). The relationship of women's role strain to social support, role satisfaction, and self-efficacy. *Family Relations, 50,* 230–238. doi:10.1111/j.1741-3729.2001.00230.x

Etzioni, A. (1961). *A comparative analysis of complex organizations.* New York, NY: Free Press.

Farh, J. L., Hackett, R. D., & Liang, J. (2007). Individual-level cultural values as moderators of perceived organizational support–employee outcome relationships in China: Comparing the effects of power distance and traditionality. *Academy of Management Journal, 50,* 715–729. doi:10.2307/20159880

Featherstone, L. (2005, January 3). Down and out in discount America. *Nation, 280,* 11–15.

Feldman, D. C., Doerpinghaus, H. I., & Turnley, W. H. (1994). Managing temporary workers: A permanent HRM challenge. *Organizational Dynamics, 23,* 49–63. doi:10.1016/0090-2616(94)90068-X

Feldman, D. C., Doerpinghaus, H. I., & Turnley, W. H. (1995). Employee reactions to temporary jobs. *Journal of Managerial Issues, 7,* 127–141.

Ferris, G. R., & Kacmar, K. M. (1992). Perceptions of organizational politics. *Journal of Management, 18,* 93–116. doi:10.1177/014920639201800107

Fishbein, M., & Ajzen, I. (1975). *Belief, attitude, intention and behavior: An introduction to theory and research.* Reading, MA: Addison-Wesley.

Fishman, C. (2006). *The Wal-Mart effect.* New York, NY: Penguin Press.

Flanigan, J. (2004, February 15). Costco sees value in higher pay. *The Los Angeles Times.* Retrieved from http://www.latimes.com

Foa, E. B., & Foa, U. G. (1980). Resource theory: Interpersonal behavior as exchange. In K. Gergen, M. S. Greenberg, & R. Willis (Eds.), *Social exchange: Advances in theory and research* (pp. 77–94). New York, NY: Plenum Press.

Foa, U. G., & Foa, E. B. (1974). *Societal structures of the mind.* Springfield, IL: Charles C. Thomas.

Folkman, S., & Lazarus, R. (1991). Coping and emotion. In A. Monat & R. Lazarus (Eds.), *Stress and coping: An anthology* (3rd ed., pp. 207–227). New York, NY: Columbia University Press.

Ford, W. S. Z. (2003). Communication practices of professional service providers: Predicting customer satisfaction and loyalty. *Journal of Applied Communication Research, 31,* 189–211. doi:10.1080/00909880305383

Frey, C. (2004, March 29). Costco's love of labor: Employees' well-being key to its success. *seattlepi.com.* Retrieved from http://www.seattlepi.com

Frone, M. R. (2003). Work–family balance. In J. C. Quick & L. E. Tetrick (Eds.), *Handbook of occupational health psychology* (pp. 143–162). Washington, DC: American Psychological Association. doi:10.1037/10474-007

Frone, M. R., Russell, M., & Cooper, M. L. (1992). Antecedents and outcomes of work–family conflict: Testing a model of the work–family interface. *Journal of Applied Psychology, 77,* 65–78. doi:10.1037/0021-9010.77.1.65

Gakovic, A., & Tetrick, L. E. (2003). Perceived organizational support and work status: A comparison of the employment relationships of part-time and full-time employees attending university classes. *Journal of Organizational Behavior, 24,* 649–666. doi:10.1002/job.206

Gecas, V. (1982). The self-concept. *Annual Review of Sociology, 8,* 1–33. doi:10.1146/annurev.so.08.080182.000245

Gellatly, I. R. (1995). Individual and group determinants of employee absenteeism: Test of a causal model. *Journal of Organizational Behavior, 16,* 469–485. doi:10.1002/job.4030160507

Gellatly, I. R., Hunter, K. H., Luchak, A. A., & Meyer, J. P. (2007, April). *Predicting commitment profile membership: The role of perceived organizational support and autonomy.* Paper presented at the 22nd annual meeting of the Society for Industrial and Organizational Psychology, New York, NY.

Geller, L. (1982). The failure of self-actualization therapy: A critique of Carl Rogers and Abraham Maslow. *Journal of Humanistic Psychology, 22,* 56–73. doi:10.1177/0022167882222004

Gentry, W. A., Kuhnert, K. W., Mondore, S. P., & Page, E. E. (2007). The influence of supervisory-support climate and unemployment rate on part-time employee retention: A multilevel analysis. *Journal of Management Development, 26,* 1005–1022. doi:10.1108/02621710710833432

George, J. M. (1989). Mood and absence. *Journal of Applied Psychology, 74,* 317–324. doi:10.1037/0021-9010.74.2.317

George, J. M., & Brief, A. P. (1992). Feeling good—doing good: A conceptual analysis of the mood at work–organizational spontaneity relationship. *Psychological Bulletin, 112,* 310–329. doi:10.1037/0033-2909. 112.2.310

George, J. M., Reed, T. F., Ballard, K. A., Colin, J., & Fielding, J. (1993). Contact with AIDS patients as a source of work-related distress: Effects of organizational and social support. *Academy of Management Journal, 36,* 157–171. doi:10.2307/256516

Gergen, K., Ellsworth, P., Maslach, C., & Seipel, M. (1975). Obligation, donor resources, and reactions to aid in three cultures. *Journal of Personality and Social Psychology, 31,* 390–400. doi:10.1037/h0076482

Gibson, J. L. (2006). *Employees and work–life resources: Influences on attraction, spillover, and commitment* (Unpublished doctoral dissertation). George Mason University, Fairfax, VA.

Gibson, J. L., & Tremble, T. R. (2006). Influences of work–life support of officers' organizational commitment and negative work–family spillover. *ARI Research Note, 2006-02.*

Gist, M. E., & Mitchell, T. R. (1992). Self-efficacy: A theoretical analysis of its determinants and malleability. *Academy of Management Review, 17,* 183–211. doi:10.2307/258770

Gittell, J. H. (2002). *The Southwest Airlines way: Using the power of relationships to achieve high performance.* New York, NY: McGraw-Hill.

Glazer, M. P., & Glazer, P. M. (1986). Whistleblowing. *Psychology Today, 39.*

Goldner, F. H., Ritti, R. R., & Ference, T. P. (1977). The production of cynical knowledge in organizations. *American Sociological Review, 42,* 539–551. doi:10.2307/2094553

González-Roma, V., Schaufeli, W. B., Bakker, A. B., & Lloret, S. (2006). Burnout and work engagement: Independent factors or opposite poles? *Journal of Vocational Behavior, 68,* 165–174. doi:10.1016/j.jvb.2005. 01.003

Goranson, R. E., & Berkowitz, L. (1966). Reciprocity and responsibility reactions to prior help. *Journal of Personality and Social Psychology, 3,* 227–232. doi:10.1037/h0022895

Gosserand, R. H. (2003). An examination of individual and organizational factors related to emotional labor. *Dissertation Abstracts International: Section B. The Sciences and Engineering, 64,* 1533.

Gould, S. (1979). An equity-exchange model of organizational involvement. *Academy of Management Review, 4,* 53–62. doi:10.2307/257403

Gouldner, A. W. (1958). Cosmopolitans and locals: Toward an analysis of latent social roles. Part II. *Administrative Science Quarterly, 2,* 444–480. doi:10.2307/2390795

Gouldner, A. W. (1960). The norm of reciprocity: A preliminary statement. *American Sociological Review, 25,* 161–178. doi:10.2307/2092623

Graen, G., & Scandura, T. (1987). Towards a psychology of dyadic organizing. *Research in Organizational Behavior, 9,* 175–208.

Graham, J. W. (1991). An essay on organizational citizenship behavior. *Employee Responsibilities and Rights Journal, 4,* 249–270. doi:10.1007/ BF01385031

Grant-Vallone, E. J., & Ensher, E. A. (2001). An examination of work and personal life conflict, organizational support, and employee health among international expatriates. *International Journal of Intercultural Relations, 25,* 261–278. doi:10.1016/S0147-1767(01)00003-7

Great Places to Work Institute, Inc. (2007). *Why is Google so great?.* Retrieved from http://resources.greatplacetowork.com/article/pdf/why_google_is_no._1.pdf

Great workplaces outperform their peers. (2010). *Great Place to Work.* Retrieved from http://www.greatplacetowork.com/what_we_believe/graphs.php?page=1

Greenberg, J. (1979). Group vs. individual equity judgments: Is there a polarization effect? *Journal of Experimental Social Psychology, 15,* 504–512. doi:10.1016/0022-1031(79)90012-X

Greenberg, J. (1990). Employee theft as a reaction to underpayment inequity: The hidden cost of pay cuts. *Journal of Applied Psychology, 75,* 561–568. doi:10.1037/0021-9010.75.5.561

Greenberg, J. (1997). The STEAL motive: Managing the social determinants of employee theft. In R. A. Giacalone & J. Greenberg (Eds.), *Antisocial behavior in organizations* (pp. 85–108). Newbury Park, CA: Sage.

Greenberg, M. S. (1980). A theory of indebtedness. In K. Gergen, M. S. Greenberg, & R. Willis (Eds.), *Social exchange: Advances in theory and research* (pp. 3–26). New York, NY: Plenum Press.

Greenberg, M. S., & Bar-Tal, D. (1976). Indebtedness as a motive for acquisition of "helpful" information. *Representative Research in Social Psychology, 7,* 19–27.

Greenberg, M. S., & Frisch, D. M. (1972). Effect of intentionality on willingness to reciprocate a favor. *Journal of Experimental Social Psychology, 8,* 99–111. doi:10.1016/0022-1031(72)90028-5

Greenberg, M. S., & Westcott, D. R. (1983). Indebtedness as mediator of reactions to aid. In J. D. Fisher, A. Nadler, & B. M. DePaulo (Eds.), *New directions in helping* (pp. 85–112). San Diego, CA: Academic Press.

Greenhaus, J. H., & Beutell, N. J. (1985). Sources of conflict between work and family roles. *Academy of Management Review, 10,* 76–88. doi:10.2307/258214

Greenhaus, J. H., Parasuraman, S., & Wormley, W. M. (1990). Effects of race on organizational experience, job performance evaluations, and career outcomes. *Academy of Management Journal, 33,* 64–86. doi:10.2307/256352

Greenleaf, R. K. (1977). *Servant-leadership: A journey into the nature of legitimate power and greatness.* Mahwah, NJ: Paulist Press.

Gross, A. E., & Latane, J. G. (1974). Receiving help, reciprocation, and interpersonal attraction. *Journal of Applied Social Psychology, 4,* 210–223. doi:10.1111/j.1559-1816.1974.tb02641.x

Gustafsson, A., Johnson, M. D., & Roos, I. (2005). The effects of customer satisfaction, relationship commitment dimensions, and triggers on customer retention. *Journal of Marketing, 69,* 210–218. doi:10.1509/jmkg.2005.69.4.210

Guzzo, R. A., Noonan, K. A., & Elron, E. (1994). Expatriate managers and the psychological contract. *Journal of Applied Psychology, 79,* 617–626. doi:10.1037/0021-9010.79.4.617

Haines, V. Y., Merrheim, G., & Roy, M. (2001). Understanding reactions to safety incentives. *Journal of Safety Research, 32,* 17–30. doi:10.1016/S0022-4375(00)00051-7

Han, X. Y., Kwortnik, R. J., & Wang, C. X. (2008). Service loyalty: An integrative model and examination across service contexts. *Journal of Service Research, 11,* 22–42. doi:10.1177/1094670508319094

Hayton, J. C., Carnabuci, G., & Eisenberger, R. (2009). *With a little help from my colleagues: A social embeddedness approach to perceived organizational support.* Unpublished manuscript, Bocconi University, Milano, Italy.

Head, S. (2004, December 16). Inside the leviathan. *The New York Review of Books, 51,* 80–89.

Head, S. (2005). *The new ruthless economy: Work & power in the digital age.* New York, NY: Oxford University Press.

Heider, F. (1958). *The psychology of interpersonal relations.* New York, NY: Wiley. doi:10.1037/10628-000

Helm, B., Bonoma, T., & Tedeschi, J. (1972). Reciprocity for harm done. *The Journal of Social Psychology, 87,* 89–98.

Henberg, M. (1990). *Retribution: Evil for evil in ethics, law, and literature.* Philadelphia, PA: Temple University Press.

Hennessey, B. A., & Amabile, T. M. (1988). The conditions of creativity. In R. J. Sternberg (Ed.), *The nature of creativity* (pp. 11–38). Cambridge, MA: Cambridge University Press.

Hill, C. A. (1987). Affiliation motivation: People who need people . . . but in different ways. *Journal of Personality and Social Psychology, 52,* 1008–1018. doi:10.1037/0022-3514.52.5.1008

Hill, C. A. (1991). Seeking emotional support: The influence of affiliative need and partner warmth. *Journal of Personality and Social Psychology, 60,* 112–121. doi:10.1037/0022-3514.60.1.112

Hirschfeld, R. R., & Feild, H. S. (2000). Work centrality and work alienation: Distinct aspects of a general commitment to work. *Journal of Organizational Behavior, 21,* 789–800. doi:10.1002/1099-1379(200011)21:7<789::AID-JOB59>3.0.CO;2-W

Hochwarter, W. A., James, M., Johnson, D., & Ferris, G. R. (2004). The interactive effects of politics perceptions and trait cynicism on work outcomes. *Journal of Leadership & Organizational Studies, 10,* 44–57. doi:10.1177/107179190401000404

Hochwarter, W. A., Kacmar, C., Perrewé, P. L., & Johnson, D. (2003). Perceived organizational support as a mediator of the relationship between politics perceptions and work outcomes. *Journal of Vocational Behavior, 63,* 438–456. doi:10.1016/S0001-8791(02)00048-9

Hoffman, C., Mischel, W., & Baer, J. S. (1984). Language and person cognition: Effects of communicative set on trait attribution. *Journal of Personality and Social Psychology, 46,* 1029–1043. doi:10.1037/0022-3514.46.5.1029

Hofmann, D. A., & Morgeson, F. P. (1999). Safety-related behavior as a social exchange: The role of perceived organizational support and leader–member exchange. *Journal of Applied Psychology, 84,* 286–296. doi:10.1037/0021-9010.84.2.286

Hogan, R. (1975). Theoretical egocentrism and the problem of compliance. *American Psychologist, 30,* 533–540. doi:10.1037/h0076638

Hogg, M. A. (2001). A social identity theory of leadership. *Personality and Social Psychology Review, 5,* 184–200. doi:10.1207/S15327957PSPR0503_1

Holmes, S., & Zellner, W. (2004, April 12). The Costco way. *Business Week,* 76–77.

Homans, G. C. (1950). *The Human Group.* New York, NY: Harcourt, Brace and World.

Homans, G. C. (1974). *Social behavior: Its elementary forms.* New York, NY: Harcourt Brace Jovanovich.

Howell, J. M. (1988). Two faces of charisma: Socialized and personalized leadership in organizations. In J. A. Conger & R. N. Kanungo (Eds.), *Charismatic leadership: The elusive factor in organizational effectiveness* (pp. 213–236). San Francisco, CA: Jossey-Bass.

Hrebiniak, L. G. (1974). Effects of job level and participation on employee attitudes and perceptions of influence. *Academy of Management Journal, 17,* 649–662. doi:10.2307/255644

Hui, C., Wong, A., & Tjosvold, D. (2007). Turnover intention and performance in China: The role of Positive Affectivity, Chinese values, perceived organizational support and constructive controversy. *Journal of Occupational and Organizational Psychology, 80,* 735–751. doi:10.1348/096317906X171037

Hui, C. H., Chiu, W. C. K., Yu, P. L. H., Cheng, K., & Tse, H. H. M. (2007). The effects of service climate and the effective leadership behaviour of supervisors on frontline employee service quality: A multi-level analysis. *Journal of Occupational and Organizational Psychology, 80,* 151–172. doi:10.1348/096317905X89391

Hutchison, S. (1997). A path model of perceived organizational support. *Journal of Social Behavior and Personality, 12,* 159–174.

Hutchison, S., & Garstka, M. L. (1996). Sources of perceived organizational support: Goal setting and feedback. *Journal of Applied Social Psychology, 26,* 1351–1366. doi:10.1111/j.1559-1816.1996.tb00075.x

Hyatt, K. (2007). *The influence of leadership practices on subordinates' perceived organizational support in MBA students* (Unpublished doctoral dissertation). Nova Southeastern University, Fort Lauderdale, FL.

Igbaria, M., Guimaraes, T., & Davis, G. B. (1995). Testing the determinants of microcomputer usage via a structural equation model. *Journal of Management Information Systems, 11,* 87–114.

Irwin, N. (2010, January 2). Aughts were a lost decade for U.S. economy, workers. *Washington Post.* Retrieved from http://www.washington post.com

James, M. (2005). *Antecedents and consequences of cynicism in organizations: An examination of the potential positive and negative effects on school systems* (Unpublished doctoral dissertation). The Florida State University, Tallahasse.

Jana, R. (2000). Doing a double take. *InfoWorld, 22,* 100–101.

Janis, I. L. (1983). *Groupthink* (2nd ed.). Boston, MA: Houghton Mifflin.

Jawahar, I. M., Stone, T. H., & Kisamore, J. L. (2007). Role conflict and burnout: The direct and moderating effects of political skill and perceived organizational support on burnout dimensions. *International Journal of Stress Management, 14,* 142–159. doi:10.1037/1072-5245.14.2.142

Johnson, J., & O'Leary-Kelly, A. (2003). The effects of psychological contract breach and organizational cynicism: Not all social exchange violations are created equal. *Journal of Organizational Behavior, 24,* 627–647. doi:10.1002/job.207

Jones, B., Flynn, D. M., & Kelloway, E. K. (1995). Perception of support from the organization in relation to work stress, satisfaction, and commitment. In S. L. Sauter & L. R. Murphy (Eds.), *Organizational risk factors for job stress* (pp. 41–52). Washington, DC: American Psychological Association. doi:10.1037/10173-002

Jones, E. E., & Davis, K. E. (1965). From acts to dispositions: The attribution process in person perception. In L. Berkowitz (Ed.), *Advances in experimental social psychology* (Vol. 2, pp. 219–266). New York, NY: Academic Press. doi:10.1016/S0065-2601(08)60107-0

Jones, E. E., & Nisbett, R. E. (1972). The actor and the observer: Divergent perceptions of the causes of behavior. In E. E. Jones, D. E. Kanouse, H. H. Kelley, R. E. Nisbett, S. Valins, & B. Weiner (Eds.), *Attributions: Perceiving the causes of behavior* (pp. 79–94). Morristown, NJ: General Learning Press.

Jones, J. R., & Eisenberger, R. (2004). *Understanding the relationships between perceived organizational support and social accounts.* Unpublished manuscript, University of Delaware, Newark.

Judge, T. A., Cable, D. M., Boudreau, J. W., & Bretz, R. D. (1995). An empirical investigation of the predictors of executive career success. *Personnel Psychology, 48,* 485–519. doi:10.1111/j.1744-6570.1995.tb01767.x

Judge, T. A., & Piccolo, R. F. (2004). Transformational and transactional leadership: A meta-analytic test of their relative validity. *Journal of Applied Psychology, 89,* 755–768. doi:10.1037/0021-9010.89.5.755

Kacmar, K. M., Andrews, M. C., Van Rooy, D. L., Steilberg, R. C., & Cerrone, S. (2006). Sure everyone can be replaced . . . but at what cost? Turnover as a predictor of unit-level performance. *Academy of Management Journal, 49,* 133–144. doi:10.2307/20159750

Kacmar, K. M., & Carlson, D. S. (1997). Further validation of the perceptions of politics scale (POPS): A multiple sample investigation. *Journal of Management, 23,* 627–658. doi:10.1177/014920639702300502

Kahn, R., Wolfe, D., Quinn, R., Snoek, J., & Rosenthal, R. (1964). *Organizational stress: Studies in role conflict and ambiguity.* Oxford, England: Wiley.

Kahn, W. A. (1990). Psychological conditions of personal engagement and disengagement at work. *Academy of Management Journal, 33,* 692–724. doi:10.2307/256287

Kanter, D., & Mirvis, P. (1989). *The cynical Americans: Living and working in an age of discontent and disillusion.* San Francisco, CA: Jossey-Bass.

Kanungo, R. N. (1979). The concepts of alienation and involvement revisited. *Psychological Bulletin, 86,* 119–138. doi:10.1037/0033-2909.86.1.119

Kanungo, R. N. (1982). Measurement of job and work involvement. *Journal of Applied Psychology, 67,* 341–349. doi:10.1037/0021-9010.67.3.341

Kaplan, D. (2000). *Structural equation modeling: Foundations and extensions.* Thousand Oaks, CA: Sage.

Kaplan, D. A. (2010, January 21). SAS: A new no. 1 best employer. *Fortune.* Retrieved from http://money.cnn.com

Karagonlar, G., Eisenberger, R., & Steiger-Mueller, M. (2009). *Influences of supervisors' POS and reciprocation wariness on LMX.* Unpublished manuscript, University of Delaware, Newark.

Kark, R., Shamir, B., & Chen, G. (2003). The two faces of transformational leadership: Empowerment and dependency. *Journal of Applied Psychology, 88,* 246–255. doi:10.1037/0021-9010.88.2.246

Kelman, H. (1961). Processes of opinion change. *Public Opinion Quarterly, 25,* 57–78. doi:10.1086/266996

Kiesler, S. B. (1966). The effect of perceived role requirements on reactions to favor doing. *Journal of Experimental Social Psychology, 2,* 198–210. doi:10.1016/0022-1031(66)90079-5

Kinnunen, U., Feldt, T., & Makikangas, A. (2008). Testing the effort–reward imbalance model among Finnish managers: The role of perceived organizational support. *Journal of Occupational Health Psychology, 13,* 114–127. doi:10.1037/1076-8998.13.2.114

Kinnunen, U., Geurts, S., & Mauno, S. (2004). Work-to-family conflict and its relationship with satisfaction and well-being: A one-year longitudinal study on gender differences. *Work and Stress, 18,* 1–22. doi:10.1080/02678370410001682005

Klein, J., Becker, T. E., & Meyer, J. P. (2009). *Commitment in organizations: Accumulated wisdom and new directions.* New York, NY: Routledge/Taylor and Francis.

Knudsen, H. K., Johnson, J. A., Martin, J. K., & Roman, P. M. (2003). Downsizing survival: The experience of work and organizational commitment. *Sociological Inquiry, 73*, 265–283. doi:10.1111/1475-682X.00056

Kochan, T., & Weinstein, M. (1994). Recent developments in U.S. industrial relations. *British Journal of Industrial Relations, 32*, 483–504. doi:10.1111/j.1467-8543.1994.tb01047.x

Konik, J. A. (2005). Harassment as a system for policing traditional gender norms in the workplace: The structure and process of sexual harassment and heterosexist harassment. *Dissertation Abstracts International: Section B. The Sciences and Engineering, 66*, 1207.

Konovsky, M. A., & Organ, D. W. (1996). Dispositional and contextual determinants of organizational citizenship behavior. *Journal of Organizational Behavior, 17*, 253–266. doi:10.1002/(SICI)1099-1379(199605)17:3<253::AID-JOB747>3.0.CO;2-Q

Kopelman, R. E., Greenhaus, J. H., & Connolly, T. F. (1983). A model of work, family, and interrole conflict: A construct-validation study. *Organizational Behavior and Human Performance, 32*, 198–215. doi:10.1016/0030-5073(83)90147-2

Kossek, E. E., & Lambert, S. (2005). "Work–family scholarship": Voice and context. In E. E. Kossek & S. Lambert (Eds.), *Work and life integration: Organizational, cultural, and individual perspectives* (pp. 3–17). Mahwah, NJ: Erlbaum.

Kossek, E. E., Noe, R. A., & DeMarr, B. J. (1999). Work–family role synthesis: Individual and organizational determinants. *International Journal of Conflict Management, 10*, 102–129. doi:10.1108/eb022820

Kottke, J. L., & Sharafinski, C. E. (1988). Measuring perceived supervisory and organizational support. *Educational and Psychological Measurement, 48*, 1075–1079. doi:10.1177/0013164488484024

Koys, D. (1991). Fairness, legal compliance, and organizational commitment. *Employee Responsibilities and Rights Journal, 4*, 283–291. doi:10.1007/BF01385033

Kraimer, M. L., & Wayne, S. J. (2004). An examination of perceived organizational support as a multidimensional construct in the context of an expatriate assignment. *Journal of Management, 30*, 209–237. doi:10.1016/j.jm.2003.01.001

Kraimer, M. L., Wayne, S. J., & Jaworski, R. A. (2001). Sources of support and expatriate performance: The mediating role of expatriate adjustment. *Personnel Psychology, 54*, 71–99. doi:10.1111/j.1744-6570.2001.tb00086.x

Kuhlman, D. M., & Marshello, A. F. (1975). Individual differences in game motivation as moderators of preprogrammed strategy effects in prisoner's dilemma. *Journal of Personality and Social Psychology, 32,* 922–931. doi:10.1037/0022-3514.32.5.922

Kurtessis, J. N., Ford, M. T., Buffardi, L. C., & Stewart, K. A. (2009, April). *Perceived organizational support: An updated meta-analytic review.* Poster presented at the 24th annual meeting of the Society for Industrial and Organizational Psychology, New Orleans.

Ladd, D., & Henry, R. A. (2000). Helping coworkers and helping the organization: The role of support perceptions, exchange ideology, and conscientiousness. *Journal of Applied Social Psychology, 30,* 2028–2049. doi:10.1111/j.1559-1816.2000.tb02422.x

Larsen, R. J., & Diener, E. (1992). Problems and promises with the circumplex model of emotion. *Review of Personality and Social Psychology, 13,* 25–59.

Lawler, E., & Hall, D. (1970). Relationship of job characteristics to job involvement, satisfaction, and intrinsic motivation. *Journal of Applied Psychology, 54,* 305–312. doi:10.1037/h0029692

Lazarova, M., & Caligiuri, P. (2001). Retaining repatriates: The role of organizational support practices. *Journal of World Business, 36,* 389–401. doi:10.1016/S1090-9516(01)00063-3

Lazarova, M., & Cerdin, J. L. (2007). Revisiting repatriation concerns: Organizational support versus career and contextual influences. *Journal of International Business Studies, 38,* 404–429. doi:10.1057/palgrave.jibs.8400273

Lazarova, M., & Tarique, I. (2005). Knowledge transfer upon repatriation. *Journal of World Business, 40,* 361–373. doi:10.1016/j.jwb.2005.08.004

Lazarus, R. S., & Folkman, S. (1984). *Stress, appraisal, and coping.* New York, NY: Springer.

Leather, P., Lawrence, C., Beale, D., Cox, T., & Dickson, R. (1998). Exposure to occupational violence and the buffering effects of intra-organizational support. *Work and Stress, 12,* 161–178. doi:10.1080/02678379808256857

Leavy, R. L. (1983). Social support and psychological disorder: A review. *Journal of Community Psychology, 11,* 3–21. doi:10.1002/1520-6629(198301)11:1<3::AID-JCOP2290110102>3.0.CO;2-E

Lee, J., & Pecce, R. (2007). Perceived organizational support and affective commitment: The mediating role of organization-based self-esteem in the context of job insecurity. *Journal of Organizational Behavior, 28,* 661–685. doi:10.1002/job.431

Leonhardt, D. (2007, April 3). One safety net is disappearing: What will follow? *The New York Times.* Retrieved from http://www.nytimes.com

LePine, J. A., Erez, A., & Johnson, D. E. (2002). The nature and dimensionality of organizational citizenship behavior: A critical review and meta-analysis. *Journal of Applied Psychology, 87*, 52–65. doi:10.1037/0021-9010.87.1.52

LePine, J. A., LePine, M. A., & Jackson, C. L. (2004). Challenge and hindrance stress: Relationships with exhaustion, motivation to learn, and learning performance. *Journal of Applied Psychology, 89*, 883–891. doi:10.1037/0021-9010.89.5.883

LePine, J. A., Podsakoff, N. P., & LePine, M. A. (2005). A meta-analytic test of the challenge stressor–hindrance stressor framework: An explanation for inconsistent relationships among stressors and performance. *Academy of Management Journal, 48*, 764–775. doi:10.2307/20159696

Levering, R., & Moskowitz, M. (2006). *What it takes to be #1.* San Francisco, CA: Great Place to Work Institute. Retrieved from http://resources.greatplacetowork.com/article/pdf/why_genentech_is_1.pdf

Levinson, H. (1965). Reciprocation: The relationship between man and organization. *Administrative Science Quarterly, 9*, 370–390. doi:10.2307/2391032

Liao, H., Toya, K., Lepak, D. P., & Hong, Y. (2009). Do they see eye to eye? Management and employee perspectives of high-performance work systems and influence processes on service quality. *Journal of Applied Psychology, 94*, 371–391. doi:10.1037/a0013504

Liden, R. C., & Graen, G. (1980). Generalizability of the vertical dyad linkage model of leadership. *Academy of Management Journal, 23*, 451–465. doi:10.2307/255511

Liden, R. C., & Maslyn, J. M. (1998). Multidimensionality of leader–member exchange: An empirical assessment through scale development. *Journal of Management, 24*, 43–72. doi:10.1016/S0149-2063(99)80053-1

Liden, R. C., Sparrowe, R. T., & Wayne, S. J. (1997). Leader–member exchange theory: The past and potential for the future. In G. R. Ferris (Ed.), *Research in personnel and human resources management* (Vol. 15, pp. 47–119). Greenwich, CT: JAI Press.

Liden, R. C., Wayne, S. J., Kraimer, M. L., & Sparrowe, R. T. (2003). The dual commitments of contingent workers: An examination of contingents' commitment to the agency and the organization. *Journal of Organizational Behavior, 24*, 609–625. doi:10.1002/job.208

Liden, R. C., Wayne, S. J., & Stilwell, D. (1993). A longitudinal study on the early development of leader–member exchanges. *Journal of Applied Psychology, 78*, 662–674. doi:10.1037/0021-9010.78.4.662

Liden, R. C., Wayne, S. J., Zhao, H., & Henderson, D. (2008). Servant leadership: Development of a multidimensional measure and multi-level assessment. *The Leadership Quarterly, 19*, 161–177. doi:10.1016/j.leaqua.2008.01.006

Lieberman, T. (2009, June 24). Excluded voices: An interview with Wendell Potter. *Columbia Journalism Review.* Retrieved from http://www.cjr.org/campaign_desk/excluded_voices_6.php?page=all

Lind, E. A., Kray, L., & Thompson, L. (1998). The social construction of injustice: Fairness judgments in response to own and others unfair treatment by authorities. *Organizational Behavior and Human Decision Processes, 75,* 1–22. doi:10.1006/obhd.1998.2785

Locke, E. A., & Latham, G. P. (2002). Building a practically useful theory of goal setting and task motivation: A 35-year odyssey. *American Psychologist, 57,* 705–717. doi:10.1037/0003-066X.57.9.705

Lowe, K. B., Kroeck, K. G., & Sivasubramaniam, N. (1996). Effectiveness correlates of transformational and transactional leadership: A meta-analytic review of the MLQ literature. *The Leadership Quarterly, 7,* 385–425. doi:10.1016/S1048-9843(96)90027-2

Lyman, A. (2009). Net App—Culture, values, leadership #1 on the 2009 list of the 100 best companies to work for. San Francisco, CA: Great Place to Work Institute. Retrieved from http://resources.greatplace towork.com/article/pdf/2009-best-company-netapp.pdf

Lynch, P. D., Eisenberger, R., & Armeli, S. (1999). Perceived organizational support: Inferior versus superior performance by wary employees. *Journal of Applied Psychology, 84,* 467–483. doi:10.1037/0021-9010.84.4.467

MacKenzie, S. B., Podsakoff, P. M., & Rich, G. A. (2001). Transformational and transactional leadership and sales performance. *Journal of the Academy of Marketing Science, 29,* 115–134. doi:10.1177/0307945 9994506

Mael, F. (1988). *Organizational identification: Construct redefinition and a field application with organizational alumni* (Unpublished doctoral dissertation). Wayne State University, Detroit, MI.

Mael, F. A., & Ashforth, B. E. (1992). Alumni and their alma-mater: A partial test of the reformulated model of organizational identification. *Journal of Organizational Behavior, 13,* 103–123. doi:10.1002/job.4030130202

Mael, F. A., & Tetrick, L. E. (1992). Identifying organizational identification. *Educational and Psychological Measurement, 52,* 813–824. doi:10.1177/0013164492052004002

Magni, M., & Pennarola, F. (2008). Intra-organizational relationships and technology acceptance. *International Journal of Information Management, 28,* 517–523. doi:10.1016/j.ijinfomgt.2008.01.002

Malatesta, R. M. (1995). *Understanding the dynamics of organizational and supervisory commitment using a social exchange framework* (Unpublished doctoral dissertation). Wayne State University, Detroit, MI.

March, J. G., & Simon, H. A. (1958). *Organizations.* New York, NY: Wiley.

Markus, H. R., & Kitayama, S. (1991). Culture and the self-implications for cognition, emotion, and motivation. *Psychological Review, 98,* 224–253. doi:10.1037/0033-295X.98.2.224

Mars, G. (1974). Dock pilferage: A case study in occupational theft. In M. Warner (Ed.), *The sociology of the workplace* (pp. 200–210). New York, NY: Halsted.

Martin, H. J. (1984). A revised measure of approval motivation and its relationship to social desirability. *Journal of Personality Assessment, 48,* 508–519. doi:10.1207/s15327752jpa4805_10

Mason, P. (2002). Canadian forces recruitment. *FMI Journal, 14,* 12–14.

Masterson, S. S. (2001). A trickle-down model of organizational justice: Relating employees' and customers' perceptions of and reactions to fairness. *Journal of Applied Psychology, 86,* 594–604. doi:10.1037/0021-9010.86.4.594

Masterson, S. S., Lewis, K., Goldman, B. M., & Taylor, M. S. (2000). Integrating justice and social exchange: The differing effects of fair procedures and treatment on work relationships. *Academy of Management Journal, 43,* 738–748. doi:10.2307/1556364

Mathieu, J. E., & Kohler, S. S. (1990). A cross-level examination of group absence influences on individual absence. *Journal of Applied Psychology, 75,* 217–220. doi:10.1037/0021-9010.75.2.217

Mathieu, J. E., & Zajac, D. M. (1990). A review and meta-analysis of the antecedents, correlates, and consequences of organizational commitment. *Psychological Bulletin, 108,* 171–194. doi:10.1037/0033-2909.108.2.171

Mauseth, K. B. (2008). *The influence of perceived organizational support and school culture on positive workplace outcomes for teachers in private schools* (Unpublished doctoral dissertation). Seattle Pacific University, Seattle, WA.

Mayer, R. C., Davis, J. H., & Schoorman, D. (1995). An integrative model of organizational trust. *Academy of Management Review, 20,* 709–734. doi:10.2307/258792

McClelland, D. C. (1985). *Human motivation.* Glenview, IL: Scott, Foresman.

McDonald, L. G., & Robinson, P. (2009). *A colossal failure of common sense: The inside story of the collapse of Lehman Brothers.* New York, NY: Crown Business.

McHenry, L. (2007). Commercial influences on the pursuit of wisdom. *London Review of Education, 5,* 131–142. doi:10.1080/14748460701440665

McLean Parks, J., & Kidder, D. L. (1994). "Till death do us part . . . ": Changing work relationships in the 1990s. In C. L. Cooper & D. M. Rousseau (Eds.), *Trends in organizational behavior* (pp. 111–136). New York, NY: Wiley.

McLean Parks, J., Kidder, D. L., & Gallagher, D. G. (1998). Fitting square pegs into round holes: Mapping the domain of contingent work arrangements onto the psychological contract. *Journal of Organizational Behavior, 19,* 697–730. doi:10.1002/(SICI)1099-1379(1998)19:1+<697::AID-JOB974>3.0.CO;2-I

McWilliams, A., & Siegel, D. (2001). Corporate social responsibility: A theory of the firm perspective. *Academy of Management Review, 26,* 117–127. doi:10.2307/259398

Mearns, K. J., & Reader, T. (2008). Organizational support and safety outcomes: An un-investigated relationship? *Safety Science, 46,* 388–397. doi:10.1016/j.ssci.2007.05.002

Mettee, D. R., Taylor, S. E., & Friedman, H. (1973). Affect conversion and the gain–loss liking effect. *Sociometry, 36,* 494–513. doi:10.2307/2786246

Meyer, J. P., & Allen, N. J. (1991). A three-component conceptualization of organizational commitment. *Human Resource Management Review, 1,* 61–89. doi:10.1016/1053-4822(91)90011-Z

Meyer, J. P., & Allen, N. J. (1997). *Commitment in the workplace: Theory, research, and application.* Thousand Oaks, CA: Sage.

Meyer, J. P., Becker, T. E., & Van Dick, R. (2006). Social identities and commitments at work: Toward an integrative model. *Journal of Organizational Behavior, 27,* 665–683. doi:10.1002/job.383

Meyer, J. P., & Herscovitch, L. (2001). Commitment in the workplace: Toward a general model. *Human Resource Management Review, 11,* 299–326. doi:10.1016/S1053-4822(00)00053-X

Meyer, J. P., Stanley, D. J., Herscovitch, L., & Topolnytsky, L. (2002). Affective, continuance, and normative commitment to the organization: A meta-analysis of antecedents, correlates, and consequences. *Journal of Vocational Behavior, 61,* 20–52. doi:10.1006/jvbe.2001.1842

Michael, J. H., Evans, D. D., Jansen, K. J., & Haight, J. M. (2005). Management commitment to safety as organizational support: Relationships with non-safety outcomes in wood manufacturing employees. *Journal of Safety Research, 36,* 171–179. doi:10.1016/j.jsr.2005.03.002

Milgram, S. (1974). *Obedience to authority: An experimental view.* New York, NY: Harper & Row.

Mirvis, P. H., & Kanter, D. L. (1992). Beyond demography: A psychographic profile of the workforce. *Human Resource Management Review, 30,* 45–68.

Mitchell, M. S., & Ambrose, M. L. (2007). Abusive supervision and workplace deviance and the moderating effects of negative reciprocity beliefs. *Journal of Applied Psychology, 92,* 1159–1168. doi:10.1037/0021-9010.92.4.1159

Mitchell, T. R., & Lee, T. W. (2001). The unfolding model of voluntary turnover and job embeddedness: Foundations for a comprehensive theory of attachment. *Research in Organizational Behavior, 23,* 189–246. doi:10.1016/S0191-3085(01)23006-8

Moideenkutty, U., Blau, G., Kumar, R., & Nalakath, A. (2001). Perceived organisational support as a mediator of the relationship of perceived situational factors to affective organisational commitment. *Applied Psychology: An International Review, 50,* 615–634.

Moorman, R. H., Blakely, G. L., & Niehoff, B. P. (1998). Does perceived organizational support mediate the relationship between procedural justice and organizational citizenship behavior? *Academy of Management Journal, 41,* 351–357. doi:10.2307/256913

Moorman, R. H., & Harland, L. K. (2002). Temporary employees as good citizens: Factors influencing their OCB performance. *Journal of Business and Psychology, 17,* 171–187. doi:10.1023/A:1019629330766

Morgenson, G. (2004, April 4). Two pay packages, two different galaxies. *New York Times.* Retrieved from http://www.nytimes.com

Morrow, P. C., & Goetz, J. F. (1988). Professionalism as a form of work commitment. *Journal of Vocational Behavior, 32,* 92–111. doi:10.1016/0001-8791(88)90008-5

Mossholder, K. W., Bennett, N., & Martin, C. L. (1998). A multilevel analysis of procedural justice context. *Journal of Organizational Behavior, 19,* 131–141. doi:10.1002/(SICI)1099-1379(199803)19:2<131::AID-JOB878>3.0.CO;2-P

Mottola, G. R., Bachman, B. A., Gaertner, S. L., & Dovidio, J. F. (1997). How groups merge: The effects of merger integration patterns on anticipated commitment to the merged organization. *Journal of Applied Social Psychology, 27,* 1335–1358. doi:10.1111/j.1559-1816.1997.tb01809.x

Mowday, R. T., Porter, L. W., & Steers, R. M. (1982). *Organizational linkages: The psychology of commitment, absenteeism, and turnover.* San Diego, CA: Academic Press.

Mumford, M. D., & Gustafson, S. B. (1988). Creativity syndrome: Integration, application, and innovation. *Psychological Bulletin, 103,* 27–43. doi:10.1037/0033-2909.103.1.27

Murphy, K. R. (1993). *Honesty in the workplace.* Belmont, CA: Brooks/Cole.

Murphy, S. M., Wayne, S. J., Liden, R. C., & Erdogan, B. (2003). Understanding social loafing: The role of justice perceptions and exchange relationships. *Human Relations, 56,* 61–84. doi:10.1177/0018726703056001450

National Association of Professional Employer Organizations. (2005). *PEO industry facts.* Retrieved from http://www.napeo.org/peoindustry/industryfacts.cfm

Narayandas, D. (1998). Measuring and managing the benefits of customer retention: An empirical investigation. *Journal of Service Research, 1,* 108–128. doi:10.1177/109467059800100202

Naumann, S. E., & Bennett, N. (2000). A case for procedural justice climate: Development and test of a multilevel model. *Academy of Management Journal, 43,* 881–889. doi:10.2307/1556416

Naus, F., van Iterson, A., & Roe, R. (2007). Organizational cynicism: Extending the exit, voice, loyalty, and neglect model of employees' response to adverse conditions in the workplace. *Human Relations, 60,* 683–718. doi:10.1177/0018726707079198

Nelson, D. L., & Simmons, B. L. (2003). Health psychology and work stress: A more positive approach. In J. C. Quick & L. E. Tetrick (Eds.), *Handbook of occupational health psychology* (pp. 97–119). Washington, DC: American Psychological Association. doi:10.1037/10474-005

Nemeth, C. (1970). Effects of free versus constrained behavior on attraction between people. *Journal of Personality and Social Psychology, 15,* 302–311. doi:10.1037/h0029605

Netemeyer, R. G., Boles, J. S., & McMurrian, R. (1996). Development and validation of work–family conflict and family–work conflict scales. *Journal of Applied Psychology, 81,* 400–410. doi:10.1037/0021-9010.81.4.400

Ng, T. W. H., & Sorensen, K. L. (2008). Toward a further understanding of the relationships between perceptions of support and work attitudes: A meta-analysis. *Group & Organization Management, 33,* 243–268. doi:10.1177/1059601107313307

Nollen, S., & Axel, H. (1996). *Managing contingent workers: How to reap the benefits and reduce the risks.* New York, NY: American Management Association.

Now bringing home the leaner bacon. (2006, September 3). *The New York Times,* pp. 1,12.

Nye, L. G., & Witt, L. A. (1993). Dimensionality and construct-validity of the Perceptions of Organizational Politics Scale (POPS). *Educational and Psychological Measurement, 53,* 821–829. doi:10.1177/001316449 3053003026

O'Driscoll, M. P. (1996). The interface between job and offjob roles: Enhancement and conflict. In I. T. Robertson & C. L. Cooper (Eds.), *International review of industrial and organisational psychology* (pp. 279–306). Chichester, UK: Wiley.

Oliver, S. (2010, September 21). PC industry customer satisfaction again dominated by Apple. *Apple Insider.* Retrieved from http://www.apple insider.com/articles/10/09/21/pc_industry_customer_satisfaction_ again_dominated_by_apple.html

O'Toole, J., & Lawler, E. E. (2006). *The new American workplace.* New York, NY: Palgrave-Macmillan.

Organ, D. W. (1988). *Organizational citizenship behavior: The good soldier syndrome.* Lexington, MA, England: Lexington Books/D. C. Heath and Com.

Organ, D. W., & Konovsky, M. (1989). Cognitive versus affective determinants of organizational citizenship behavior. *Journal of Applied Psychology, 74,* 157–164. doi:10.1037/0021-9010.74.1.157

Osterman, P. (1994). Supervision, discretion, and work organization. *The American Economic Review, 84,* 380–384.

Oyserman, D., Coon, H. M., & Kemmelmeier, M. (2002). Rethinking individualism and collectivism: Evaluation of theoretical assumptions and meta-analyses. *Psychological Bulletin, 128,* 3–72. doi:10.1037/0033-2909.128.1.3

Parasuraman, A., Zeithaml, V. A., & Berry, L. L. (1988). Servqual: A multiple-item scale for measuring consumer perceptions of service quality. *Journal of Retailing, 64,* 12–40.

Pearce, C. L., & Giacalone, R. A. (2003). Teams behaving badly: Factors associated with anti-citizenship behavior in teams. *Journal of Applied Social Psychology, 33,* 58–75. doi:10.1111/j.1559-1816.2003.tb02073.x

Pearce, J. L. (1993). Toward an organizational behavior of contract laborers: Their psychological involvement and effects on employee coworkers. *Academy of Management Journal, 36,* 1082–1096. doi:10.2307/256646

Perrewé, P. L., & Hochwarter, W. A. (2001). Can we really have it all? The attainment of work and family values. *Current Directions in Psychological Science, 10,* 29–33. doi:10.1111/1467-8721.00108

Phillips, A. S., & Bedeian, A. G. (1994). Leader–follower exchange quality: The role of personal and interpersonal attributes. *Academy of Management Journal, 37,* 990–1001. doi:10.2307/256608

Piasecki, A. (2002). The habits of scoundrels. *Critical Quarterly, 44,* 21–24. doi:10.1111/1467-8705.00450

Pierce, J. L., Gardner, D. G., Cummings, L. L., & Dunham, R. B. (1989). Organization-based self-esteem: Construct definition, measurement, and validation. *Academy of Management Journal, 32,* 622–648. doi:10.2307/256437

Podolny, J. M., & Baron, J. N. (1997). Resources and relationships: Social networks and mobility in the workplace. *American Sociological Review, 62,* 673–693. doi:10.2307/2657354

Podsakoff, P. M., MacKenzie, S. B., Paine, J. B., & Bachrach, D. G. (2000). Organizational citizenship behaviors: A critical review of the theoretical and empirical literature and suggestions for future research. *Journal of Management, 26,* 513–563. doi:10.1177/014920630002600307

Poe, A. C. (2000). Welcome back. *HRMagazine, 45,* 94–105.

Porter, L. W., Steers, R. M., Mowday, R. T., & Boulian, P. V. (1974). Organizational commitment, job satisfaction, and turnover among psychiatric technicians. *Journal of Applied Psychology, 59,* 603–609. doi:10.1037/h0037335

Pruitt, D. G. (1968). Reciprocity and credit building in a laboratory dyad. *Journal of Personality and Social Psychology, 8,* 143–147. doi:10.1037/h0025323

Pugh, S. D., Skarlicki, D. P., & Passell, B. S. (2003). After the fall: Layoff victims' trust and cynicism in re-employment. *Journal of Occupational and Organizational Psychology, 76,* 201–212. doi:10.1348/096317903765913704

Quillian-Wolever, R., & Wolever, M. (2003). Stress management at work. In J. C. Quick & L. E. Tetrick (Eds.), *Handbook of occupational health psychology* (pp. 355–375). Washington, DC: American Psychological Association. doi:10.1037/10474-017

Rabinowitz, S., & Hall, D. (1977). Organizational research on job involvement. *Psychological Bulletin, 84,* 265–288. doi:10.1037/0033-2909.84.2.265

Rachlin, H., Battalio, R., Kagel, J., & Green, L. (1981). Maximization theory in behavioral psychology. *The Behavioral and Brain Sciences, 4,* 371–417. doi:10.1017/S0140525X00009407

Randall, M. L., Cropanzano, R., Borman, C. A., & Birjulin, A. (1999). Organizational politics and organizational support as predictors of work attitudes, job performance, and organizational citizenship behavior. *Journal of Organizational Behavior, 20,* 159–174. doi:10.1002/(SICI)1099-1379(199903)20:2<159::AID-JOB881>3.0.CO;2-7

Reichfield, F. (1996). *The loyalty effect, the hidden force behind growth, profits and long lasting value.* Boston, MA: Harvard Business School Press.

Rempel, J. K., Holmes, J. G., & Zanna, M. P. (1985). Trust in close relationships. *Journal of Personality and Social Psychology, 49,* 95–112. doi:10.1037/0022-3514.49.1.95

Rhee, E., Uleman, J. S., & Lee, H. K. (1996). Variations in collectivism and individualism by ingroup and culture: Confirmatory factor analyses. *Journal of Personality and Social Psychology, 71,* 1037–1054. doi:10.1037/0022-3514.71.5.1037

Rhoades, L., & Eisenberger, R. (2002). Perceived organizational support: A review of the literature. *Journal of Applied Psychology, 87,* 698–714. doi:10.1037/0021-9010.87.4.698

Rhoades, L., Eisenberger, R., & Armeli, S. (2001). Affective commitment to the organization: The contribution of perceived organizational support. *Journal of Applied Psychology, 86,* 825–836. doi:10.1037/0021-9010.86.5.825

Riketta, M. (2005). Organizational identification: A meta-analysis. *Journal of Vocational Behavior, 66,* 358–384. doi:10.1016/j.jvb.2004.05.005

Robblee, M. A. (1998). Confronting the threat of organizational downsizing: Coping and health. *Dissertation Abstracts International: Section B. The Sciences and Engineering, 59,* 3072.

Roberts, K., Varki, S., & Brodie, R. (2003). Measuring the quality of relationships in consumer services: An empirical study. *European Journal of Marketing, 37,* 169–196. doi:10.1108/03090560310454037

Robinson, S. L., & Bennett, R. J. (1997). Workplace deviance: Its definition, its manifestations, and its causes. In R. J. Lewicki & R. J. Bies (Eds.), *Research on negotiation in organizations* (Vol. 6, pp. 3–27). Greenwich, CT: JAI Press.

Roch, S. G., & Shanock, L. R. (2006). Organizational justice in an exchange framework: Clarifying organizational justice distinctions. *Journal of Management, 32,* 299–322. doi:10.1177/0149206305280115

Rogelberg, S. G., Barnes-Farrell, J. L., & Creamer, V. (1999). Customer service behavior: The interaction of service predisposition and job characteristics. *Journal of Business and Psychology, 13,* 421–435. doi:10.1023/A:1022934618445

Rosenblatt, Z., & Ruvio, A. (1996). A test of a multidimensional model of job insecurity: The case of Israeli teachers. *Journal of Organizational Behavior, 17,* 587–605. doi:10.1002/(SICI)1099-1379(199612)17:1+ <587::AID-JOB825>3.0.CO;2-S

Rousseau, D. M. (1989). Psychological and implied contracts in organizations. *Employee Responsibilities and Rights Journal, 2,* 121–139. doi:10. 1007/BF01384942

Rousseau, D. M. (1995). *Psychological contracts in organizations: Understanding written and unwritten agreements.* Thousand Oaks, CA: Sage.

Rousseau, D. M. (1997). Organizational behaviour in the new organizational era. *Annual Review of Psychology, 48,* 515–546. doi:10.1146/ annurev.psych.48.1.515

Rousseau, D. M., & McLean Parks, J. (1993). The contracts of individuals and organizations. *Research in Organizational Behavior, 15,* 1–43.

Rousseau, D. M., Sitkin, S. B., Burt, R. S., & Camerer, C. (1998). Not so different after all: A cross-discipline view of trust. *Academy of Management Review, 23,* 393–404.

Rupp, D. E., & Cropanzano, R. (2002). The mediating effects of social exchange relationships in predicting workplace outcomes from multifoci organizational justice. *Organizational Behavior and Human Decision Processes, 89,* 925–946. doi:10.1016/S0749-5978(02)00036-5

Rusbult, C. E., & Farrell, D. (1983). A longitudinal test of the investment model: The impact on job satisfaction, job commitment, and turnover of variations in rewards, costs, alternatives, and investments. *Journal of Applied Psychology, 68,* 429–438. doi:10.1037/0021-9010.68.3.429

Sabini, J., & Silver, M. (1982). *Moralities of everyday life.* Oxford, England: Oxford University Press.

Salancik, G. R., & Pfeffer, J. (1978). A social information processing approach to job attitudes and task design. *Administrative Science Quarterly, 23,* 224–253. doi:10.2307/2392563

Saporito, B. (2007, November 7). *Restoring Wal-Mart.* Retrieved from http://www.time.com/time/magazine/article/0,9171,1680166,00.html

SAS ranks No. 1 on *Fortune* 'Best Companies to Work For' list in America. (2010, January 21). *SAS.* Retrieved from http://www.sas.com/ news/preleases/2010fortuneranking.html

Scandura, T. A., & Graen, G. B. (1984). Moderating effects of initial leader–member exchange status on the effects of a leadership intervention. *Journal of Applied Psychology, 69,* 428–436. doi:10.1037/0021-9010. 69.3.428

Schaufeli, W., Salanova, M., González-Romá, V., & Bakker, A. (2002). The measurement of engagement and burnout: A two sample confirmatory factor analytic approach. *Journal of Happiness Studies, 3,* 71–92. doi:10.1023/A:1015630930326

Schneider, B., Ehrhart, M. G., Mayer, D. M., Saltz, J. L., & Niles-Jolly, K. (2005). Understanding organization-customer links in service settings. *Academy of Management Journal, 48,* 1017–1032. doi:10.2307/20159727

Schneider, B., Holcombe, K. M., & White, S. E. (1997). Lessons learned about service quality: What it is, how to manage it, and how to become a service quality organization. *Consulting Psychology Journal: Practice and Research, 49,* 35–50. doi:10.1037/1061-4087.49.1.35

Schneider, B., White, S. S., & Paul, M. C. (1997). Relationship marketing: An organizational perspective. In T. A. Swartz, D. E. Bowen, & S. W. Brown (Eds.), *Advances in services marketing and management* (Vol. 6, pp. 1–22). Greenwich, CT: JAI Press.

Schopler, J. (1970). An attribution analysis of some determinants of reciprocating a benefit. In J. Macaulay & L. Berkowitz (Eds.), *Altruism and helping behavior* (pp. 231–238). New York, NY: Academic Press.

Scott, S. G., & Bruce, R. A. (1994). Determinants of innovative behavior: A path model of individual innovation in the workplace. *Academy of Management Journal, 37,* 580–607. doi:10.2307/256701

Seligman, M. E. P., & Csikszentmihalyi, M. (2000). Positive psychology: An introduction. *American Psychologist, 55,* 5–14. doi:10.1037/0003-066X.55.1.5

Sergeant, A., & Frenkel, S. (2000). When do customer contact employees satisfy customer? *Journal of Service Research, 3,* 18–34. doi:10.1177/109467050031002

Settoon, R. P., Bennett, N., & Liden, R. C. (1996). Social exchange in organizations: Perceived organizational support, leader–member exchange, and employee reciprocity. *Journal of Applied Psychology, 81,* 219–227. doi:10.1037/0021-9010.81.3.219

Shaffer, M. A., Harrison, D. A., Gilley, K. M., & Luk, D. M. (2001). Struggling for balance amid turbulence on international assignments: Work–family conflict, support and commitment. *Journal of Management, 27,* 99–121. doi:10.1177/014920630102700106

Shalley, C. E., Zhou, J., & Oldham, G. R. (2004). The effects of personal and contextual characteristics on creativity: Where should we go from here? *Journal of Management, 30,* 933–958. doi:10.1016/j.jm.2004.06.007

Shanock, L. R., & Eisenberger, R. (2006). When supervisors feel supported: Relationships with subordinates' perceived supervisor support, perceived organizational support, and performance. *Journal of Applied Psychology, 91,* 689–695. doi:10.1037/0021-9010.91.3.689

Shanock, L. R., & Eisenberger, R. (2009). *Perceived customer support.* Unpublished manuscript, Department of Psychology, University of North Carolina, Charlotte.

Shore, L. M., & Barksdale, K. (1998). Examining degree of balance and level of obligation in the employment relationship: A social exchange approach. *Journal of Organizational Behavior, 19*, 731–744. doi:10.1002/(SICI)1099-1379(1998)19:1+<731::AID-JOB969>3.0.CO;2-P

Shore, L. M., Ehrhart, M. G., & Coyle-Shapiro, J. A. M. (2009). *POS in teams: Support for all or support for on.* Unpublished manuscript, San Diego State University, San Diego, CA.

Shore, L. M., Porter, L. W., & Zahra, S. A. (2004). Employer-oriented strategic approaches to the employee–organization relationship (EOR). In J. Coyle-Shapiro, L. M. Shore, S. Taylor, & L. E. Tetrick (Eds.), *The employment relationship: Examining psychological and contextual perspectives* (pp. 135–160). Oxford, England: Oxford University Press.

Shore, L. M., & Shore, T. H. (1995). Perceived organizational support and organizational justice. In R. S. Cropanzano & K. M. Kacmar (Eds.), *Organizational politics, justice, and support: Managing the social climate of the workplace* (pp. 149–164). Westport, CT: Quorum.

Shore, L. M., & Tetrick, L. E. (1991). A construct-validity study of the Survey of Perceived Organizational Support. *Journal of Applied Psychology, 76*, 637–643. doi:10.1037/0021-9010.76.5.637

Shore, L. M., & Tetrick, L. E. (1994). The psychological contract as an explanatory framework in the employment relationship. In C. L. Cooper & D. M. Rousseau (Eds.), *Trends in organizational behavior* (Vol. 1, 91–109). London, England: Wiley.

Shore, L. M., Tetrick, L. E., Lynch, P., & Barksdale, K. (2006). Social and economic exchange: Construct development and validation. *Journal of Applied Social Psychology, 36*, 837–867.

Shore, L. M., Tetrick, L. E., Sinclair, R. R., & Newton, L. A. (1994). Validation of a measure of perceived union support. *Journal of Applied Psychology, 79*, 971–977. doi:10.1037/0021-9010.79.6.971

Shore, L. M., & Wayne, S. J. (1993). Commitment and employee behavior: Comparison of affective commitment and continuance commitment with perceived organizational support. *Journal of Applied Psychology, 78*, 774–780. doi:10.1037/0021-9010.78.5.774

Silverman, S. (2004, August 20). Biography: Sam Walton. *Online NewsHour.* Retrieved from http://www.pbs.org/newshour/bb/business/wal-mart/sam-walton.html

Sisodia, R. S., Wolfe, D. B., & Sheth, J. N. (2007). *Firms of endearment.* Upper Saddle River, NJ: Wharton School Publishing.

Sitkin, S. B., & Bies, R. J. (1993). Social accounts in conflict situations: Using explanations to manage conflict. *Human Relations, 46*, 349–370. doi:10.1177/001872679304600303

Skarlicki, D. P., & Latham, G. P. (2005). Can leaders be trained to be fair? In J. Greenberg & J. Colquitt (Eds.), *Handbook of organizational justice* (pp. 499–524). Mahwah, NJ: Erlbaum.

Sluss, D. M., Klimchak, M., & Holmes, J. J. (2008). Perceived organizational support as a mediator between relational exchange and organizational identification. *Journal of Vocational Behavior, 73,* 457–464. doi:10.1016/j.jvb.2008.09.001

Sonnentag, S. (2003). Recovery, work engagement, and proactive behavior: A new look at the interface between nonwork and work. *Journal of Applied Psychology, 88,* 518–528. doi:10.1037/0021-9010.88.3.518

Spielberger, C., Vagg, P., & Wasala, C. (2003). Occupational stress: Job pressures and lack of support. In J. C. Quick & L. E. Tetrick (Eds.), *Handbook of occupational health psychology* (pp. 185–200). Washington, DC: American Psychological Association. doi:10.1037/10474-009

Spitzmüller, C., Glenn, D. M., Barr, C. D., Rogelberg, S. G., & Daniel, P. (2006). "If you treat me right, I reciprocate": Examining the role of exchange in organizational survey response. *Journal of Organizational Behavior, 27,* 19–35. doi:10.1002/job.363

Spreitzer, G. M. (1995). Psychological empowerment in the workplace: Dimensions, measurement, and validation. *Academy of Management Journal, 38,* 1442–1465. doi:10.2307/256865

Spreitzer, G. M. (1996). Social structural characteristics of psychological empowerment. *Academy of Management Journal, 39,* 483–504. doi:10.2307/256789

Stamper, C. L., & Van Dyne, L. (2001). Work status and organizational citizenship behavior: A field study of restaurant employees. *Journal of Organizational Behavior, 22,* 517–536. doi:10.1002/job.100

Steers, R. M. (1977). Antecedents and outcomes of organizational commitment. *Administrative Science Quarterly, 22,* 46–56. doi:10.2307/2391745

Stellard, M. L. (2010, June 18). Has SAS chairman Jim goodnight cracked the code of the corporate culture? *The Economic Times.* Retrieved from http://economictimes.indiatimes.com/Features/Corporate-Dossier/Has-SAS-chairman-Jim-Goodnight-cracked-the-code-of-corporate-culture/articleshow/6060110.cms?curpg=1

Stinglhamber, F., & De Cremer, D. (2008). Co-workers' justice judgments, own justice judgments and employee commitment: A multifoci approach. *Psychologica Belgica, 48,* 197–218.

Stinglhamber, F., De Cremer, D., & Mercken, L. (2006). Perceived support as a mediator of the relationship between justice and trust: A multiple foci approach. *Group & Organization Management, 31,* 442–468. doi:10.1177/1059601106286782

Stinglhamber, F., Eisenberger, R., Aselage, J., Becker, T. E., Sucharski, I. L., & Eder, P. (2010). *Supervision support and perceived organizational support: The contribution of supervisor's organizational embodiment.* Unpublished manuscript, Université catholique de Louvain-la-Neuve, Belgium, and University of Houston, Houston, TX.

Stinglhamber, F., Eisenberger, R., Stewart, R., & Hanin, D. (2010). *The impact of personnel selection procedure on applicants' attitudes and inten-*

tions: The role of anticipated organizational support. Manuscript in preparation.

Stinglhamber, F., & Vandenberghe, C. (2003). Organizations and supervisors as sources of support and targets of commitment: A longitudinal study. *Journal of Organizational Behavior, 24,* 251–270. doi:10.1002/job.192

Stinglhamber, F., & Vandenberghe, C. (2004). Favorable job conditions and perceived support: The role of organizations and supervisors. *Journal of Applied Social Psychology, 34,* 1470–1493. doi:10.1111/j.1559-1816.2004.tb02015.x

Stokols, D., Clitheroe, C., & Zmuidzinas, M. (2002). Qualities of work environments that promote perceived support for creativity. *Creativity Research Journal, 14,* 137–147. doi:10.1207/S15326934CRJ1402_1

Stone, R. W., & Good, D. J. (2002). The impacts of computer use on marketing operations. *Journal of Marketing Theory and Practice, 10,* 38–45.

Suazo, M. M. (2003). An examination of antecedents and consequences of psychological contract breach. *Dissertation Abstracts International: Section: A. Humanities and Social Sciences, 64,* 988.

Susskind, A. M., Kacmar, K. M., & Borchgrevink, C. P. (2003). Customer service providers' attitudes relating to customer service and customer satisfaction in the customer–server exchange. *Journal of Applied Psychology, 88,* 179–187. doi:10.1037/0021-9010.88.1.179

Swanson, E. B. (1988). *Information system implementation.* Homewood, IL: Irwin.

Szymanski, D. M., & Henard, D. H. (2001). Customer satisfaction: A meta-analysis of the empirical evidence. *Journal of the Academy of Marketing Science, 29,* 16–35.

Tajfel, H. (1978). *Differentiation between social groups: Studies in the social psychology of intergroup relations.* London, England: Academic Press.

Tajfel, H., & Turner, J. C. (1979). An integrative theory of intergroup conflict. In W. G. Austin & S. Worchel (Eds.), *The social psychology of intergroup relations* (pp. 33–47). Monterey, CA: Brooks/Cole.

Tan, H. H., & Tan, C. S. F. (2000). Toward the differentiation of trust in supervisor and trust in organization. *Genetic, Social, and General Psychology Monographs, 126,* 241–260.

Tansky, J. W., & Cohen, D. J. (2001). The relationship between organizational support, employee development, and organizational commitment: An empirical study. *Human Resource Development Quarterly, 12,* 285–300. doi:10.1002/hrdq.15

Tedeschi, J. T. (1983). Social influence theory and aggression. In R. G. Green & E. I. Donnerstein (Eds.), *Aggression: Theoretical and empirical reviews* (Vol. 1, pp. 135–162). New York, NY: Academic Press.

Tepper, B. J. (2000). Consequences of abusive supervision. *Academy of Management Journal, 43,* 178–190. doi:10.2307/1556375

Tepper, B. J., & Taylor, E. C. (2003). Relationships among supervisors' and subordinates' procedural justice perceptions and organizational citizenship behaviors. *Academy of Management Journal, 46,* 97–105. doi:10.2307/30040679

Tesser, A., Gatewood, R., & Driver, M. (1968). Some determinants of gratitude. *Journal of Personality and Social Psychology, 9,* 233–236. doi:10.1037/h0025905

Tetrick, L. E. (1995). Developing and maintaining union commitment: A theoretical framework. *Journal of Organizational Behavior, 16,* 583–595. doi:10.1002/job.4030160606

Tetrick, L. E., Shore, L. M., McClurg, L. N., & Vandenberg, R. J. (2007). Model of union participation: The impact of perceived union support, union instrumentality, and union loyalty. *Journal of Applied Psychology, 92,* 820–828. doi:10.1037/0021-9010.92.3.820

The J. M. Smucker company named to *Fortune*'s list of '100 Best Companies to Work For' for fourth year in a row; fruit spread company receives #23 ranking. (2000, December 28). *PR Newswire.* Retrieved from http://www.highbeam.com/doc/1G1-68500203.html

Thibaut, J., & Kelley, H. (1959). *The social psychology of groups.* New York, NY: Wiley.

Thibaut, J., & Riecken, H. W. (1955). Some determinants and consequences of social causality. *Journal of Personality, 24,* 113–133. doi:10.1111/j.1467-6494.1955.tb01178.x

Thomas, K. W., & Velthouse, B. A. (1990). Cognitive elements of empowerment: An "interpretive" model of intrinsic task motivation. *Academy of Management Review, 15,* 666–681. doi:10.2307/258687

Thompson, C. A., Beauvais, L. L., & Lyness, K. S. (1999). When work–family benefits are not enough: The influence of work–family culture on benefit utilization, organizational attachment, and work–family conflict. *Journal of Vocational Behavior, 54,* 392–415. doi:10.1006/jvbe.1998.1681

Thompson, C. A., & Prottas, D. J. (2005). Relationships among organizational family support, job autonomy, perceived control, and employee well-being. *Journal of Occupational Health Psychology, 10,* 100–118.

Treadway, D. C., Hochwarter, W. A., Ferris, G. R., Kacmar, C. J., Douglas, C., Ammeter, A. P., . . . Buckley, M. R. (2004). Leader political skill and employee reactions. *The Leadership Quarterly, 15,* 493–513. doi:10.1016/j.leaqua.2004.05.004

Triandis, H. C. (1995). *Individualism and collectivism.* Boulder, CO: Westview.

Triandis, H. C., & Gelfand, M. J. (1998). Converging measurement of horizontal and vertical individualism and collectivism. *Journal of*

Personality and Social Psychology, 74, 118–128. doi:10.1037/0022-3514. 74.1.118

Tsui, A. S., Pearce, J. L., Porter, L. W., & Hite, J. P. (1995). Choice of employee–organization relationship: Influence of external and internal organizational factors. In G. R. Ferris (Ed.), *Research in personnel and human resource management* (Vol. 13, pp. 117–151). Greenwich, CT: JAI Press.

Tsui, A. S., Pearce, J. L., Porter, L. W., & Tripoli, A. M. (1997). Alternative approaches to the employee–organization relationship: Does investment in employees pay off? *Academy of Management Journal, 40,* 1089–1121. doi:10.2307/256928

Tucker, S., Chmiel, N., Turner, N., Hershcovis, M. S., & Stride, C. B. (2008). Perceived organizational support for safety and employee safety voice: The mediating role of coworker support for safety. *Journal of Occupational Health Psychology, 13,* 319–330. doi:10.1037/1076-8998.13.4.319

Tung, R. (1988). *The new expatriates: Managing human resources abroad.* New York, NY: Ballinger/Harper & Row.

Turner, J. C. (1984). Social identification and psychological group formation. In H. Tajfel (Ed.), *The social dimension: European developments in social psychology* (Vol. 2, pp. 518–538). Cambridge, UK: Cambridge University Press.

Uhl-Bien, M., & Maslyn, J. M. (2003). Reciprocity in manager–subordinate relationships: Components, configurations, and outcomes. *Journal of Management, 29,* 511–532.

Van Dick, R., Hirst, G., Grojean, M. W., & Wieseke, J. (2007). Relationships between leader and follower organizational identification and implications for follower attitudes and behaviour. *Journal of Occupational and Organizational Psychology, 80,* 133–150. doi:10.1348/ 096317905X71831

van Knippenberg, D., & Sleebos, E. (2006). Organizational identification versus organizational commitment: Self-definition, social exchange, and job attitudes. *Journal of Organizational Behavior, 27,* 571–584. doi: 10.1002/job.359

van Knippenberg, D., van Dick, R., & Tavares, S. (2007). Social identity and social exchange: Identification, support, and withdrawal from the job. *Journal of Applied Social Psychology, 37,* 457–477. doi:10.1111/ j.1559-1816.2007.00168.x

Van Lange, P. A. M. (2000). Self-determination in interpersonal situations. *Psychological Inquiry, 11,* 310–312.

Vance, A. (June 29, 2010). In faulty computer suit, Window to Dell decline. *New York Times,* pp. B1.

Vandenberghe, C., Bentein, K., Michon, R., Chebat, J. C., Tremblay, M., & Fils, J. F. (2007). An examination of the role of perceived support and employee commitment in employee-customer encounters. *Journal of Applied Psychology, 92,* 1177–1187. doi:10.1037/0021-9010.92.4.1177

Vardaman, J. M., Hancock, J. I., Allen, D. G., & Shore, L. M. (2009). *Group-level POS and the relationship between individual-level POS and outcomes.* Unpublished manuscript, Mississippi State University, Starkville.

Venkatachalam, M. (1995). Personal hardiness and perceived organizational support as links in the role stress–outcome relationship: A person–environment fit model. *Dissertation Abstracts International: Section A. Humanities and Social Sciences, 56,* 2328.

Vidmar, N. (2002). Retributive justice: Its social context. In M. Ross & D. T. Miller (Eds.), *The justice motive in everyday life* (pp. 291–313). New York, NY: Cambridge University Press. doi:10.1017/CBO9780511499975.016

Wadsworth, L. L., & Owens, B. P. (2007). The effects of social support on work–family enhancement and work–family conflict in the public sector. *Public Administration Review, 67,* 75–86. doi:10.1111/j.1540-6210.2006.00698.x

Wallace, J. C., Arnold, T., Finch, D. M., Edwards, B. D., & Frazier, M. L. (2009). Work stressors, role-based performance, and the moderating influence of organizational support. *Journal of Applied Psychology, 94,* 254–262. doi:10.1037/a0013090

Wallace, J. C., Edwards, B. D., Arnold, T., Frazier, M.L., & Finch, D. M. (2009). Work stressors, role-based performance and the moderating influence of organizational support. *Journal of Applied Psychology, 94,* 254–262.

Wang, M., & Takeuchi, R. (2007). The role of goal orientation during longitudinal expatriation: A cross-sectional and investigation. *Journal of Applied Psychology, 92,* 1437–1445. doi:10.1037/0021-9010.92.5.1437

Watson, D., & Clark, L. A. (1984). Negative affectivity: The disposition to experience aversive emotional states. *Psychological Bulletin, 96,* 465–490. doi:10.1037/0033-2909.96.3.465

Watson, D., Clark, L. A., & Tellegen, A. (1988). Development and validation of brief measures of Positive and Negative Affect: The PANAS Sates. *Journal of Personality and Social Psychology, 54,* 1063–1070. doi:10.1037/0022-3514.54.6.1063

Wayne, S. J., Coyle-Shapiro, J. A. M., Eisenberger, R., Liden, R. C., Rousseau, D. M., & Shore, L. M. (2009). Social influences. In H. J. Klein, T. E. Becker & J. P. Meyer (Eds.), *Commitment in organizations: Accumulated wisdom and new directions* (pp. 253–284). New York, NY: Routledge/Taylor and Francis.

Wayne, S. J., & Ferris, G. R. (1990). Influence tactics, affect, and exchange quality in supervisor–subordinate interactions: A laboratory experiment and field study. *Journal of Applied Psychology, 75,* 487–499.

Wayne, S. J., Shore, L. M., Bommer, W. H., & Tetrick, L. E. (2002). The role of fair treatment and rewards in perceptions of organizational support and leader–member exchange. *Journal of Applied Psychology, 87,* 590–598. doi:10.1037/0021-9010.87.3.590

Wayne, S. J., Shore, L. M., & Liden, R. C. (1997). Perceived organizational support and leader–member exchange: A social exchange perspective. *Academy of Management Journal, 40,* 82–111. doi:10.2307/257021

Weiner, B. (1985). Spontaneous' causal thinking. *Psychological Bulletin, 97,* 74–84. doi:10.1037/0033-2909.97.1.74

White, J. (2004, December 28). US Airways workers stage Christmas job action. *World Socialist Web.* Retrieved from http://www.wsws.org

Whitener, E. M. (2001). Do "high commitment" human resource practices affect employee commitment? A cross-level analysis using hierarchical linear modeling. *Journal of Management, 27,* 515–535.

Wiseman, R. M., & Gomez-Mejia, L. R. (1998). A behavioral agency model of managerial risk taking. *Academy of Management Review, 23,* 133–153. doi:10.2307/259103

Witt, L. A. (1991). Exchange ideology as a moderator of job attitudes: Organizational citizenship behaviors relationships. *Journal of Applied Social Psychology, 21,* 1490–1501. doi:10.1111/j.1559-1816.1991.tb00483.x

Witt, L. A., & Carlson, D. S. (2006). The work–family interface and job performance: Moderating effects of conscientiousness and perceived organizational support. *Journal of Occupational Health Psychology, 11,* 343–357. doi:10.1037/1076-8998.11.4.343

Witt, L. A., & Hellman, C. M. (1992). Effects of subordinate feedback to the supervisor and participation in decision-making in the prediction of organizational support. In K. A. Vaverek (Ed.), *Proceedings of the Southwest Academy of Management* (pp. 191–195). Houston, TX: The Mescon Group.

Yoon, J., Han, N. C., & Seo, Y. J. (1996). Sense of control among hospital employees: An assessment of choice process, empowerment, and buffering hypotheses. *Journal of Applied Social Psychology, 26,* 686–716. doi:10.1111/j.1559-1816.1996.tb02739.x

Yoon, J., & Lim, J. C. (1999). Organizational support in the workplace: The case of Korean hospital employees. *Human Relations, 52,* 923–945. doi:10.1177/001872679905200704

Yoon, J., & Thye, S. (2000). Supervisor support in the workplace: Legitimacy and Positive Affectivity. *The Journal of Social Psychology, 140,* 295–316. doi:10.1080/00224540009600472

Young, T. R. (1984). The lonely micro. *Datamation, 30,* 100–114.

Youngs, G. A. (1986). Patterns of threat and punishment reciprocity in a conflict setting. *Journal of Personality and Social Psychology, 51,* 541–546. doi:10.1037/0022-3514.51.3.541

Zagenczyk, T. J., Scott, K. D., Gibney, R., Murrell, A. J., & Thatcher, J. B. (2010). Social influence and perceived organizational support: A social networks analysis. *Organizational Behavior and Human Decision Processes, 111,* 127–138. doi:10.1016/j.obhdp.2009.11.004

Zhou, J., & George, J. M. (2001). When job dissatisfaction leads to creativity: Encouraging the expression of voice. *Academy of Management Journal, 44,* 682–696. doi:10.2307/3069410

Zimmerman, A. (2004, March 26). Costco's dilemma: Be kind to its workers, or Wall Street? *The Wall Street Journal,* B1.

Index

About the Authors

Robert Eisenberger, PhD, is a professor in the psychology department and a professor of management in the Bauer College of Business at the University of Houston. His organizational support theory, with its central concept of perceived organizational support, is one the most frequently cited views of employee–organization relationships, leading to over 350 scholarly studies and 600,000 references on the Internet. His article introducing perceived organizational support was the most cited article in organizational behavior during the last studied 5-year period. Dr. Eisenberger is the author of 70 publications on motivation and organizational behavior. His research was recognized with the Psi Chi Distinguished Lectureship, and he is a fellow of a number of scientific societies. Two special reports focusing on his research were carried nationally on National Public Radio, and reports on his research have appeared in the American Psychological Association's *Monitor on Psychology, Encylopaedia Britannica Science and the Future Yearbook, Science News, Report on Educational Research,* and *School Board Notes.* Dr. Eisenberger's research has been supported by grants from the U.S. Army Research Institute for the Social and Behavioral Sciences, the National Institutes of Health, and the National Park Service.

Florence Stinglhamber, PhD, is an associate professor of organizational psychology and human resource management in the psychology department at the Université Catholique de Louvain (Louvain-la-Neuve, Belgium). She is a member of the Psychological Sciences Research Institute at the same university. Perceived organizational support has been one of her main research interests for 10 years. Her other research interests include employees' identification and commitment in the workplace, perceived justice and trust, leadership and managerial skills, and employer branding. Dr. Stinglhamber is the author or coauthor of a number of scientific articles on organizational psychology and organizational behavior.